REPEAT PERFORMANCES

By Doris Milberg

Repeat Performances

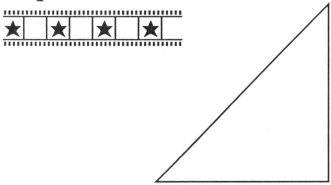

By

Doris Milberg

A Guide to Hollywood Movie Remakes

ISBN: 0-911747-21-4

Printed in the United States of America

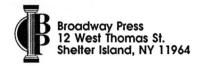

Broadway Press
12 West Thomas St.
Shelter Island, NY 11964

To Ted
My husband and best friend,
whose love and encouragement have helped
me to see the light at the end of a long tunnel.

TABLE OF CONTENTS

Note: Two common abbreviations are used throughout the book. TCF stands for Twentieth Century-Fox, and MMTV denotes Movie Made for Television. Also, the symbol ★AOV★ indicates a film is *available on video*..

☆ ☆ ☆ ☆ ☆ ☆ ☆

PROLOGUE

AN OVERVIEW

Many a famous writer has, at one time or another, stated that there are only six or seven original stories to be told—all the rest are variations upon a theme. This fact of life also holds true for the motion picture industry—ergo, we have the movie remake, a phenomenon which has been in evidence since the embryonic stages of Hollywood's growth. "Let's redo such and such," remarks a producer to his cohorts. "Why not?" answer the latter and, with a minimum of change (in some cases), another film is in the can.

From silents such as THE HUNCHBACK OF NOTRE DAME (1923) and THE MERRY WIDOW (1925), to the various versions of THE FRONT PAGE (1988's SWITCHING CHANNELS is the latest in the series), the films remade have either been virtual replicas of the original or have undergone some change in location and/or character names. In almost sixty of the films discussed during the course of this book, the original genre has been changed, creating a new look for an old chestnut.

Casting from original to remake is also very interesting to contemplate. A fascinating aspect of this, which surfaced during my research, is the fact that several stars have reprised their roles in remakes of their original films, among them Clark Gable in RED DUST (1932) and MOGAMBO (1953), also Betty Grable in both CONEY ISLAND (1943) and WABASH AVENUE (circa 1950). Four hits, each in their time. All parts of movie magic.

As television and its offspring, cable television, became part and parcel of everyday living, more and more material was needed to satisfy the millions who daily demanded instant entertainment. Improvements in the medium, which at first was live in its presentations, gave rise to taped and then filmed versions of favorite shows. Movies Made for Television (MMTV) was only one step beyond. The realization that an old movie script, given a facelift and a different cast, could capture a generation unfamiliar with the original evolved from this and gave a whole new meaning to the word "remake"—the many films revisited in this way, therefore, warrant inclusion in these pages.

Repeat Performances is a compilation of the film remake. Each chapter begins with a short introduction to the genre examined and then goes on to list the representative body of film.

Information in each listing includes:

name of film (year of release)

production company • director

stars

Also I give a brief description of the plotline, and wherever possible, I have interpolated information and bits of trivia about stars and films culled from years of reading and writing about the movies. Another piece of information I have included in each listing is whether or not a film is *available on video*. Where this is the case, the symbol ★AOV★ follows the name. Of course, films are being released on video more and more every day and just because my research in 1990 didn't show a film was available yet, doesn't mean it never will. Be sure to check with your video store.

It is, of course, virtually impossible to know about each and every film that has ever been remade. While being as comprehensive as possible, I have also tried to list films that I think will strike responsive chords in my readers. Where a film has been remade more than once, credits are given for the original production and for the most important redo—the others are named, but without credits. For example,the previously mentioned HUNCHBACK OF NOTRE DAME has been filmed four times. The first version, a silent, stars Lon Chaney Sr in the title role, giving what is considered the greatest performance in that part. Charles Laughton, playing the tortured Quasimodo in the 1939 remake,was also praised by critics and movie fans of that era for his efforts.Credits are listed for these two productions—the other films, not half good as their predecessors, which feature Anthony Quinn and Anthony Hopkins in the title roles, are merely mentioned. Also, many films can be considered as belonging to more than one genre. In my capacity as author, I have placed them in what I consider the more representative category.

Here then is my compilation. For me, this book has been a true labor of love—if the reader has even half as much fun in turning its pages as I did in researching its material, I will be very happy.

★   ★   ★   ★   ★   ★   ★

CHAPTER ONE

ONCE MORE WITH FEELING: DRAMA REMAKES

The big screen has always been interested in the long green. Money is the name of the game in Hollywood and filmmakers, at the same time purveyors of dreams and also eminently realistic, have seen that a highly profitable source of the movie remake has been of a dramatic nature.

Interesting characterization, well-paced plot development, some conflict and logical resolution of same—most people would agree that these are the key ingredients of good drama. Stir into the batter some potent performers and voila—a box-office bonanza. When this occurs, can a remake be far away? "Let's try it again, maybe lightning will strike twice," becomes the operative phrase for filmmakers of all genres. And since there have been more remakes of popular dramas than any other kind of films, it seems that for this particular genre, lightning has struck again and again.

☆   ☆   ☆   ☆   ☆   ☆   ☆

▶ ADVICE TO THE LOVELORN (1933)
Fox • Alfred Werker

Lee Tracy, Sally Blaine

▷ LONELY HEARTS (1958)★AOV★
United Artists • Vincent Donehue

Montgomery Clift, Robert Ryan, Myrna Loy,
Maureen Stapleton

Plot: A columnist, assigned to the "Lonely hearts" desk of a newspaper, deals with affairs of the heart.

Notes: LONELY HEARTS was the debut film for Maureen Stapleton. Also featured in the 1958 production is former child star Jackie Coogan.

★ ★ ★

▶ AND GOD CREATED WOMAN (1957)★AOV★
Ilena/UCIL/Cocinor • Roger Vadim

Brigitte Bardot, Curt Jurgens, Jean-Louis Trintignant

▷ AND GOD CREATED WOMAN (1988)★AOV★
Vestron/Crow • Roger Vadim

Rebecca De Mornay, Frank Langella, Vincent Spano

Plot: The "adventures" of a girl who uses her sex appeal to get what she wants.

Notes: The 1957 production brought Bardot and her then husband Vadim international fame. He later was married to and divorced from Jane Fonda.

★ ★ ★

▶ ANIMAL KINGDOM, THE (1932)
RKO • Edward H. Griffith

Leslie Howard, Ann Harding, Myrna Loy

▷ ONE MORE TOMORROW (1946)
Warners • Peter Godfrey

Dennis Morgan, Alexis Smith, Ann Sheridan, Jane Wyman

Plot: A publisher is torn between his selfish wife and the girl he really loves.

Notes: Both films are based upon the play "The Animal Kingdom" by Philip Barry.

★ ★ ★

▶ ANNA LUCASTA (1949)
Columbia • Irving Rapper

Paulette Goddard, Broderick Crawford

▷ ANNA LUCASTA (1958)
United Artists • Arnold Laven

Eartha Kitt, Sammy Davis Jr., Frederick O'Neal

Plot: The life and loves of a promiscuous woman.

Notes: Philip Yordan wrote the play upon which the films are based. The Broadway version had an all-black cast as does the 1958 production.

★ ★ ★

▶ BAD SEED, THE (1956)★AOV★
Warners • Mervyn Le Roy

Patty McCormack, Nancy Kelly, Henry Jones, Eileen Heckart

▷ BAD SEED, THE (1985)
MMTV • Paul Wendkos

Carrie Wells, Lynn Redgrave, David Carradine, Richard Kiley

Plot: A young girl's evil tendencies lead to death and tragedy.

Notes: The four principal players of the 1956 production were also starred in the Broadway play. Featured in the first film is William Hopper, son of gossip columnist Hedda Hopper, also known to TV fans as detective Paul Drake on the "Perry Mason" series.

★ ★ ★

★   ★   ★   ★   ★   ★   ★

▶ BILL OF DIVORCEMENT, A (1932)   ▷ BILL OF DIVORCEMENT, A (1940)
RKO • George Cukor   RKO • John Farrow

Katharine Hepburn, John Barrymore, Billie Burke   Maureen O'Hara, Adolphe Menjou, Fay Bainter

Plot: A man, released from a mental institution, comes home to his wife and daughter.

Notes: BILL OF DIVORCEMENT was Katharine Hepburn's first film. She plays John Barrymore's daughter. She had been signed to a one picture deal at RKO as a result of her performance in a Broadway play titled "The Warrior's Husband." Billie Burke, featured in the 1932 production, was the widow of famed showman Florenz Ziegfeld.

Both Geraldine Fitzgerald and Bette Davis are smiling up at Ronald Reagan in a close-up from DARK VICTORY. A portent of things to come? Not likely, as both actresses were Democrats.

▶ BISCUIT EATER, THE (1940)   ▷ BISCUIT EATER, THE (1972)
Paramount • Stuart Heisler   Disney • Vincent McEveety

Billy Lee, Richard Lane   Johnny Whitaker, Earl Holliman

Plot: Two boys turn a stray dog into a champion hunter.

Notes: Earl Holliman and Johnny Whitaker each appeared on a prime-time television show—Holliman co-starred with Angie Dickinson in "Police Woman" and Johnny Whitaker was featured in "Family Affair."

▶ CAGED (1950)   ▷ HOUSE OF WOMEN (1962)
Warners • John Cromwell   Warners • Walter Doniger

Eleanor Parker, Jan Sterling, Agnes Moorehead   Shirley Knight, Constance Ford

Plot: The harrowing lives of women in prison.

Notes: Jan Sterling was the wife of the late actor Paul Douglas.

☆   ☆   ☆   ☆   ☆   ☆   ☆

▶ CAT ON A HOT TIN ROOF (1958)★AOV★
MGM • Richard Brooks
Elizabeth Taylor, Paul Newman, Burl Ives

▷ CAT ON A HOT TIN ROOF (1984)★AOV★
MMTV • Jack Y. Hofsiss
Jessica Lange, Tommy Lee Jones, Rip Torn

Plot: Two problematic sons face up to the death of their plantation-owning father.

Notes: Burl Ives recreates his stage role in the 1958 screen adaptation of the Tennessee Williams drama.

★ ★ ★

▶ CHALLENGE TO LASSIE (1949)
MGM • Richard Thorpe
Edmund Gwenn, Donald Crisp, Lassie

▷ GREYFRIARS BOBBY (1961)★AOV★
Disney • Don Chaffey
Donald Crisp, Kay Walsh, Gordon Jackson

Plot: A dog keeps vigil over his master's grave.

Notes: The original based on fact story is about a Skye terrier. Donald Crisp plays a different role in each version. Some "wag" once called Lassie the world's greatest female impersonator ever—all "her" roles have been played by males.

★ ★ ★

▶ CHAMP, THE (1931)
MGM • King Vidor
Wallace Beery, Jackie Cooper

▷ CHAMP, THE (1979)★AOV★
MGM • Franco Zeffirelli
Jon Voight, Faye Dunaway, Ricky Schroder

Plot: Drama of a young boy's abiding love for his washed-up boxer father.

Notes: In THE CLOWN★AOV★, Red Skelton and Tim Considine play a father and son very similar to the two in THE CHAMP. Young Ricky was also the star of the television series "Silver Spoons."

★ ★ ★

▶ CHIENNE, LA (1931)★AOV★
French • Jean Renoir
Michel Simon, Janie Mareze

▷ SCARLET STREET (1945)★AOV★
Universal • Fritz Lang
Edward G. Robinson, Joan Bennett, Dan Duryea

Plot: A mild-mannered man is led into a web of murder and intrigue by a seductress and her no-good lover.

Notes: The previous year, Lang had directed THE WOMAN IN THE WINDOW, which stars the same trio of performers from SCARLET STREET. Joan Bennett was the wife of the late Walter Wanger, producer of the 1945 film.

★ ★ ★

▶ COMMON CLAY (1930)
Fox • Victor Fleming
Constance Bennett, Lew Ayres

▷ PRIVATE NUMBER (1936)
TCF • Roy Del Ruth
Loretta Young, Robert Taylor

Plot: Complications set in as a young girl, hired as a maid, falls in love with her employer's son.

Notes: Constance Bennett was the daughter of stage and silent screen star Richard Bennett and the sister of actress Joan. A top performer during the late twenties, thirties and forties, she died in 1965.

★ ★ ★

▶ CORN IS GREEN, THE (1945)★AOV★
Warners • Irving Rapper
Bette Davis, John Dall, Joan Lorring

▷ CORN IS GREEN, THE (1979)
MMTV • George Cukor
Katharine Hepburn, Bill Fraser

Plot: A spinster teacher brings education to a talented young Welsh coal miner.

Notes: The MMTV version was shot on location in Northern Wales, giving the production an air of authenticity.

★ ★ ★

*Jane Wyman in THE GLASS
MENAGERIE—Wyman's only foray into
the realm of Tennessee Williams.*

★ ★ ★

▶ CRAIG'S WIFE (1936)★AOV★
Columbia • Dorothy Arzner
Rosalind Russell, John Boles

▷ HARRIET CRAIG (1950)
Columbia • Vincent Sherman
Joan Crawford, Wendell Corey

Plot: A wife's home and material possessions take precedence over the needs of her husband.

Notes: A silent version starring Irene Rich was released in 1928. Rosalind Russell was twenty-five when she played "Harriet Craig." Many critics felt that she was too young for the part. Joan Crawford was well into her forties when assigned the role. Dorothy Arzner was one of the few woman directors of her era— she worked on at least fifteen films during her career. George Kelly, upon whose play the films were based, was the uncle of Grace Kelly.

★ ★ ★

☆   ☆   ☆   ☆   ☆   ☆   ☆

▶ DANGEROUS (1935)
Warners • Alfred E. Green
Bette Davis, Franchot Tone

▷ SINGAPORE WOMAN (1941)
Warners • Jean Negulesco
Brenda Marshall, David Bruce

Plot: The redemption of a woman by a good man.

Notes: Oscar number one for Davis, who had lost out the year before.

★ ★ ★

▶ DARK MIRROR, THE (1946) ★AOV★
International • Robert Siodmak
Olivia de Havilland, Lew Ayres, Thomas Mitchell

▷ DARK MIRROR, THE (1984)
MMTV • Richard Lang
Jane Seymour, Stephen Collins

Plot: Twin sisters, one good, one disturbed, become involved in murder.

Notes: Olivia de Havilland won her first Oscar in 1946, not for THE DARK MIRROR, but for TO EACH HIS OWN.

★ ★ ★

▶ DARK VICTORY (1939) ★AOV★
Warners • Edmund Goulding
Bette Davis, George Brent, Humphrey Bogart, Geraldine Fitzgerald

▷ STOLEN HOURS (1963)
United Artists • Daniel Petrie
Susan Hayward, Michael Craig, Diane Baker

Plot: A doomed heiress falls in love with her doctor.

Notes: Also featured in the 1939 production is an actor named Ronald Reagan. The film was remade in 1978 under its original title. This third version, directed by Robert Butler, stars Elizabeth Montgomery, Anthony Hopkins and Michele Lee.

★ ★ ★

▶ DAUGHTERS COURAGEOUS (1939)
Warners • Michael Curtiz
John Garfield, The Lane Sisters, Gale Page, Claude Rains

▷ ALWAYS IN MY HEART (1942)
Warners • Jo Graham
Walter Huston, Kay Francis, Gloria Warren

Plot: A prodigal father returns to his family after a long absence.

Notes: The 1939 release followed on the heels of the very successful FOUR DAUGHTERS (See Chapter Eight) and used the same cast. Although only one daughter appears in the 1942 production, both films are adapted from a play titled "Fly Away Home."

★ ★ ★

▶ DAVID COPPERFIELD (1935) ★AOV★
MGM • George Cukor
Freddie Bartholomew, W.C. Fields, Lionel Barrymore

▷ DAVID COPPERFIELD (1970)
British • Delbert Mann
Ralph Richardson, Michael Redgrave, Robin Phillips

Plot: The life of David Copperfield, from boyhood to manhood, as written by Charles Dickens.

Notes: Freddie Bartholomew was discovered while director Cukor and producer David Selznick were scouting locations in England. W.C. Fields replaced Charles Laughton as Micawber. Also in the cast of the 1935 film are Basil Rathbone and Maureen O'Sullivan.

★ ★ ★

☆   ☆   ☆   ☆   ☆   ☆   ☆

▶ DEATH OF A SALESMAN (1951)
Columbia/Stanley Kramer • Laslo Benedek

Fredric March, Kevin McCarthy, Mildred Dunnock,
Cameron Mitchell

▷ DEATH OF A SALESMAN (1985)★AOV★
MMTV • Volker Schlondorff

Dustin Hoffman, Kate Reid, John Malkovich,
Charles Durning

Plot: The life and times of an aging and despondent salesman via flashback.

Notes: Kevin McCarthy's debut film. He, Fredric March and Mildred Dunnock were Oscar-nominated. None of the three won.

★   ★   ★

An All-Star Metro line-up in the 1932 Academy Award-winning film GRAND HOTEL.

★   ★   ★

▶ DOG OF FLANDERS, A (1935)
RKO • Edward Sloman

Frankie Thomas, Helen Parrish

▷ DOG OF FLANDERS, A (1959)★AOV★
TCF • James B. Clark

David Ladd, Donald Crisp

Plot: A boy picks up a stray dog and meets an artist who encourages him to enter an amateur art contest.

Notes: The 1959 production, which stars Alan Ladd's son, is the third version of the heart-warming tale. The first, a 1924 silent starring Jackie Coogan, was made at Metro.

★   ★   ★

☆   ☆   ☆   ☆   ☆   ☆   ☆

▶ DOLL'S HOUSE, A (1973)
British/Elkins • Patrick Garland

Claire Bloom, Anthony Hopkins, Ralph Richardson

▷ DOLL'S HOUSE, A (1973)★AOV★
World Film Service • Joshua Losey

Jane Fonda, David Warner, Trevor Howard

Plot: During the last years of the nineteenth century, a woman trapped in a stultifying marriage strives to become liberated.

Notes: Both films released in 1973 are based upon a play by Henrik Ibsen.

★ ★ ★

▶ DUST BE MY DESTINY (1939)
Warners • Louis Seiler

John Garfield, Priscilla Lane

▷ I WAS FRAMED (1942)
Warners • D. Ross Lederman

Michael Ames

Plot: An alienated young man tries to find himself with the help of a girl he meets.

Notes: John Garfield and Priscilla Lane made three films together within two years: FOUR DAUGHTERS (1938), DAUGHTERS COURAGEOUS and DUST BE MY DESTINY, both 1939 releases.

★ ★ ★

▶ ENTERTAINER, THE (1960)★AOV★
BL/Bryanston/Woodfall/Holly • Tony Richardson

Laurence Olivier, Joan Plowright

▷ ENTERTAINER, THE (1976)
MMTV • Donald Wrye

Jack Lemmon, Sada Thompson

Plot: An entertainer on the skids reflects upon both his professional and private lives.

Notes: The location of the first film is Brighton, England. The second takes place in Santa Cruz, California. Joan Plowright is Lady Olivier in private life.

★ ★ ★

▶ ESCAPE ME NEVER (1935)
B and D/ Herbert Wilcox • Paul Czinner

Elizabeth Bergner, Hugh Sinclair

▷ ESCAPE ME NEVER (1947)
Warners • Peter Godfrey

Ida Lupino, Errol Flynn, Eleanor Parker

Plot: A composer marries one woman though he is in love with another.

Notes: Elizabeth Bergner received an Oscar nomination for her role in the 1935 film. She was also married to its director.

★ ★ ★

▶ FLAME OF NEW ORLEANS (1941)
Universal • Rene Clair

Marlene Dietrich, Bruce Cabot, Roland Young

▷ SCARLET ANGEL (1952)
Universal-International • Sidney Salkow

Yvonne De Carlo, Rock Hudson, Amanda Blake

Plot: A dance hall girl must choose between a wealthy business man and an adventurous rogue.

Notes: Amanda Blake played Miss Kitty in television's long running "Gunsmoke" series.

★ ★ ★

▶ FREE SOUL, A (1935)
MGM • Clarence Brown
Norma Shearer, Clark Gable, Lionel Barrymore,
Leslie Howard

▷ GIRL WHO HAD EVERYTHING, THE (1953)
MGM • Richard Thorpe
Elizabeth Taylor, William Powell, Fernando Lamas

Plot: A lawyer's daughter falls in love with her father's gangster client.

Notes: Lionel Barrymore, who delivers a fourteen minute speech in the 1935 production, may have won the year's Best Actor Oscar, but it was Clark Gable who scored the film's biggest hit.

★ ★ ★

Jane Wyman in JOHNNY BELINDA. Her portrayal of a deaf-mute brought the actress her only Academy Award. A far cry from the very verbal Angela Channing of "Falcon Crest."

★ ★ ★

▶ GALLANT LADY (1933)
Twentieth Century • Gregory La Cava
Ann Harding, Clive Brook, Otto Kruger

▷ ALWAYS GOODBYE (1938)
TCF • Sidney Lanfield
Barbara Stanwyck, Herbert Marshall, Ian Hunter

Plot: A mother allows her illegitimate child to be adopted, but later marries the adoptive father.

★ ★ ★

▶ GLASS MENAGERIE, THE (1950)
Warners • Irving Rapper
Gertrude Lawrence, Jane Wyman, Kirk Douglas

▷ GLASS MENAGERIE, THE (1973)
MMTV • Anthony Harvey
Katharine Hepburn, Sam Waterston, Joanna Miles

Plot: A shy crippled girl, her faded Southern belle mother and idealistic brother all dream of escape from reality.

Notes: A third version of the Tennessee Williams play stars Joanne Woodward and John Malkovich. Released in 1987★AOV★, Paul Newman receives credit as its director.

★ ★ ★

☆   ☆   ☆   ☆   ☆   ☆   ☆

▶ GRAND HOTEL (1932)⋆AOV⋆
MGM • Edmund Goulding

▷ WEEKEND AT THE WALDORF (1945)
MGM • Robert Z. Leonard

Greta Garbo, John Barrymore, Lionel Barrymore,
Joan Crawford, Wallace Beery

Ginger Rogers, Lana Turner, Walter Pidgeon, Van
Johnson, Edward Arnold

Plot: The lives of various guests at a fashionable hotel become intertwined.

Notes: GRAND HOTEL was chosen Best Film of 1932. Another Vicki Baum originated film, HOTEL
BERLIN, similar in plot to GRAND HOTEL, takes place during the declining days of World War
II—it stars Raymond Massey, Peter Lorre, Faye Emerson and Helmut Dantine.

★ ★ ★

▶ GREAT GATSBY, THE (1949)
Paramount • Elliott Nugent

▷ GREAT GATSBY, THE (1974)⋆AOV⋆
Paramount • Jack Clayton

Alan Ladd, Betty Field, Barry Sullivan, MacDonald
Carey

Robert Redford, Mia Farrow, Sam Waterston

Plot: A mystery man crashes into Long Island society during the nineteen twenties.

Notes: A silent version of F. Scott Fitzgerald's popular novel was made, also by Paramount, in
1926. It stars Warner Baxter, Lois Wilson and William Powell, who plays "the villain in the piece."

★ ★ ★

▶ HEIDI (1937)⋆AOV⋆
TCF • Alan Dwan

▷ HEIDI (1968)⋆AOV⋆
MMTV • Delbert Mann

Shirley Temple, Jean Hersholt, Arthur Treacher

Jennifer Edwards, Jean Simmons, Maximilian
Schell, Michael Redgrave

Plot: A young orphan, living with her grandfather in a Swiss mountain village, is suddenly taken
from him and sent to live with someone else.

Notes: A Swiss version of the popular children's story by Joanna Spyri was made in 1953⋆AOV⋆
and a fourth, filmed in Austria, was released in 1965⋆AOV⋆.

★ ★ ★

▶ HOUSE OF STRANGERS (1949)
TCF • Joseph L. Mankiewicz

▷ BROKEN LANCE (1954)
TCF • Edward Dmytryk

Edward G. Robinson, Susan Hayward, Richard
Conte, Luther Adler

Spencer Tracy, Richard Widmark, Jean Peters,
Robert Wagner

Plot: An autocratic father is the cause of much dissension among his sons.

Notes: In a switch of genre (and locale) HOUSE OF STRANGERS, a straight drama, becomes
BROKEN LANCE, a Western.

★ ★ ★

▶ ILLICIT (1931)   ▷ EX-LADY (1933)
Warners • Archie Mayo   Warners • Robert Florey
Barbara Stanwyck, Ricardo Cortez, Joan Blondell   Bette Davis, Gene Raymond, Frank McHugh

Plot: An unhappily married wife leaves her husband and seeks love elsewhere.

Notes: The two films feature three of Warner Brothers top female stars of the nineteen thirties: Stanwyck, Blondell and Davis.

★ ★ ★

Paul Douglas and Linda Darnell in a close-up from A LETTER TO THREE WIVES—a former radio announcer and a great beauty of the silver screen.

★ ★ ★

▶ IMITATION OF LIFE (1934)   ▷ IMITATION OF LIFE (1959)★AOV★
Universal • John Stahl   Universal-International • Douglas Sirk
Claudette Colbert, Warren William, Louise Beavers   Lana Turner, John Gavin, Juanita Moore

Plot: Two mothers, one black, one white, come up against overwhelming odds as they struggle to raise their daughters.

Notes: Both films are based upon a novel by Fannie Hurst, a prolific best-selling author during the nineteen twenties and thirties.

★ ★ ★

▶ INFORMER, THE (1935)★AOV★   ▷ UP TIGHT (1968)
RKO • John Ford   Paramount • Jules Dassin
Victor McLaglen, Heather Angel, Preston Foster   Raymond St. Jacques, Roscoe Lee Browne, Ruby Dee

Plot: One man is hounded when he betrays another for money.

Notes: THE INFORMER is set in Ireland during the Irish Rebellion. Its remake was updated to portray the Black Struggle.

★ ★ ★

★   ★   ★   ★   ★   ★   ★

▶ INHERIT THE WIND (1960)★AOV★
United Artists • Stanley Kramer
Spencer Tracy, Fredric March, Gene Kelly

▷ INHERIT THE WIND (1988)
MMTV • David Greene
Kirk Douglas, Jason Robards, Darren McGavin

Plot: A fictionalized account of the famous Scopes "Monkey Trial" of 1925, during which a teacher was tried for teaching about evolution.

Notes: Playing Fredric March's wife on screen is his off-screen wife, actress Florence Eldridge. The 1968 film was filmed by Kirk Douglas' Bryna Productions (named for his mother).

★ ★ ★

▶ IRON MAN (1931)
Universal • Tod Browning
Lew Ayres, Jean Harlow

▷ IRON MAN (1951)
Universal-International • Joseph Pevney
Jeff Chandler, Evelyn Keyes

Plot: A prize fighter's head is turned by money, success and a scheming wife.

Notes: Brooklyn-born Jeff Chandler co-starred with Eve Arden in the radio version of "Our Miss Brooks." Seen in the 1951 film are James Arness and Rock Hudson.

★ ★ ★

▶ JOHNNY BELINDA (1948)★AOV★
Warners • Jean Negulesco
Jane Wyman, Lew Ayres, Stephen McNally

▷ JOHNNY BELINDA (1982)★AOV★
MMTV • Anthony Page
Richard Thomas, Rosanna Arquette, Dennis Quaid

Plot: A deaf-mute is raped and becomes pregnant. The doctor who befriends her is wrongly suspected of being the baby's father.

Notes: Jane Wyman clutched her Best Actress Academy Award and said, "I accept this very gratefully for keeping my mouth shut. I think I'll do it again."

★ ★ ★

▶ JOUR SE LEVE, LE (1939)★AOV★
(American Title: DAYBREAK)
French/Sigma • Marcel Carne
Jean Gabin, Arletty

▷ LONG NIGHT, THE (1947)

RKO • Anatole Litvak
Henry Fonda, Vincent Price, Barbara Bel Geddes

Plot: Via flashbacks, a killer, hiding in an attic, relives his past.

Notes: Fans of "Dallas" can see Miss Ellie (Barbara Bel Geddes) as she looked in the late nineteen forties.

★ ★ ★

▶ JUDGE PRIEST (1934)★AOV★
Fox • John Ford
Will Rogers, Anita Louise, Tom Brown

▷ SUN SHINES BRIGHT, THE (1953)
Republic/Argosy • John Ford
Charles Winninger, Arlene Whelan, John Russell

Plot: The life and times of a small town judge— a slice of Americana.

Notes: Oklahoma-born actor and humorist Will Rogers died in 1935 as the result of a plane crash. Star of vaudeville, screen and radio, he was beloved by millions.

★ ★ ★

★   ★   ★   ★   ★   ★   ★

▶ KID FROM LEFT FIELD, THE (1953)
TCF • Harmon Jones

Dan Dailey, Anne Bancroft, Billy Chapin

▷ KID FROM LEFT FIELD, THE (1979)★ᴬᴼⱽ★
MMTV • Adell Aldrich

Robert Guillaume, Gary Coleman

Plot: A former big league baseball player gives advice to a team through his son.

Notes: The two stars of the 1979 film are television veterans: Gary Coleman portrayed Arnold on "Different Strokes" and Robert Guillaume was Benson.

★ ★ ★

Jean Parker, Katharine Hepburn, Joan Bennett and Frances Dee as Beth, Jo, Amy and Meg (left to right), in Louisa May Alcott's LITTLE WOMEN.

★ ★ ★

▶ LADIES IN RETIREMENT (1941)
Columbia • Charles Vidor

Ida Lupino, Louis Hayward, Elsa Lanchester

▷ MAD ROOM, THE (1969)
Columbia • Bernard Girard

Shelley Winters, Skip Ward, Stella Stevens

Plot: A housekeeper murders her employer so that her mentally disturbed siblings will have a home.

Notes: At the time they made the 1941 movie, Ida Lupino was married to co-star Louis Hayward. They were divorced in 1945. She later married screen and radio actor Howard Duff and became a respected movie and television director.

★ ★ ★

▶ LADIES OF LEISURE (1930)
Columbia • Frank Capra

Barbara Stanwyck, Lowell Sherman, Marie Provost

▷ WOMEN OF GLAMOUR (1937)
Columbia • Gordon Wiles

Melvyn Douglas, Virginia Bruce

Plot: A man must chose between a rich society girl and one who is out for his money.

Notes: Lowell Sherman did double duty in several of his films as both director and actor. Marie Provost became famous as Charlie Chaplin's leading lady.

★ ★ ★

☆   ☆   ☆   ☆   ☆   ☆   ☆

▶ LAST ANGRY MAN, THE (1959)★AOV★
Columbia • Daniel Mann
Paul Muni, David Wayne, Betsy Palmer, Luther
Adler

▷ LAST ANGRY MAN, THE (1974)
MMTV • Jerrold Freedman
Pat Hingle, Lynn Carlin, Andrew Duggan

Plot: A dedicated old Brooklyn doctor is made the subject of a television documentary.

Notes: The 1959 release was Paul Muni's last film. He and featured actor Luther Adler began their careers in New York's Yiddish Theater. Also seen in this version is Billy Dee Williams.

★ ★ ★

▶ LAST HURRAH, THE (1958)★AOV★
Columbia • John Ford
Spencer Tracy, Jeffrey Hunter, Pat O'Brien

▷ LAST HURRAH, THE (1977)
MMTV • Vincent Sherman
Carroll O'Connor, Burgess Meredith, Dana
Andrews

Plot: An old New England politician fights his last campaign.

Notes: Others players in the 1958 film form a veritable "Who's Who" of character actors: Basil Rathbone, Donald Crisp, James Gleason, John Carradine, Frank McHugh and Jane Darwell.

★ ★ ★

▶ LEAVE HER TO HEAVEN (1946)
TCF • John Stahl
Gene Tierney, Cornel Wilde, Jeanne Crain, Vincent
Price

▷ TOO GOOD TO BE TRUE (1988)
MMTV • Christian I. Nyby II
Loni Anderson, Patrick Duffy, Julie Harris

Plot: A mentally disturbed, overly possessive woman plots to have her suicide investigated as a murder.

Notes: Gene Tierney received an Oscar nomination for her performance in the 1946 production, adapted from the Ben Ames Williams novel.

★ ★ ★

▶ LETTER, THE (1940)★AOV★
Warners • William Wyler
Bette Davis, Herbert Marshall, Gale Sondergaard

▷ LETTER, THE (1982)
MMTV • John Erman
Lee Remick, Ian McShane

Plot: A married woman kills her lover in a fit of passion, but claims self-defense.

Notes: An early sound version (1929) of the Somerset Maugham novel features Broadway star Jeanne Eagels. Herbert Marshall, who appears as the lover in this production, plays the husband in the 1940 film. THE UNFAITHFUL (1947), starring Ann Sheridan, Zachary Scott and Lew Ayres, deals with a similar plot.

★ ★ ★

▶ LETTER TO THREE WIVES, A (1949)★AOV★
TCF • Joseph L. Mankiewicz

Ann Sothern, Linda Darnell, Paul Douglas, Kirk Douglas, Jeanne Crain

▷ LETTER TO THREE WIVES, A (1985)
MMTV • Larry Elikann

Loni Anderson, Michele Lee, Ben Gazzara, Michael Gross

Plot: Three wives receive a letter from an erstwhile friend saying that she has run away with one of their husbands.

Notes: Academy Awards went to Mankiewicz as writer and director. Ann Sothern, one of the three wives in the original film, plays Loni Anderson's mother in the remake.

★ ★ ★

LITTLE WOMEN revisited—(left to right) Margaret O'Brien (Beth), Janet Leigh (Meg), June Allyson (Jo) and Elizabeth Taylor (Amy) gather around Mary Astor in the role of their beloved Marmee.

★ ★ ★

▶ LIFE BEGINS (1932)
Warners • James Flood

Loretta Young, Eric Linden, Preston Foster

▷ CHILD IS BORN, A (1939)
Warners • Lloyd Bacon

Geraldine Fitzgerald, Jeffrey Lynn, Gale Page

Plot: As life goes on in and around it, a child is born in a maternity ward.

Notes: Two young ladies in the supporting cast of A CHILD IS BORN went on to bigger things: Eve Arden and Nanette Fabray.

★ ★ ★

★   ★   ★   ★   ★   ★   ★

▶ LITTLE MEN (1935)★AOV★
Mascot • Phil Rosen

Ralph Morgan, Junior Durkin, Erin O'Brien-Moore

▷ LITTLE MEN (1940)★AOV★
RKO • Norman Z. McLeod

Jack Oakie, Kay Francis, James Lydon

Plot: An adolescent boy finds happiness at a school run by a professor and his wife.

Notes: LITTLE MEN is the sequel to LITTLE WOMEN (See below). Film buffs will remember James Lydon from the "Henry Aldrich" movies.

★   ★   ★

▶ LITTLE WOMEN (1933)★AOV★
MGM • George Cukor

Katharine Hepburn, Joan Bennett, Frances Dee, Jean Parker, Paul Lukas

▷ LITTLE WOMEN (1949)★AOV★
MGM • Mervyn Le Roy

June Allyson, Elizabeth Taylor, Janet Leigh, Peter Lawford, Margaret O'Brien

Plot: Four girls come of age in pre-Civil War New England.

Notes: A Movie Made for Television was released in 1978. Among its stars are Robert Young, Dorothy McGuire and Greer Garson. "Little Women" is the first and most popular book in Louisa May Alcott's trilogy of life in New England. "Little Men" and "Jo's Boys" never attained the popularity of their predecessor.

★   ★   ★

▶ LONG HOT SUMMER, THE (1958)★AOV★
TCF • Martin Ritt

Paul Newman, Orson Welles, Joanne Woodward, Lee Remick

▷ LONG HOT SUMMER, THE (1985)★AOV★
MMTV • Stuart Cooper

Don Johnson, Jason Robards, Ava Gardner, Judith Ivey

Plot: The members of a family are dominated by their strong willed patriarch until a wanderer comes to town and changes the course of their lives.

Notes: Both productions are adaptations of William Faulkner's novel of life in rural Mississippi.

★   ★   ★

▶ MADAME X (1937)
MGM • Sam Wood

Gladys George, John Beal, Warren William

▷ MADAME X (1965)★AOV★
Universal • David Lowell Rich

Lana Turner, John Forsythe, Ricardo Montalban

Plot: A woman, who has disappeared for several years after accidently killing someone, is defended by her son who does not recognize his mother.

Notes: A 1929 version of MADAME X stars Ruth Chatterton—it was directed by Lionel Barrymore who received an Academy Award nomination for his efforts. The old chestnut was also done as a silent on two occasions and as a Movie Made for Television in 1981 with Tuesday Weld, Len Cariou and Eleanor Parker.

★   ★   ★

▶ MAEDCHEN IN UNIFORM (1931)★AOV★
German • Leontine Sagon

Dorothea Wieck, Hertha Thiele

▷ MAEDCHEN IN UNIFORM (1958)
German • Geza von Radvanyi

Lilli Palmer, Romy Schneider

Plot: A girl in a boarding school has a lesbian relationship with her teacher—a truly shocking theme in 1931.

★   ★   ★

★   ★   ★   ★   ★   ★   ★

▶ MAYBE IT'S LOVE (1935)
Warners • William McGann
Gloria Stuart, Ross Alexander

▷ SATURDAY'S CHILDREN (1940)
Warners • Vincent Sherman
John Garfield, Anne Shirley

Plot: Two young people fall in love and face the vicissitudes of life together.

Notes: A silent version of the Maxwell Anderson play was filmed in 1929. Directed by Gregory La Cava, it stars the then popular Corinne Griffith and was released under the title of SATURDAY'S CHILDREN.

★   ★   ★

Anne Bancroft as Annie Sullivan and Patty Duke as blind-deaf-mute Helen Keller in THE MIRACLE WORKER. A grown-up Duke, in a switch of roles, plays teacher Sullivan to Melissa Gilbert's Helen Keller in the 1979 remake.

★   ★   ★

▶ MEN ARE NOT GODS (1936)
London/Korda • Walter Reisch
Miriam Hopkins, Rex Harrison, Gertrude Lawrence

▷ DOUBLE LIFE, A (1947) ⋆AOV⋆
Universal • George Cukor
Ronald Colman, Shelley Winters, Signe Hasso

Plot: An actor playing Othello nearly strangles his actress-wife while on stage.

Notes: In later years, Rex Harrison would star in the film version of ANNA AND THE KING OF SIAM and Gertrude Lawrence would play Anna in its Broadway incarnation, "The King and I."

★   ★   ★

▶ MIDSHIPMAN JACK (1933)
RKO • Christy Cabanne
Bruce Cabot, Betty Furness

▷ ANNAPOLIS SALUTE (1937)
RKO • Christy Cabanne
James Ellison, Marsha Hunt, Van Heflin

Plot: A young man grows to maturity during his years at the U.S. Naval Academy in Annapolis.

Notes: Over a half century later, Betty Furness is still to be seen on the NBC television network.

★   ★   ★

☆   ☆   ☆   ☆   ☆   ☆   ☆

▶ MIRACLE WORKER, THE (1962)★AOV★
United Artists • Arthur Penn

Anne Bancroft, Patty Duke

▷ MIRACLE WORKER, THE (1979)★AOV★
MMTV • Paul Aaron

Patty Duke, Melissa Gilbert

Plot: Annie Sullivan teaches blind deaf mute Helen Keller to become a productive citizen.

Notes: Both Anne Bancroft and Patty Duke won Oscars in 1962. The latter plays Helen Keller in the first film—in the second, she portrays Annie Sullivan, Keller's teacher.

★   ★   ★

▶ MORNING GLORY (1933)★AOV★
RKO • Lowell Sherman

Katharine Hepburn, Adolphe Menjou, Douglas Fairbanks Jr.

▷ STAGE STRUCK (1957)★AOV★
RKO • Sidney Lumet

Henry Fonda, Christopher Plummer, Susan Strasberg

Plot: A young actress comes to New York to seek fame and fortune on Broadway.

Notes: Katharine Hepburn won her first Oscar for her performance as the stage struck would-be star.

★   ★   ★

▶ MR. LUCKY (1943)★AOV★
RKO • H. C. Potter

Cary Grant, Laraine Day, Charles Bickford

▷ GAMBLING HOUSE (1950)
RKO • Ted Tetzlaff

Victor Mature, Terry Moore, William Bendix

Plot: The reformation of a gambler, through love, from shady character to responsible citizen.

Notes: MR. LUCKY inspired a television series of the same name. Starring John Vivyan, it ran on CBS from 1959 through 1960.

★   ★   ★

▶ NANA (1934)
Samuel Goldwyn • Dorothy Arzner

Anna Sten, Lionel Atwill

▷ NANA (1980)★AOV★
Italian • Don Walman

Katya Berger, Jean-Pierre Aumont

Plot: A high living street walker from Paris becomes involved in a tragic love affair.

Notes: "Nana" was written by the great novelist Emile Zola. The 1934 film was to have made a great star of Anna Sten. It didn't. A French version starring Charles Boyer and Martine Carol was released in 1957.

★   ★   ★

▶ NATIVE SON (1950)★AOV★
Argentine • Pierre Chenal

Richard Wright, Jean Wallace

▷ NATIVE SON (1986)★AOV★
Cinecom • Jerrold Freedman

Carroll Baker, Geraldine Page, Victor Love, Oprah Winfrey

Plot: A black man's life takes a tragic turn when he unintentionally kills a white woman.

Notes: Richard Wright, who stars in the 1950 production, wrote the novel upon which the films are based. Jean Wallace was married to actors Franchot Tone and Cornel Wilde.

★   ★   ★

☆   ☆   ☆   ☆   ☆   ☆   ☆

▶ NO MAN OF HER OWN (1949)
Paramount • Mitchell Leisen
Barbara Stanwyck, Jane Cowl, John Lund

▷ I MARRIED A SHADOW (1982)★AOV★
French • Robin Davis
Nathalie Baye, Francis Huster

Plot: After a train wreck, a pregnant woman assumes the identity of a dead passenger's wife.

Notes: Though making very few films, Jane Cowl was a celebrated star of the Broadway stage.

★   ★   ★

Victorian England—Laurence Harvey exiting a cab for a scene from OF HUMAN BONDAGE. This was the third production of the Somerset Maugham novel.

★   ★   ★

▶ ODD MAN OUT (1947)★AOV★
GDF/Two Cities • Carol Reed
James Mason, Robert Newton, Kathleen Ryan

▷ LOST MAN, THE (1969)
Universal • Robert Alan Arthur
Sidney Poitier, Joanna Shimkus

Plot: A man hunted by the police is helped and hindered by the various people he meets.

Notes: Joanna Shimkus is Mrs. Sidney Poitier in private life. ODD MAN OUT takes place during the Irish Rebellion while THE LOST MAN, updated to more modern times, revolves around the civil rights movement of the nineteen sixties.

★   ★   ★

▶ OF HUMAN BONDAGE (1934)★AOV★
RKO • John Cromwell
Bette Davis, Leslie Howard, Frances Dee

▷ OF HUMAN BONDAGE (1946)
Warners • Edmund Goulding
Paul Henreid, Eleanor Parker, Alexis Smith

Plot: A well-to-do English doctor becomes infatuated with a slatternly waitress.

Notes: The 1934 version of the Somerset Maugham novel is the definitive film with the Davis performance one that is still talked about over a half-century later. A third production released by MGM in 1964★AOV★ stars Laurence Harvey and Kim Novak.

★   ★   ★

☆   ☆   ☆   ☆   ☆   ☆   ☆

▶ OF MICE AND MEN (1939)
Hal Roach • Lewis Milestone

Burgess Meredith, Betty Field, Lon Chaney Jr.

▷ OF MICE AND MEN (1981)★AOV★
MMTV • Reza Badiyi

Robert Blake, Randy Quaid, Lew Ayres, Cassie Yates

Plot: A migrant farm worker watches over his mentally retarded co-worker.

Notes: Television aficionados will recognize producer-star Robert Blake from "Baretta." To film his own version of the John Steinbeck novel was a dream come true for the veteran actor.

★ ★ ★

▶ OLD ACQUAINTANCE (1943)
Warners • Vincent Sherman

Bette Davis, Miriam Hopkins, Gig Young

▷ RICH AND FAMOUS (1981)★AOV★
MGM • George Cukor

Candice Bergen, David Selby, Jaqueline Bisset

Plot: Two women maintain a long time friendship despite a personal and professional rivalry.

Notes: Bette Davis and Miriam Hopkins loathed each other! This was not the usual Hollywood "feud." They did, however, realize their box-office clout and co-starred in this film and in THE OLD MAID. George Cukor was eighty-one when he directed RICH AND FAMOUS.

★ ★ ★

▶ PANAMA FLO (1932)
RKO • Ralph Murphy

Charles Bickford, Helen Twelvetrees

▷ PANAMA LADY (1939)
RKO • Jack Hively

Lucille Ball, Allan Lane, Steffi Duna

Plot: A cabaret girl is marooned in the tropics and meets up with an oil prospector and a gun-running aviator.

★ ★ ★

▶ PORT OF SEVEN SEAS (1938)
MGM • James Whale

Wallace Beery, Frank Morgan, Maureen O'Sullivan

▷ FANNY (1961)★AOV★
Warners • Joshua Logan

Charles Boyer, Leslie Caron, Maurice Chevalier

Plot: Life and love on the Marseille waterfront as a young girl falls in love with a handsome sailor.

Notes: The Broadway musical "Fanny," like both films, is based upon the original story by the French writer Marcel Pagnol. An earlier cinema version was released in 1932★AOV★.

★ ★ ★

▶ RAIN (1932)★AOV★
United Artists • Lewis Milestone

Joan Crawford, Walter Huston, William Gargan

▷ MISS SADIE THOMPSON (1953)★AOV★
Columbia • Curtis Bernhardt

Rita Hayworth, José Ferrer, Aldo Ray

Plot: A "fallen woman" is lusted after by a "god fearing man."

Notes: SADIE THOMPSON (1928), starring Gloria Swanson and Lionel Barrymore, is the silent version of the Somerset Maugham novel. Raoul Walsh, who co-stars in the film, was also its director. In the 1953 version, Sadie's image is a softer one—the script portrays her as a stranded showgirl.

★ ★ ★

▶ RAINS CAME, THE (1939)
TCF • Clarence Brown
Myrna Loy, George Brent, Tyrone Power

▷ RAINS OF RANCHIPUR, THE (1955)
TCF • Jean Negulesco
Lana Turner, Richard Burton, Fred MacMurray

Plot: The wife of an Englishman falls in love with a Hindu doctor in the wake of a devastating earthquake.

Notes: The special effects (flood and earthquake scenes) of the 1939 production won an Academy Award.

★ ★ ★

Bette Davis and Gig Young in a close-up from OLD ACQUAINTANCE. The actor, whose real name was Byron Barr, took his professional name from his character in THE GAY SISTERS, a 1942 Warner Brothers release.

★ ★ ★

▶ RASHOMON (1951) ★AOV★
Japanese • Akiro Kurosawa
Toshiro Mifone, Machiko Kyo, Masayuki Mori

▷ OUTRAGE, THE (1964)
MGM • Martin Ritt
Paul Newman, Edward G. Robinson, Laurence Harvey

Plot: Four people have differing views of a violent crime.

Notes: In an interesting change of genre, RASHOMON, which takes place in Japan, becomes THE OUTRAGE, a western.

★ ★ ★

☆ ☆ ☆ ☆ ☆ ☆ ☆

▶ RAZOR'S EDGE, THE (1946)★AOV★
TCF • Edmund Goulding

Tyrone Power, Gene Tierney, Anne Baxter, John
Payne, Herbert Marshall

▷ RAZOR'S EDGE, THE (1984)★AOV★
Columbia • John Byrum

Bill Murray, Denholm Elliott, Catherine Hicks,
Theresa Russell

Plot: A young American survives the first World War and begins to question the meaning of life.

Notes: Anne Baxter won a Best Supporting Actress award for her performance in the 1946
production. Both films are based upon a novel by the prolific Somerset Maugham.

★ ★ ★

▶ RED PONY, THE (1949)★AOV★
Republic • Lewis Milestone

Myrna Loy, Robert Mitchum, Peter Miles, Louis
Calhern

▷ RED PONY, THE (1973)
MMTV • Robert Totten

Henry Fonda, Maureen O'Hara, Ben Johnson

Plot: A farmer's son has a troubled relationship with his father and seeks solace in his pet pony.

Notes: The films are based upon a best selling novella by John Steinbeck. Interestingly enough,
Henry Fonda had one of his greatest roles in another Steinbeck film, THE GRAPES OF WRATH.

★ ★ ★

▶ ROMAN HOLIDAY (1953)★AOV★
Paramount • William Wyler

Audrey Hepburn, Gregory Peck, Eddie Albert

▷ ROMAN HOLIDAY (1987)
MMTV • Noel Nosseck

Catherine Oxenberg, Tom Conti, Ed Begley Jr.

Plot: A princess, running away from her palace duties, has a brief romance with a newspaper man.

Notes: Audrey Hepburn won an Academy Award for her ROMAN HOLIDAY role. Eddie Albert and
the film were also Oscar nominated but lost to Frank Sinatra and FROM HERE TO ETERNITY.

★ ★ ★

▶ SECRET GARDEN, THE (1949)
MGM • Fred M. Wilcox

Margaret O'Brien, Herbert Marshall, Dean
Stockwell

▷ SECRET GARDEN, THE (1987)
MMTV • Alan Grint

Gennie James, Derek Jacobi

Plot: A young girl, coming to live with her uncle, changes the lives of those around her.

Notes: Margaret O'Brien, child star of the nineteen forties, began her career in 1941 at the age of
four. It has been said, and never denied, that she was able to cry on demand.

★ ★ ★

▶ SENTIMENTAL JOURNEY (1946)
TCF • Walter Lang
Maureen O'Hara, John Payne, William Bendix,
Connie Marshall

▷ GIFT OF LOVE (1958)
TCF • Jean Negulesco
Lauren Bacall, Robert Stack, Evelyn Rudie

Plot: A dying woman meets a little girl whom she hopes will be a comfort to her husband when she is
gone.

Notes: In 1984, a loosely based version of the above was a Movie Made for Television called
SENTIMENTAL JOURNEY. Directed by James Goldstone, it stars Jaclyn Smith and David Dukes.

★ ★ ★

▶ SMILIN' THROUGH (1932)
MGM • Sidney Franklin
Norma Shearer, Leslie Howard, Fredric March

▷ SMILIN' THROUGH (1941)★AOV★
MGM • Frank Borzage
Jeanette MacDonald, Gene Raymond, Brian Aherne

Plot: An elderly man, whose fiancee had been slain on their wedding day, raises a niece who falls in love with the son of the murderer.

Notes: Although many fans thought that if Jeanette MacDonald and Nelson Eddy were not married, they should be, the movie diva was married to Gene Raymond. SMILIN' THROUGH was the only film they made together.

★ ★ ★

Aldo Ray's temperature soars when confronted by Rita Hayworth as Somerset Maugham's questionable heroine in MISS SADIE THOMPSON.

★ ★ ★

▶ SO BIG (1932)
Warners • William Wellman
Barbara Stanwyck, George Brent, Bette Davis

▷ SO BIG (1953)
Warners • Robert Wise
Jane Wyman, Sterling Hayden, Nancy Olson

Plot: A farmer's widow, a schoolteacher as a young girl, raises her only son to be a self-reliant and productive citizen.

Notes: The Edna Ferber novel was first filmed as a silent in 1925 starring Colleen Moore.

★ ★ ★

▶ SPLENDOR IN THE GRASS (1961)★AOV★
Warners • Elia Kazan
Natalie Wood, Warren Beatty, Pat Hingle

▷ SPLENDOR IN THE GRASS (1981)
MMTV • Richard Sarafian
Melissa Gilbert, Eva Marie Saint, Ned Beatty

Plot: Two young people find love in a small Kansas town during the late nineteen twenties.

Notes: The earlier production marked the film debut of Warren Beatty. No relation to Ned Beatty, he is the brother of Shirley MacLaine.

★ ★ ★

▶ STOLEN LIFE, A (1939)
Paramount • Paul Czinner
Elizabeth Bergner, Michael Redgrave

▷ STOLEN LIFE, A (1946)
Warners • Curtis Bernhardt
Bette Davis, Glenn Ford, Dane Clark

Plot: A woman exchanges identities with her dead twin.

Notes: The locale of the first film is France, the setting of the second is a New England town. Bette Davis is listed as a producer on the later version.

★ ★ ★

▶ STORY OF TEMPLE DRAKE, THE (1933)
Paramount • Stephen Roberts
Miriam Hopkins, William Gargan, Jack La Rue

▷ SANCTUARY (1960)
TCF • Tony Richardson
Lee Remick, Yves Montand, Bradford Dillman

Plot: Degradation, rape and murder are the ingredients in this nineteen twenties tale of a southern belle kidnapped from her home.

Notes: The films are adaptations of "Sanctuary," William Faulkner's best-selling novel. The producer of the 1960 version is Richard Zanuck, son of TCF head Darryl.

★ ★ ★

▶ STREETCAR NAMED DESIRE, A (1951)★AOV★
Feldman/Kazan • Elia Kazan
Vivien Leigh, Marlon Brando, Karl Malden, Kim Hunter

▷ STREETCAR NAMED DESIRE, A (1984)
MMTV • John Erman
Ann-Margret, Randy Quaid, Treat Williams

Plot: A repressed Southern woman comes to stay with her younger sister and is both repelled and attracted by the latter's brutish husband.

Notes: Malden and the Misses Leigh and Hunter won Oscars for their performances in the 1951 film. The screen play of that production was written by Tennessee Williams, who wrote the Broadway success.

★ ★ ★

▶ SUN ALSO RISES, THE (1957)
TCF • Henry King
Tyrone Power, Ava Gardner, Errol Flynn, Mel Ferrer

▷ SUN ALSO RISES, THE (1984)
MMTV • James Goldstone
Jane Seymour, Hart Bochner, Robert Carradine

Plot: A veteran of World War I becomes part of an expatriate group wandering around Europe during the nineteen twenties.

Notes: Both films are based upon the novel by Ernest Hemingway. Featured in the 1957 film is Robert Evans, who some decades later, became the head of Paramount Pictures.

★ ★ ★

▶ SWEEPINGS (1933)
RKO • John Cromwell
Lionel Barrymore, Eric Linden, William Gargan

▷ THREE SONS (1939)
RKO • Jack Hively
Edward Ellis, Kent Taylor, William Gargan

Plot: A self-made man builds a large store and wants his children to carry on in the business.

Notes: William Gargan plays the man's son in the first film and the man's brother in the remake.

★ ★ ★

⋆　　⋆　　⋆　　⋆　　⋆　　⋆　　⋆

▶ THERE'S ALWAYS TOMORROW (1934)
Universal • Edward Sloman

Frank Morgan, Binnie Barnes, Lois Wilson

▷ THERE'S ALWAYS TOMORROW (1956)
Universal • Douglas Sirk

Barbara Stanwyck, Fred MacMurray, Joan Bennett

Plot: A man, taken for granted by his family, finds comfort in the arms of another woman.

Notes: Frank Morgan divided his time between radio and movies. He is best remembered in the title role of THE WIZARD OF OZ.

★　★　★

▶ THESE THREE (1936)⋆AOV⋆
Samuel Goldwyn • William Wyler

Merle Oberon, Joel McCrea, Miriam Hopkins, Bonita Granville

▷ CHILDREN'S HOUR, THE (1961)
United Artists • William Wyler

Shirley MacLaine, Audrey Hepburn, James Garner, Miriam Hopkins

Plot: A vicious young girl accuses two teachers in the boarding school she attends of scandalous behavior.

Notes: When Wyler directed the 1936 version of Lillian Hellman's stage hit, he couldn't use the original theme of suspected lesbianism. In the remake he could and did. Miriam Hopkins, star of the first film, plays a featured role in the second.

★　★　★

▶ THREE COINS IN THE FOUNTAIN (1954)⋆AOV⋆
TCF • Jean Negulesco

Clifton Webb, Dorothy McGuire, Louis Jourdan, Rossano Brazzi

▷ PLEASURE SEEKERS, THE (1964)
TCF • Jean Negulesco

Ann-Margret, Carole Lynley, Gene Tierney, Brian Keith

Plot: Three American girls go abroad in search of love and romance.

Notes: The locale of the 1954 film is Rome. For his second go-round, director Negulesco went on location to Madrid. The title song of the 1954 production, was recorded by the Four Aces, a popular singing group of the day. Sales of the record were in the millions which helped win the song an Oscar.

★　★　★

▶ THREE ON A MATCH (1932)
Warners • Mervyn Le Roy

Bette Davis, Joan Blondell, Ann Dvorak

▷ BROADWAY MUSKETEERS (1935)
Warners • John Farrow

Ann Sheridan, Marie Wilson, Margaret Lindsay, John Litel

Plot: Three childhood friends meet again after many years with melodramatic results.

Notes: Ann Sheridan was known as "The Oomph Girl" during the early part of her career.

★　★　★

▶ TOM BROWN OF CULVER (1932)
Universal • William Wyler

Tom Brown, H. B. Warner

▷ SPIRIT OF CULVER (1939)
Universal • Joseph Santley

Jackie Cooper, Henry Hull

Plot: A boy goes to military school on scholarship because his father was a war hero.

Notes: Playing a bit role in the 1932 version is future super star Tyrone Power.

★　★　★

☆   ☆   ☆   ☆   ☆   ☆   ☆

▶ TOM BROWN'S SCHOOL DAYS (1940)★ÀOV★
RKO • Robert Stevenson

James Lydon, Cedric Hardwicke, Freddie
Bartholomew

▷ TOM BROWN'S SCHOOL DAYS (1951)
British/Renown • Gordon Parry

Robert Newton, Diana Wynyard, John Howard
Davies

Plot: Tom Brown goes to a boy's school in Victorian England.

★ ★ ★

▶ TREE GROWS IN BROOKLYN, A (1945)★AOV★
TCF • Elia Kazan

Dorothy McGuire, Peggy Ann Garner, James Dunn,
Joan Blondell

▷ TREE GROWS IN BROOKLYN, A (1974)
MMTV • Joseph Hardy

Cliff Robertson, Diane Baker, James Olson

Plot: A family struggles to make ends meet in turn-of-the-century Brooklyn.

Notes: James Dunn won Best Supporting Actor award for playing a loveable but not very
dependable head of family while thirteen year old Peggy Ann Garner won a special Oscar for her
performance as his daughter, Francie, in the same production.

★ ★ ★

▶ TRESPASSER, THE (1929)
United Artists • Edmund Goulding

Gloria Swanson, Robert Ames, Kay Hammond

▷ THAT CERTAIN WOMAN (1937)
Warners • Edmund Goulding

Bette Davis, Henry Fonda, Ian Hunter

Plot: A gangster's widow, going straight, finds true love.

Notes: The 1929 production was Gloria Swanson's first talking film— she also had a hand in
writing the screenplay.

★ ★ ★

▶ UNDER MY SKIN (1949)
TCF • Jean Negulesco

John Garfield, Luther Adler, Micheline Presle

▷ MY OLD MAN (1979)★AOV★
MMTV • John Erman

Eileen Brennan, Warren Oates, Kristy McNichol

Plot: A crooked jockey tries to reform for the sake of his child.

Notes: The films are based upon a short story by Ernest Hemingway.

★ ★ ★

▶ YANK AT OXFORD, A (1938)
MGM • Jack Conway

Robert Taylor, Vivien Leigh, Maureen O'Sullivan

▷ OXFORD BLUES (1984)★AOV★
Winkast/Baltic Industrial • Robert Boris

Rob Lowe, Ally Sheedy

Plot: A cocky American goes to Oxford and gets into all sorts of scrapes.

Notes: A YANK AT OXFORD was shot on location in England by a combined Anglo-American MGM
team. A few more American financed films were made in England before the start of World War II.

★ ★ ★

★   ★   ★   ★   ★   ★   ★

CHAPTER TWO

I LOVE YOU AGAIN: REDOS OF SPECIAL LOVE STORIES

"Love is a many splendored thing." The name of a song, the title of a film. For some, an impossible dream, for others more fortunate, a fact of life.

Love is a strong emotion for us humans because each of us has experienced it in some way or another. Beautiful, tawdry, tender, simple, difficult, obsessive, right or wrong—all of those adjectives apply—love means different things to different people—it takes on many forms and colorations, flourishing or withering in various climes and locations.

Hollywood has made and remade several love stories with varying degrees of success throughout the years. Often these tales of unrequited love were taken from the pens of popular novelists of the day such as Theodore Dreiser, Leo Tolstoy, Fanny Hurst, Alexandre Dumas, the Brontes (Emily and Charlotte) and Ernest Hemingway. For those of a younger generation, in these days of television, it may be difficult to comprehend the impact of writers, but before the small screen held sway, there was lots of reading going on.

And movie going. Among the most popular film fare were the love stories, the ones for which men were dragged into theaters. The movie moguls, as will be emphasized in several instances throughout this book, were not fools—they knew it was "the little woman" who was the ticket buyer in the family—and what was her preference? Good old fashioned love stories in every shape and form—and she didn't care how many times one story was refilmed.

To paraphrase an old popular ballad, "Love, Its Magic Spell is Everywhere"—this is so in the movies. According to Hollywood, a LOVE AFFAIR can take place aboard a trans-Atlantic liner. Love can also be found in a tawdry German night club called THE BLUE ANGEL, as a BRIEF ENCOUNTER on a London-bound commuter train, in the Yorkshire moors surrounding WUTHERING HEIGHTS and against the backdrop of WATERLOO BRIDGE.

Love is indeed a many splendored thing.

★   ★   ★   ★   ★   ★   ★

▶ AMERICAN TRAGEDY, AN (1931)
Paramount • Josef von Sternberg
Phillips Holmes, Sylvia Sidney, Frances Dee

▷ PLACE IN THE SUN, A (1951)★AOV★
Paramount • George Stevens
Montgomery Clift, Elizabeth Taylor, Shelley
Winters

Plot: A young man murders his pregnant girlfriend when he has a chance to marry into a wealthy family.

Notes: Both Montgomery Clift and Shelley Winters were Oscar-nominated for their performances in the 1951 version of the novel by Theodore Dreiser. Neither won.

★   ★   ★

▶ BACK STREET (1932)
Universal • John M. Stahl
Irene Dunne, John Boles

▷ BACK STREET (1941)
Universal • Robert Stevenson
Margaret Sullavan, Charles Boyer, Richard Carlson

Plot: A woman has a long-lasting affair with a married man.

Notes: A third version of the Fanny Hurst tear-jerker was released in 1961★AOV★. It stars Susan Hayward, John Gavin and Vera Miles.

★   ★   ★

▶ BARRETTS OF WIMPOLE STREET, THE (1934)
MGM • Sidney Franklin
Norma Shearer, Fredric March, Charles Laughton

▷ BARRETTS OF WIMPOLE STREET, THE (1956)
MGM • Sidney Franklin
Jennifer Jones, Bill Travers, John Gielgud

Plot: Elizabeth Barrett plans to marry fellow poet Robert Browning against the wishes of her father.

Notes: Elizabeth Browning is most famous for the poem which begins "How do I love thee, Let me count the ways..."

★   ★   ★

▶ BLUE ANGEL, THE (1930)★AOV★
Germany/UFA • Josef von Sternberg
Emil Jannings, Marlene Dietrich

▷ BLUE ANGEL, THE (1959)
TCF • Edward Dmytryk
Curt Jurgens, Mai Britt, Theodore Bikel

Plot: A professor becomes infatuated with a singer, marries her, is humiliated by her and goes back to his classroom to die.

Notes: The 1930 version of THE BLUE ANGEL made Marlene Dietrich an international star. The remake did nothing for Mai Britt who played the Dietrich role almost thirty years later. Britt was once married to entertainer Sammy Davis Jr.

★   ★   ★

★   ★   ★   ★   ★   ★   ★

▶ BRIEF ENCOUNTER (1945)★AOV★   ▷ BRIEF ENCOUNTER (1975)
Cineguild • David Lean   MMTV • Alan Bridge
Celia Johnson, Trevor Howard, Stanley Holloway   Richard Burton, Sophia Loren

Plot: A suburban wife has a tender love affair with the doctor she has met on the London commuter train.

Notes: BRIEF ENCOUNTER was written by Noel Coward. Stanley Holloway went on to play Eliza Doolitle's father in both the stage and screen versions of MY FAIR LADY.

Marlene Dietrich performing at THE BLUE ANGEL. The film of the same name made Dietrich an international star and brought her to America.

★ ★ ★

▶ CAMILLE (1936)★AOV★   ▷ CAMILLE (1984)
MGM • George Cukor   MMTV • Desmond Davis
Greta Garbo, Robert Taylor, Lionel Barrymore   Greta Scacchi, Colin Firth, John Gielgud, Ben Kingsley

Plot: A French courtesan falls in love with a well-born man but soon realizes that she must give him up.

Notes: Three silent versions of the Dumas novel were filmed—in 1915 with Clara Kimball Young, in 1917 with Theda Bara and in 1921 with Nazimova and Rudolph Valentino. Greta Garbo was Oscar-nominated for CAMILLE but lost. Just before completion of the 1936 film, its thirty-seven year old producer Irving Thalberg, MGM head of production, died.

★ ★ ★

▶ CONSTANT NYMPH, THE (1933)
British/ Gaumont • Basil Dean
Brian Aherne, Victoria Hopper

▷ CONSTANT NYMPH, THE (1943)
Warners • Edmund Goulding
Charles Boyer, Joan Fontaine, Alexis Smith, Charles Coburn

Plot: A composer becomes infatuated with a sickly young girl and leaves his wife for her.

Notes: A silent version of THE CONSTANT NYMPH was filmed in 1928. Brian Aherne, star of the 1933 film and Joan Fontaine, star of the later one, were married during the nineteen forties.

★ ★ ★

Ambulance driver Gary Cooper (left) is introduced to nurse Helen Hayes (extreme right) by Adolphe Menjou as an extra looks on in FAREWELL TO ARMS.

★ ★ ★

▶ CYRANO de BERGERAC (1950)⋆AOV⋆
United Artists • Michael Gordon
José Ferrer, Mala Powers, William Prince

▷ ROXANNE (1987)
Columbia • Fred Schepisi
Steve Martin, Darryl Hannah, Shelley Duval, Rick Rossivich

Plot: A sensitive long-nosed man uses his writings to court a lovely woman for another man.

Notes: José Ferrer won an Oscar for his "Cyrano." Steve Martin's updated version is set in an American ski town.

★ ★ ★

▶ FAREWELL TO ARMS, A (1932)⋆AOV⋆
Paramount • Frank Borzage
Gary Cooper, Helen Hayes, Adolphe Menjou

▷ FAREWELL TO ARMS, A (1957)⋆AOV⋆
TCF/Selznick • Charles Vidor
Rock Hudson, Jennifer Jones, Vittorio de Sica

Plot: During World War I, a wounded American ambulance driver falls in love with his nurse.

Notes: Jennifer Jones, star of the 1957 version, was married to its producer David Selznick. FORCE OF ARMS is a World War II updating of the Hemingway novel. Directed by Michael Curtiz, the 1951 film stars William Holden and Nancy Olson.

★ ★ ★

▶ JANE EYRE (1943)★AOV★
TCF • Robert Stevenson
Joan Fontaine, Orson Welles

▷ JANE EYRE (1971)
MMTV • Delbert Mann
George C. Scott, Susannah York

Plot: An orphan, grown up, becomes a governess in a mysterious house.

Notes: During the nineteen thirties and forties, several studios, called "Poverty Row" production companies, made movies on the cheap. One, Monogram by name, produced a version of the Emily Bronte novel in 1934★AOV★ starring Virginia Bruce. A trio of famous child stars appear in the 1943 film: Peggy Ann Garner, Margaret O'Brien and Elizabeth Taylor.

★ ★ ★

A quarter of a century later, when David Selznick produced the remake of A FAREWELL TO ARMS, he cast his wife, Jennifer Jones, in the Helen Hayes role and Rock Hudson (center) in the one played by Gary Cooper.

★ ★ ★

▶ LADY TO LOVE, A (1930)

MGM • Victor Seastrom
Edward G. Robinson, Vilma Banky, Robert Ames

▷ THEY KNEW WHAT THEY WANTED
(1940)★AOV★
RKO • Garson Kanin
Charles Laughton, Carole Lombard, William Gargan

Plot: An elderly vineyard owner proposes to a young waitress by mail, sending her a picture of his handsome foreman.

Notes: This unique love story was the basis of the Broadway hit, "The Most Happy Fella."

★ ★ ★

▶ LOVE AFFAIR (1939)★AOV★
RKO • Leo McCarey
Charles Boyer, Irene Dunne

▷ AFFAIR TO REMEMBER, AN (1957)
TCF • Leo McCarey
Cary Grant, Deborah Kerr

Plot: A shipboard romance almost ends through a misunderstanding, but all live happily ever after.

Notes: LOVE AFFAIR and Irene Dunne were Oscar nominated. Both "Wishing," the song played in the first film and the title tune of the remake, were also nominated. None of the above won.

★ ★ ★

▶ MAGNIFICENT OBSESSION (1935)
Universal • John M. Stahl
Irene Dunne, Robert Taylor, Ralph Morgan

▷ MAGNIFICENT OBSESSION (1954)⋆AOV⋆
Universal • Douglas Sirk
Jane Wyman, Rock Hudson, Agnes Moorehead

Plot: A reckless playboy, responsible for accidently blinding a woman and killing her husband, becomes a surgeon and cures her.

Notes: Jane Wyman was Oscar nominated for her 1954 performance. MAGNIFICENT OBSESSION was the second film within a span of two years in which Wyman played an Irene Dunne role—the first was LET'S DO IT AGAIN (1953), a remake of THE AWFUL TRUTH (see Chapter Three).

★ ★ ★

Man Meets Woman, Man Loses Woman, Man Gets Woman— Deborah Kerr and Cary Grant in AN AFFAIR TO REMEMBER.

★ ★ ★

▶ MAYERLING (1936)⋆AOV⋆
French/Nero Film • Anatole Litvak
Charles Boyer, Danielle Darrieux

▷ MAYERLING (1968)
Corona/Winchester • Terence Young
Omar Shariff, Catherine Deneuve, Ava Gardner

Plot: In 1888, the heir to the Hapsburg Empire and his mistress commit suicide in a country house.

Notes: Both films, based on fact, were shot in France.

★ ★ ★

▶ ONE ROMANTIC NIGHT (1930)
United Artists • Paul Stein
Lillian Gish, Conrad Nagel, Rod La Rocque

▷ SWAN, THE (1956)
MGM • Charles Vidor
Grace Kelly, Alec Guinness, Louis Jourdan

Plot: A Princess is betrothed to a foreign Crown Prince but is really in love with the tutor of her brothers.

Notes: The 1956 movie was released just as Grace Kelly became Princess Grace of Monaco. A silent version of the story was filmed in 1925.

★ ★ ★

▶ ONE WAY PASSAGE (1932)
Warners • Tay Garnett

William Powell, Kay Francis, Aline MacMahon

▷ `TIL WE MEET AGAIN (1940)
Warners • Edmund Goulding

Merle Oberon, George Brent, Pat O'Brien,
Geraldine Fitzgerald

Plot: Aboard an ocean liner, a dying woman falls in love with a con-man on his way to prison.

Notes: Marlene Dietrich had originally been slated to play the doomed woman in the 1940 production.

★ ★ ★

William Powell and Kay Francis share some wine in ONE WAY PASSAGE. No one who has seen the film can forget its shatteed glass ending.

★ ★ ★

▶ RESURRECTION (1931)
Universal • Edwin Carewe

John Boles, Lupe Velez

▷ WE LIVE AGAIN (1934)
Samuel Goldwyn • Rouben Mamoulian

Fredric March, Anna Sten

Plot: After being seduced by an Imperial Russian prince, a peasant girl gives birth to his child.

Notes: The novel "Resurrection" was written by the Russian novelist Leo Tolstoy. The screen play of the 1934 film was the work of Preston Sturgis and Maxwell Anderson.

★ ★ ★

▶ SHOPWORN ANGEL (1938)
MGM • H. C. Potter

Margaret Sullavan, James Stewart, Walter Pidgeon

▷ THAT KIND OF WOMAN (1959)
Paramount • Sidney Lumet

Sophia Loren, Tab Hunter, George Sanders,
Keenan Wynn

Plot: A showgirl meets a naive soldier and leaves her sophisticated lover for him.

Notes: SHOPWORN ANGEL was filmed in 1928 starring Nancy Carroll, Gary Cooper and Paul Lukas. This film, though officially a silent, had some dialogue tacked on to its end.

★ ★ ★

▶ THIS LOVE OF OURS (1945)
Universal-International • William Dieterle
Merle Oberon, Charles Korvin, Claude Rains

▷ NEVER SAY GOODBYE (1955)
Universal-International • Jerry Hopper
Rock Hudson, George Sanders, Cornell Borchers

Plot: A doctor leaves his wife but returns to her years later.

Notes: Clint Eastwood has a small part in NEVER SAY GOODBYE. He plays Rock Hudson's lab assistant.

★ ★ ★

David Niven and Merle Oberon, man and wife in WUTHERING HEIGHTS. Geraldine Fitzgerald is at rear right. Can Heathcliff (Laurence Olivier), Merle's true love, be far away?

★ ★ ★

▶ WATERLOO BRIDGE (1940)★AOV★
MGM • Mervyn Le Roy
Vivien Leigh, Robert Taylor

▷ GABY (1956)
MGM • Curtis Bernhardt
Leslie Caron, John Kerr

Plot: When an army officer is reported dead, his heartbroken sweetheart sinks into prostitution.

Notes: WATERLOO BRIDGE, adapted from a play by Robert E. Sherwood, was first filmed in 1931. This early production stars Mae Clarke, Kent Douglass and features an up and coming actress named Bette Davis.

★ ★ ★

▶ WHEN TOMORROW COMES (1939)
Universal • John M. Stahl

Charles Boyer, Irene Dunne, Barbara O'Neil

▷ INTERLUDE (1957)
Universal-International • Douglas Sirk

June Allyson, Rossano Brazzi, Françoise Rosay,
Jane Wyatt

Plot: A young woman falls in love with an already married composer whose wife is on the brink of insanity.

Notes: Jane Wyatt, featured in the 1957 film, is better known for her role as Robert Young's wife on television's "Father Knows Best." The James M. Cain story was remade in 1968 starring German actor Oscar Werner.

★ ★ ★

▶ WUTHERING HEIGHTS (1939)★AOV★
Samuel Goldwyn • William Wyler

Laurence Olivier, Merle Oberon, David Niven,
Geraldine Fitzgerald

▷ WUTHERING HEIGHTS (1970)★AOV★
AIP • Robert Fuest

Anna Calder-Marshall, Timothy Dalton, Pamela
Brown

Plot: Two young people engage in a love affair that is doomed from the start by conventions in pre-Victorian England.

Notes: The film, director Wyler, musical director Alfred Newman and actors Olivier and Fitzgerald were all Oscar-nominated in 1939. They were overshadowed by GONE WITH THE WIND, which swept most of that year's awards. A Spanish-language version of the Emily Bronte classic, directed by Luis Buñuel, was released in 1954.

★ ★ ★

CHAPTER THREE

LAUGHTER TIMES TWO: COMEDY REMADE

The fledgling movie makers of the silent film era realized that one of the most precious gifts we are given in life is the ability to laugh. They also realized the fact that only a few are given an even more precious gift, the ability to *make* people laugh. It was therefore the task of these film pioneers to match properties with performers and come up on the winning side of the ledger. The vision of this group of men in tandem with the talent of the personalities they discovered resulted in some of the most innovative comedic footage ever shot. Without uttering even so much as one syllable, the genius of Chaplin, Keaton, Harold Lloyd and the Keystone Kops gave movie goers who flocked to picture palaces plenty of chuckles and a fair amount of belly laughs. Watching the antics of these loveable clowns made people forget what ailed them and in the process, they had a rip roaring good time.

Movie moguls and producers of the early talkies also acknowledged the importance of laughter and strove to give the public as much of it as they could during the dark days of the Depression and the war years which followed. Some of the most enduring films in Hollywood history were comedies made during the course of this "golden era," several of them forming a delightful sub-genre which came to be known as the "screwball" variety. Many of the screen's most beloved stars gave some of their most endearing performances in these memorable productions: the impish duo of Cary Grant and Irene Dunne in THE AWFUL TRUTH, the deliciously zany Carole Lombard cavorting with Fredric March in NOTHING SACRED, the classically comic Claudette Colbert and Clark Gable, both winning Oscars for IT HAPPENED ONE NIGHT.

Appropriately, all three films were remade in one form or another. As have the other films contained in this chapter. Each a part of the comedy genre, together they are films which, when shown for the first time, made the nation laugh, often at itself. Seen again and then viewed in their remake versions (updated in several instances to accommodate the changing scene or altered to fit a particular star), many of these stories are still able to evoke the laughter within us which often makes life seem just a little bit better.

☆   ☆   ☆   ☆   ☆   ☆   ☆

▶ ACCENT ON YOUTH (1935)
Paramount • Wesley Ruggles
Herbert Marshall, Sylvia Sidney

▷ BUT NOT FOR ME (1959)
Paramount • Walter Lang
Clark Gable, Carroll Baker, Lilli Palmer

Plot: The secretary of a Broadway producer falls for her somewhat older boss.

Notes: In between the above productions came MR. MUSIC (1950) which was revamped to fit the talents of Bing Crosby.

★   ★   ★

▶ AWFUL TRUTH, THE (1937)★AOV★
Columbia • Leo McCarey
Irene Dunne, Cary Grant, Ralph Bellamy

▷ LET'S DO IT AGAIN (1953)
Columbia • Alexander Hall
Jane Wyman, Ray Milland, Aldo Ray

Plot: A divorced couple, still in love, eventually realize that they belong together.

Notes: Two earlier versions of the comedy were filmed, a silent in 1925 with Agnes Ayres and Warner Baxter and an earlier talkie (1929)   featuring Ina Claire and Henry Daniell. Leo McCarey won an Oscar for his direction of THE AWFUL TRUTH. Irene Dunne and Ralph Bellamy were also nominated but lost.

★   ★   ★

▶ BEACHCOMBER, THE (1938)★AOV★
British • Eric Pommer
Charles Laughton, Elsa Lanchester

▷ BEACHCOMBER, THE (1954)
GDF/London Independent • Muriel Box
Robert Newton, Glynis Johns

Plot: A ne'er do well living on a South Sea island is reformed by a lady missionary.

Notes: Robert Newton, star of the 1954 film, plays a featured role in the earlier production. The story is by Somerset Maugham.

★   ★   ★

▶ BREWSTER'S MILLIONS (1945)★AOV★
Edward Small • Alan Dwan
Dennis O'Keefe, Helen Walker

▷ BREWSTER'S MILLIONS (1985)★AOV★
Universal • Walter Hill
Richard Pryor, John Candy

Plot: A man must spend a certain amount of money in order to inherit many millions more.

Notes: The earliest version of BREWSTER'S MILLIONS was filmed in 1935 starring Jack Buchanan and Lili Damita (the first Mrs. Errol Flynn). In the 1935 and 1945 films, the main character is a playboy, while in the 1985 production, he is a baseball player.

★   ★   ★

▶ DIARY OF A CHAMBERMAID (1946)★AOV★
Benedict Bogeaus • Jean Renoir
Paulette Goddard, Burgess Meredith, Francis Lederer

▷ DIARY OF A CHAMBERMAID (1964)★AOV★
French/Italian • Luis Buñuel
Jeanne Moreau, Georges Geret

Plot: A servant girl arouses different emotions in a nineteenth century country house.

Notes: Paulette Goddard and Burgess Meredith were husband and wife at the time of filming. Meredith wrote the 1946 screenplay and was its co-producer.

★   ★   ★

▶ FRONT PAGE, THE (1931)∗AOV∗
Howard Hughes • Lewis Milestone
Adolphe Menjou, Pat O'Brien, Mary Brian

▷ HIS GIRL FRIDAY (1940)∗AOV∗
Columbia • Howard Hawks
Cary Grant, Rosalind Russell, Ralph Bellamy

Plot: The editor of a newspaper pulls all sorts of stunts to keep his star reporter on the job.

Notes: In the original Ben Hecht/Charles MacArthur script, the central character of Hildy Johnson is a man. Howard Hawks turned the role into that of a woman reporter and offered it to Katharine Hepburn, Irene Dunne, Claudette Colbert and Carole Lombard. Those ladies demurred and the plum went to Rosalind Russell who who scored a hit in the part. Billy Wilder directed a third version in 1974 with Walter Matthau and Jack Lemmon as editor and reporter respectively. A 1988 remake titled SWITCHING CHANNELS∗AOV∗ takes place at a cable television station and stars Burt Reynolds, Kathleen Turner and Christopher Reeve.

Cary Grant welcomes Rosalind Russell back to the news room in HIS GIRL FRIDAY. In this remake of THE FRONT PAGE, there is a gender switch— reporter Hildy Johnson is now a woman.

★ ★ ★

▶ GHOST BREAKERS, THE (1940)
Paramount • George Marshall
Bob Hope, Paulette Goddard, Paul Lukas

▷ SCARED STIFF (1958)
Paramount • George Marshall
Dean Martin, Jerry Lewis, Lizabeth Scott

Plot: A girl inherits a castle and becomes involved with ghosts, zombies and buried treasure.

Notes: The story was filmed twice as a silent, the first time in 1914 with H.B. Warner and the second in 1922, teaming Wallace Reid and Lila Lee.

★ ★ ★

☆   ☆   ☆   ☆   ☆   ☆   ☆

▶ GOOD FAIRY, THE (1935)
Universal • William Wyler

Margaret Sullavan, Herbert Marshall, Frank
Morgan

▷ I'LL BE YOURS (1947)
Universal • William Seiter

Deanna Durbin, Tom Drake, Adolphe Menjou

Plot: A young woman uses her charms to help a neophyte lawyer win a wealthy client.

Notes: Margaret Sullavan and director William Wyler were married upon completion of the 1935 film. The union did not last.

★   ★   ★

Deanna Durbin—the youngster whose films saved Universal Studios from bankruptcy grew up to star in such films as IT STARTED WITH EVE.

★   ★   ★

▶ GOODBYE AGAIN (1933)
Warners • Michael Curtiz

Warren William, Joan Blondell

▷ HONEYMOON FOR THREE (1941)
Warners • Lloyd Bacon

George Brent, Ann Sheridan, Jane Wyman

Plot: An author's secretary is in love with him and becomes jealous of the interest he takes in another woman.

Notes: George Brent and Ann Sheridan were man and wife when HONEYMOON FOR THREE was being shot. The script of the 1941 release was written by Julius and Philip Epstein. The brother team and Howard Koch adapted a play for the screen titled "Everybody Comes to Rick's." This was the genesis of CASABLANCA.

★   ★   ★

▶ GREEKS HAD A WORD FOR THEM, THE
(1932)★AOV★
United Artists/Samuel Goldwyn • Lowell Sherman

Joan Blondell, Madge Evans, Ina Claire

▷ HOW TO MARRY A MILLIONAIRE (1953)★AOV★

TCF • Jean Negulesco

Lauren Bacall, Betty Grable, Marilyn Monroe,
William Powell

Plot: Three girls come to New York in order to snare wealthy husbands.

Notes: Betty Grable, one of the stars of HOW TO MARRY A MILLIONAIRE, plays a small role in
its predecessor.

★ ★ ★

*In IT HAPPENED ONE NIGHT,
Claudette Colbert is about to
show a skeptical Clark Gable
how one goes about the art of
hitch-hiking. The 1934 film
won five major Academy
Awards.*

★ ★ ★

▶ HI NELLIE (1934)
Warners • Mervyn Le Roy

Paul Muni, Glenda Farrell

▷ YOU CAN'T ESCAPE FOREVER (1942)
Warners • Jo Graham

George Brent, Brenda Marshall

Plot: An editor is demoted to the love-lorn column of his paper but manages to expose a leading
racketeer.

Notes: A third version of the story was filmed in 1949. Wayne Morris and Janis Paige play the
leads in HOUSE ACROSS THE STREET.

★ ★ ★

▶ HIS DOUBLE LIFE (1933)★AOV★
Paramount • Arthur Hopkins

Roland Young, Lilian Gish

▷ HOLY MATRIMONY (1943)
TCF • John Stahl

Monty Woolley, Gracie Fields

Plot: A painter, taking his valet's place when the latter dies, makes a new life for himself and his
unsuspecting bride.

Notes: In 1945, Monty Woolley and Gracie Fields were teamed for the second time—that film is
titled MOLLY AND ME.

★ ★ ★

▶ HIS GLORIOUS NIGHT (1929)
MGM • Lionel Barrymore
John Gilbert, Hedda Hopper, Catherine Dale Owen

▷ BREATH OF SCANDAL, A (1960)★AOV★
Paramount • Michael Curtiz
Sophia Loren, John Gavin, Maurice Chevalier

Plot: A princess falls for a commoner.

Notes: It has been said that HIS GLORIOUS NIGHT spelled the beginning of the end for John Gilbert's acting career. There were other postulations for his decline, as will be seen later on. Carlo Ponti, Sophia Loren's husband, was co-producer on the 1960 production.

★ ★ ★

Henry Fonda is smitten with Barbara Stanwyck in THE LADY EVE. There are a few things he doesn't know about her as yet.

★ ★ ★

▶ HOBSON'S CHOICE (1953)★AOV★
British Lion • David Lean
Charles Laughton, John Mills, Brenda de Banzie

▷ HOBSON'S CHOICE (1983)★AOV★
MMTV • Gilbert Cates
Sharon Gless, Richard Thomas, Jack Warden, Lillian Gish

Plot: The daughter of an overbearing shopkeeper goes against his wishes in choosing a husband.

Notes: The locale of the 1953 version is England, that of the 1983 production is New Orleans.

★ ★ ★

▶ HOLIDAY (1930)
RKO-Pathe • Edward H. Griffith
Ann Harding, Robert Ames, Mary Astor

▷ HOLIDAY (1938)★AOV★
Columbia George Cukor
Katharine Hepburn, Cary Grant, Lew Ayres

Plot: A free spirit falls in love with one girl but winds up with her more understanding sister.

Notes: Ann Harding received an Oscar nomination for her performance in the 1930 movie. Katharine Hepburn understudied the lead in the Broadway stage version of HOLIDAY, written by her friend Philip Barry.

★ ★ ★

▶ INDISCREET (1958)★AOV★
Grandon • Stanley Donen
Cary Grant, Ingrid Bergman

▷ INDISCREET (1988)
MMTV • Richard Michaels
Robert Wagner, Leslie-Anne Down

Plot: A man falls in love with an actress but pretends to be married in order to avoid an entangling alliance.

Notes: Besides making two highly successful films together (the other was NOTORIOUS in 1946), Cary Grant and Ingrid Bergman remained close friends until her death. It was Grant who accepted Bergman's Oscar for ANASTASIA.

★ ★ ★

William Powell takes a fishing lesson from E.E. Clive as Jean Harlow looks on in LIBELED LADY. The object of Powell's affections in the film is not Harlow, but Myrna Loy. It was the opposite, however, in real life.

★ ★ ★

▶ IT HAPPENED ONE NIGHT (1934)★AOV★
Columbia • Frank Capra
Clark Gable, Claudette Colbert, Walter Connolly

▷ YOU CAN'T RUN AWAY FROM IT (1956)
Columbia • Dick Powell
June Allyson, Jack Lemmon, Charles Bickford

Plot: A runaway heiress falls in love with a reporter during a cross country bus trip.

Notes: Both Gable and Colbert were unenthusiastic about making IT HAPPENED ONE NIGHT. Several stars including Robert Montgomery, Myrna Loy and Margaret Sullavan had turned down the roles. The film, however, won Oscars for both stars, director Capra, screenplay writer Robert Riskin and as Best Picture of 1934.

★ ★ ★

▶ IT STARTED WITH EVE (1941)
Universal • Henry Koster
Deanna Durbin, Charles Laughton, Robert
Cummings

▷ I'D RATHER BE RICH (1964)
Universal-International • Jack Smight
Maurice Chevalier, Sandra Dee, Robert Goulet

Plot: A dying millionaire wants to see his grandchild engaged and the latter obliges, with comic results.

Notes: Sandra Dee plays the Robert Cummings role in the remake.

★ ★ ★

Ten years later, in the remake, EASY TO WED, Van Johnson and Lucille Ball are married through the connivance of her boyfriend, Keenan Wynn, who with Ben Blue looking on, is waiting to kiss the reluctant bride.

★ ★ ★

▶ IT'S IN THE BAG (1945)★AOV★
United Artists • Richard Wallace
Fred Allen, Jack Benny, Binnie Barnes

▷ TWELVE CHAIRS, THE (1970)★AOV★
UMC/Crossbow • Mel Brooks
Ron Moody, Frank Langella, Dom DeLuise, Mel Brooks

Plot: A fortune in jewels is hidden in chairs which have been sold to various individuals.

Notes: Playing cameo roles in the 1945 production are Don Ameche, Victor Moore, Rudy Vallee, William Bendix and Jerry Colonna.

★ ★ ★

▶ LADIES OF THE JURY (1932)
RKO • Lowell Sherman
Edna May Oliver, Ken Murray

▷ WE'RE ON THE JURY (1937)
RKO • Ben Holman
Helen Broderick, Victor Moore

Plot: Disagreements break out during a jury trial.

Notes: Helen Broderick was the mother of actor Broderick Crawford. Ken Murray was an actor, producer and television host. His annual "Blackouts" was a popular West Coast stage presentation for many years.

★ ★ ★

▶ LADY EVE, THE (1941)★AOV★
Paramount • Preston Sturgis
Barbara Stanwyck, Henry Fonda, Charles Coburn

▷ BIRDS AND THE BEES, THE (1956)★AOV★
Paramount • Norman Taurog
George Gobel, Mitzi Gaynor, David Niven

Plot: A lady card shark falls in love with a rich young man, much to the consternation of her con-man father.

Notes: George Gobel was a popular television comedian during the nineteen fifties and sixties.

★ ★ ★

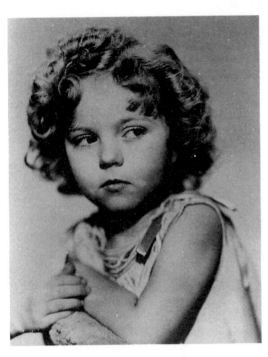

Shirley Temple, circa LITTLE MISS MARKER. What author could resist this studio still of the Depression's Dimpled Darling?

★ ★ ★

▶ LADY FOR A DAY (1933)
Columbia • Frank Capra
May Robson, Warren William, Glenda Farrell

▷ POCKETFUL OF MIRACLES, A (1961)★AOV★
United Artists • Frank Capra
Bette Davis, Glenn Ford, Hope Lange, Peter Falk

Plot: Gangland characters help an old apple seller pose as a society woman when her daughter visits her.

Notes: Peter Falk, better known to TV fans as "Columbo," received an Oscar nomination for his role in the Damon Runyan story.

★ ★ ★

☆   ☆   ☆   ☆   ☆   ☆   ☆

▶ LEMON DROP KID, THE (1934)   ▷ LEMON DROP KID, THE (1951)★ᴬᴼᵛ★
Paramount • Marshall Neilan   Paramount • Sidney Lanfield

Lee Tracy, Helen Mack, William Frawley   Bob Hope, Marilyn Maxwell, Lloyd Nolan

Plot: A racetrack tout owes a lot of money to the syndicate.

Notes: William Frawley, who died several years ago, can be seen throughout the world on any given day, through the magic of television, as Fred Mertz on the "I Love Lucy" show.

★ ★ ★

▶ LIBELED LADY (1936)   ▷ EASY TO WED (1946)
MGM • Jack Conway   MGM • Edward Buzzell

William Powell, Jean Harlow, Myrna Loy, Spencer   Van Johnson, Lucille Ball, Esther Williams, Keenan
Tracy   Wynn

Plot: When an irate heiress sues a newspaper, its editor hires an old friend to compromise her.

Notes: William Powell and Myrna Loy share an on-screen romance, but off-screen, it was Harlow who held the key to Powell's heart. The two were an "item" until her untimely death in 1937.

★ ★ ★

▶ LITTLE MISS MARKER (1934)★ᴬᴼᵛ★   ▷ SORROWFUL JONES (1949)★ᴬᴼᵛ★
Paramount • Alexander Hall   Paramount • Sidney Lanfield

Shirley Temple, Adolphe Menjou   Bob Hope, Lucille Ball, Mary Jane Saunders

Plot: A racetrack gambler is left with a little girl who proceeds to steal his heart while saving his life.

Notes: A third version of this Damon Runyan story was filmed under its original title in 1980. It stars Walter Matthau, Julie Andrews, Tony Curtis and in the role of LITTLE MISS MARKER, Sara Stimson.

★ ★ ★

▶ MAJOR AND THE MINOR, THE (1942)   ▷ YOU'RE NEVER TOO YOUNG (1955)
Paramount • Billy Wilder   Paramount • Norman Taurog

Ginger Rogers, Ray Milland, Diana Lynn   Dean Martin, Jerry Lewis, Diana Lynn

Plot: An adult posing as a child becomes involved in several amusing escapades.

Notes: Diana Lynn appears in both films, playing a teen in one and the love interest in the other. Lela Rogers, mother of Ginger in real life, is seen as her reel mother in the 1942 production. Jerry Lewis plays the Ginger Rogers part in the 1955 film.

★ ★ ★

▶ MAKE ME A STAR (1932)
Paramount • William Beaudine
Stuart Erwin, Joan Blondell

▷ MERTON OF THE MOVIES (1947)
MGM • Robert Alton
Red Skelton, Gloria Grahame

Plot: Stage struck young man goes to Hollywood and becomes a star.

Notes: Doing what we'd now call cameos in the 1932 film are "new" Paramount stars Claudette Colbert, Gary Cooper, Fredric March and Tallulah Bankhead.

★ ★ ★

William Powell is embraced by a soggy Carole Lombard in MY MAN GODFREY. Underneath the broad comedy, the film is a sharp social satire on the hard times of the Great Depression.

★ ★ ★

▶ MAN IN POSSESSION, THE (1931)
MGM • Sam Wood
Robert Montgomery, Reginald Owen, Irene Purcell

▷ PERSONAL PROPERTY (1937)
MGM • W.S. Van Dyke
Robert Taylor, Jean Harlow

Plot: A lady in financial straits falls in love with the bailiff in temporary charge of her property.

★ ★ ★

☆   ☆   ☆   ☆   ☆   ☆   ☆

▶ MAN WHO LOVED WOMEN, THE
(1977)⋆AOV⋆
French • Francois Truffaut
Charles Denner, Leslie Caron

▷ MAN WHO LOVED WOMEN, THE
(1983)⋆AOV⋆
Columbia • Blake Edwards
Burt Reynolds, Julie Andrews, Marilu Henner

Plot: To explain his obsession for women, a man writes his autobiography.

Notes: Julie Andrews, star of the 1983 version, is the wife of the film's director, Blake Edwards. Marilu Henner can be seen in reruns of the television favorite "Taxi."

★ ★ ★

Butler Bob Hope and his employer's daughter, Lucille Ball, are all set to go riding in FANCY PANTS. Tally-ho!

★ ★ ★

▶ MILLIONAIRE, THE (1931)
Warners • John Adolfi
George Arliss, Evalyn Knapp

▷ THAT WAY WITH WOMEN (1947)
Warners • Frederick de Cordova
Sydney Greenstreet, Dane Clark, Martha Vickers

Plot: A rich man retires and in his boredom, becomes involved in the lives of some people around him.

Notes: In the cast of the 1931 film is a young actor named James Cagney. Fred de Cordova, director of THAT WAY WITH WOMEN, is the same man who is at the helm of "The Tonight Show."

★ ★ ★

▶ MIRACLE OF MORGAN'S CREEK, THE
(1943)⋆AOV⋆
Paramount • Preston Sturges
Betty Hutton, Eddie Bracken, William Demarest, Diana Lynn

▷ ROCK-A-BYE BABY (1958)

Paramount • Frank Tashlin
Jerry Lewis, Marilyn Maxwell, Reginald Gardiner

Plot: A man helps a woman who has experienced a multiple birth.

Notes: Preston Sturges both wrote and directed some of the better comedies of the nineteen thirties and forties. MIRACLE OF MORGAN'S CREEK is a satire on motherhood and politics. The script of the remake was altered to fit the Jerry Lewis image.

★ ★ ★

☆   ☆   ☆   ☆   ☆   ☆   ☆

▶ MORE THE MERRIER, THE (1943)
Columbia • George Stevens

Jean Arthur, Joel McCrea, Charles Coburn

▷ WALK, DON'T RUN (1966)★AOV★
Columbia • Charles Walters

Cary Grant, Samantha Eggar, Jim Hutton

Plot: A girl rents half of her apartment to an elderly gentleman who in turn rents out part of his half to a personable young man.

Notes: Charles Coburn won a Best Supporting Actor award for his performance in the 1943 film. Film buffs remembering the rotund, cherubic yet sly-looking character actor for his fine screen emoting, will find it fascinating to note that Cary Grant plays the Coburn role in the remake.

Jack Benny, Carole Lombard, Robert Stack and "The Joseph Tura Theatrical Troupe" in TO BE OR NOT TO BE, fighting World War II in their own way.

▶ MRS. WIGGS OF THE CABBAGE PATCH (1934)★AOV★
Paramount • Norman Taurog

W.C. Fields, Pauline Lord, ZaSu Pitts

▷ MRS. WIGGS OF THE CABBAGE PATCH (1942)
Paramount • Ralph Murphy

Fay Bainter, Hugh Herbert, "Vera Vague"

Plot: A poor family faces eviction while waiting for the return of the wandering head of house.

Notes: "Vera Vague" was the character portrayed by an actress named Barbara Jo Allen who was never billed under her real name. She played the man-chasing "Vera" in movies and also on the Bob Hope radio show.

★   ★   ★

★   ★   ★   ★   ★   ★   ★

▶ MY FAVORITE WIFE (1940)★AOV★
RKO • Garson Kanin
Cary Grant, Irene Dunne, Randolph Scott

▷ MOVE OVER DARLING (1963)
TCF • Michael Gordon
Doris Day, James Garner, Polly Bergen

Plot: A wife, who has been shipwrecked for five years, returns to find that her husband has remarried—she plots to get him back.

Notes: Garson Kanin, director of MY FAVORITE WIFE, was married to writer-actress Ruth Gordon. As script-writers, the two collaborated on such films as PAT AND MIKE and ADAM'S RIB. A 1969 made for television version of MY FAVORITE WIFE, called THREE'S A CROWD, stars Larry Hagman, Jessica Walters and E.J. Peaker.

Over forty years later, in the remake of TO BE OR NOT TO BE, Anne Bancroft and Mel Brooks pay homage to the star of the original production, Jack Benny, by using his real name in their script.

▶ MY MAN GODFREY (1936)★AOV★
Universal • Gregory La Cava
Carole Lombard, William Powell, Gail Patrick

▷ MY MAN GODFREY (1957)
Universal-International • Henry Koster
June Allyson, David Niven, Martha Hyer, Eva Gabor

Plot: A "tramp" becomes butler to a zany family and in the process, teaches its members that money isn't everything.

Notes: Carole Lombard and William Powell were briefly married in the early nineteen thirties.

★   ★   ★

▶ NOTHING BUT THE TRUTH (1929)
Paramount • Victor Schertzinger
Richard Dix, Wynne Gibson

▷ NOTHING BUT THE TRUTH (1941)
Paramount • Elliott Nugent
Bob Hope, Paulette Goddard, Edward Arnold

Plot: A man makes a bet that he can tell the truth for twenty four hours.

Notes: A silent version of the story was filmed by Metro in 1920. Paulette Goddard was married to Charlie Chaplin during the late nineteen thirties and early forties.

▶ NOTHING SACRED (1937)★AOV★
Selznick-International • William Wellman

Carole Lombard, Fredric March

▷ LIVING IT UP (1954)
Paramount • Norman Taurog

Dean Martin, Jerry Lewis, Janet Leigh

Plot: A person believed to be dying of a rare disease is the focus of a series of newspaper articles.

Notes: In a switch of gender, Jerry Lewis plays the Carole Lombard role in the 1954 remake.

★ ★ ★

Spencer Tracy and Katharine Hepburn in WOMAN OF THE YEAR, the first film for the duo and the beginning of their long private and professional relationship.

★ ★ ★

▶ ONE WILD MOMENT (1977)★AOV★
French • Claude Berri

Jean-Pierre Marielle, Victor Lanoux

▷ BLAME IT ON RIO (1983)★AOV★
Sherwood • Stanley Donen

Michael Caine, Valerie Harper, Joseph Bologna

Plot: Two men go on vacation with their daughters and one of the girls "comes on" to her father's friend.

Notes: Valerie Harper made her show business mark in television as Rhoda Morgenstern on "The Mary Tyler Moore Show."

★ ★ ★

☆　☆　☆　☆　☆　☆　☆

▶ PALEFACE, THE (1948)⋆AOV⋆

Paramount • Norman Z. McLeod

Bob Hope, Jane Russell

▷ SHAKIEST GUN IN THE WEST, THE (1968)⋆AOV⋆
Universal • Alan Rafkin

Don Knotts, Jackie Coogan

Plot: A timid dentist from the East becomes a hero when he travels West.

Notes: The perky "Buttons and Bows" featured in THE PALEFACE, won Best Song Academy Awards for composers Jay Livingstone and Ray Evans. In a sequel to THE PALEFACE, aptly titled SON OF PALEFACE, Bob Hope and Jane Russell are joined by Roy Rogers and Trigger.

★　★　★

▶ PASSIONATE PLUMBER, THE (1932)
MGM • Edgar Sedgwick

Buster Keaton, Jimmy Durante, Irene Purcell

▷ HER CARDBOARD LOVER (1942)
MGM • George Cukor

Norma Shearer, Robert Taylor, George Sanders

Plot: A lady hires a lover to make her fiance jealous.

Notes: Like Greta Garbo, Norma Shearer chose to end her career while she was still on top. The 1942 film was her last.

★　★　★

▶ RICHEST GIRL IN THE WORLD, THE (1934)
RKO • William Seiter

Miriam Hopkins, Joel McCrea, Fay Wray

▷ BRIDE BY MISTAKE (1944)
RKO • Richard Wallace

Laraine Day, Alan Marshall, Marsha Hunt

Plot: A rich girl changes places with her secretary in order to find a man who will love her for herself.

Notes: The original film is typical of the depression years—the remake has been updated to World War II. Its hero is a GI.

★　★　★

▶ RUGGLES OF RED GAP (1935)⋆AOV⋆
Paramount • Leo McCarey

Charles Laughton, Charles Ruggles, Leila Hyams

▷ FANCY PANTS (1950)
Paramount • George Marshall

Bob Hope, Lucille Ball, Bruce Cabot

Plot: A butler goes out west with a nouveau riche family.

Notes: In the original, the leading character is an English butler won in a crap game. The remake has London-born Bob Hope playing a down-on-his-luck English actor who becomes a butler.

★　★　★

▶ RUSSIANS ARE COMING, THE RUSSIANS ARE COMING, THE (1966)⋆AOV⋆
United Artists/Mirsch • Norman Jewison

Alan Arkin, Carl Reiner, Brian Keith, Eva Marie Saint

▷ RUSSKIES (1987)⋆AOV⋆

New Century Entertainment • Rick Rosenthal

Whip Hubley, Leaf Phoenix, Peter Billingsley

Plot: Russians land off the coast of the United States and create a panic wherever they go.

Notes: In the first production, the Russians land off the Connecticut coastline. In the remake, they land off the Florida shore.

★　★　★

☆   ☆   ☆   ☆   ☆   ☆   ☆

▶ SLIGHT CASE OF MURDER, A (1938)
Warners • Lloyd Bacon

Edward G. Robinson, Jane Brian, Willard Parker

▷ STOP, YOU'RE KILLING ME (1953)
Warners • Roy Del Ruth

Broderick Crawford, Claire Trevor, Sheldon Leonard

Plot: An ex-prohibition bootlegger wants to go straight but runs into complications, i.e. some of his old cronies.

Notes: In his long career, Edward G. Robinson played roles on both sides of the law. In real life, he was an erudite and cultured man, a graduate of New York's Columbia University.

★   ★   ★

▶ STRICTLY DISHONORABLE (1932)
Universal • John M. Stahl

Paul Lukas, Sidney Fox, Lewis Stone

▷ STRICTLY DISHONORABLE (1951)
MGM • Melvin Frank, Norman Panama

Ezio Pinza, Janet Leigh, Millard Mitchell

Plot: A young Southern girl becomes infatuated with a sophisticated opera singer.

Notes: Metropolitan opera singer Ezio Pinza appeared on Broadway with Mary Martin in "South Pacific." Towards the end of his lengthy career, Paul Lukas co-starred on Broadway with Ethel Merman in the musical "Call Me Madam."

TALL, DARK AND HANDSOME (1941)
TCF • H. Bruce Humberstone

Cesar Romero, Virginia Gilmore, Joan Davis

LOVE THAT BRUTE (1950)
TCF • Alexander Hall

Paul Douglas, Jean Peters

Plot: A gangster is not the ruthless killer he is supposed to be, but it takes love to really reform him.

Notes: Virginia Gilmore was once married to Yul Brynner.

★   ★   ★

▶ TENDERFOOT, THE (1931)
Warners • Ray Enright

Joe E. Brown, Ginger Rogers, Lew Cody

▷ ANGEL FROM TEXAS, AN (1940)
Warners • Ray Enright

Eddie Albert, Jane Wyman, Ronald Reagan, Wayne Morris, Rosemary Lane

Plot: A cowboy comes to New York and becomes an investor in a Broadway show.

Notes: Albert, Wyman, Reagan and Morris are co-starred in two other Warner films: BROTHER RAT in 1938 (see Chapter Eight) and BROTHER RAT AND A BABY in 1940. Both productions feature Priscilla Lane, sister of Rosemary.

THREE MEN AND A CRADLE (1985)★AOV★
French • Coline Serrau

Roland Giraud, Michel Boujenah, Andrew Dussolier

THREE MEN AND A BABY (1987)★AOV★
Touchstone • Leonard Nimoy

Tom Selleck, Ted Danson, Steve Guttenberg

Plot: Three carefree bachelors find their lives immeasurably changed by a baby.

Notes: Director Leonard Nimoy as Dr. Spock on "Star Trek," and actors Tom Selleck as "Magnum, P.I." and Ted Danson as Sam on "Cheers" can all be seen on the small screen in their respective shows.

★   ★   ★

☆   ☆   ☆   ☆   ☆   ☆   ☆

▶ THREE SMART GIRLS (1936)
Universal • Henry Koster

Deanna Durbin, Charles Winninger, Ray Milland

▷ THREE DARING DAUGHTERS (1948)
MGM • Fred M. Wilcox

Jeanette MacDonald, Jane Powell, Elinor Donahue

Plot: Three girls interfere in mama's love life.

Notes: Though the original film stars Deanna Durbin and the remake boasts Jeanette MacDonald and Jane Powell, singers all, both productions are really comedies interspersed with a few musical numbers.

★ ★ ★

▶ TO BE OR NOT TO BE (1942)★AOV★
Alexander Korda • Ernst Lubitsch

Carole Lombard, Jack Benny

▷ TO BE OR NOT TO BE (1983)★AOV★
TCF • Alan Johnson

Mel Brooks, Anne Bancroft

Plot: The members of a theatrical troupe in the Poland of World War II fight their own brand of warfare.

Notes: TO BE OR NOT TO BE was Carole Lomabard's last film. She died in a plane crash en route to Hollywood after completing a successful bond career.

★ ★ ★

▶ TOPAZE (1933)★AOV★
RKO • Harry Arrast

John Barrymore, Myrna Loy

▷ I LIKE MONEY (1962)
British • Peter Sellers

Peter Sellers, Nadia Gray

Plot: A French school teacher turns the tables on some industrial sharks who are trying to exploit him.

Notes: There were three French versions of TOPAZE made, the first in 1932, the second in 1936 and the third in 1952★AOV★.

★ ★ ★

▶ TOY, THE (1976)
French • Francis Veber

Pierre Richard, Fabrice Greco, Michel Bouquet

▷ TOY, THE (1982)★AOV★
Columbia • Richard Donner

Richard Pryor, Jackie Gleason, Ned Beatty

Plot: A man is hired as a plaything for a millionaire's spoiled son.

Notes: Before becoming a television superstar, Jackie Gleason had appeared in several films, including ALL THROUGH THE NIGHT with Humphrey Bogart and ORCHESTRA WIVES with Glenn Miller.

★ ★ ★

▶ TRUE CONFESSION (1937)
Paramount • Wesley Ruggles

Carole Lombard, Fred MacMurray, John Barrymore

▷ CROSS MY HEART (1946)
Paramount • John Berry

Betty Hutton, Sonny Tufts, Michael Chekhov

Plot: In the name of love, a compulsive liar confesses to a crime she did not commit.

Notes: John Barrymore was billed over Carole Lombard in the 1934 farce, TWENTIETH CENTURY. By the time TRUE CONFESSIONS was released, Lombard's star had eclipsed Barrymore's.

★ ★ ★

☆   ☆   ☆   ☆   ☆   ☆   ☆

▶ UNFAITHFULLY YOURS (1948)✶ᴬᴼⱽ✶
TCF • Preston Sturgis
Rex Harrison, Linda Darnell, Rudy Vallee

▷ UNFAITHFULLY YOURS (1984)✶ᴬᴼⱽ✶
TCF • Howard Zieff
Dudley Moore, Nastassia Kinski, Albert Brooks

Plot: While leading his orchestra, a symphony conductor, believing his wife to be unfaithful, thinks of several ways to kill her.

Notes: Played in the 1948 film are pieces by Rossini, Wagner and Tschaikovsky.

★ ★ ★

▶ WE'RE NO ANGELS (1954)✶ᴬᴼⱽ✶
Paramount • Michael Curtiz
Humphrey Bogart, Peter Ustinov, Aldo Ray, Joan Bennett

▷ WE'RE NO ANGELS (1989)
Paramount • Neil Jordan
Robert De Niro, Sean Penn, Demi Moore

Plot: Escaped convicts on the run inadvertently help others.

Notes: In the 1954 original which takes place in France, the escapees are alumni of Devil's Island. The remake is about two American convicts, disguised as priests, trying to get to Canada.

★ ★ ★

▶ WHEN LADIES MEET (1933)
MGM • Harry Beaumont
Ann Harding, Robert Montgomery, Myrna Loy

▷ WHEN LADIES MEET (1941)
MGM • Robert Z. Leonard
Joan Crawford, Robert Taylor, Greer Garson

Plot: An authoress is in love with her married publisher.

Notes: The very popular Greer Garson was one year away from her Oscar-winning performance as MRS. MINIVER, but it was Joan Crawford, the bigger star at the time, who got top billing.

★ ★ ★

▶ WIFE, HUSBAND AND FRIEND (1938)
TCF • Gregory Ratoff
Loretta Young, Warner Baxter, Binnie Barnes

▷ EVERYBODY DOES IT (1949)
TCF • Edmund Goulding
Linda Darnell, Paul Douglas, Celeste Holm

Plot: A husband tries to thwart his wife's attempts at singing and in the process, becomes a singer himself.

Notes: In EVERYBODY DOES IT, Paul Douglas and Celeste Holm portray a married couple. 1949 also saw the release of A LETTER TO THREE WIVES (see Chapter One). In that film, Douglas is married to Linda Darnell and Celeste Holm is the catalyst of the story, albeit a disembodied voice.

★ ★ ★

▶ WOMAN OF THE YEAR (1942)✶ᴬᴼⱽ✶
MGM • George Stevens
Spencer Tracy, Katharine Hepburn, Fay Bainter

▷ WOMAN OF THE YEAR (1976)
MMTV • Jud Taylor
Renee Taylor, Joseph Bologna, Virginia Christine

Plot: A sports reporter and a political columnist, who have little in common, get married anyway.

Notes: The first Tracy/Hepburn film—he always received top billing. Renee Taylor and Joseph Bologna are married in real life.

★ ★ ★

▶ YOU BELONG TO ME (1941)　　　　　▷ EMERGENCY WEDDING (1950)
Columbia • Wesley Ruggles　　　　　　　Columbia • Edward Buzzell
Barbara Stanwyck, Henry Fonda, Edgar Buchanan　　Barbara Hale, Larry Parks, Jim Backus

Plot: A husband thinks that his doctor wife is spending too much time with her male patients.

Notes: Larry Parks played the legendary Al Jolson in two films. Jim Backus can be seen as one of the castaways in reruns of "Gilligan's Island" and can be heard as the voice of the myopic cartoon character, "Mr. Magoo."

★ ★ ★

★   ★   ★   ★   ★   ★   ★

CHAPTER FOUR

MYSTERY AND MAYHEM: THE WHODUNNIT REDONE

A shot rings out, a vial of poison is swallowed, hands are shown around a victim's neck—the body is discovered and a minion of the law is called in.

A diamond is stolen, a robbery committed, a gang of thieves is in business—again a good guy to the rescue.

Mystery, Mayhem, Suspense—all the ingredients that make up the "whodunnit," one of the more interesting of the Hollywood film genres. Whether Philip Marlowe, Sam Spade, Sherlock Holmes, Father Brown or a not-so famous public servant—have no fear—an hour or so later, the crime is solved, the culprit stands revealed. Often it doesn't take the movie goer too long to guess "who-dunnit," but every once in a while, a film comes along so well plotted that it leaves us guessing up until the very end. Dame Agatha Christie's AND THEN THERE WERE NONE is an excellent example of this—the clever lady leads us down the garden path, furnishing along the way several suspects and a few red herrings—not until the last moments is the guilty party revealed.

Good or bad, like Dame Agatha's AND THEN THERE WERE NONE, many mysteries have been remade, some more than once, while some of our most popular stars have added to their luster by performing in the genre in both originals and remakes (Bogart in THE MALTESE FALCON, Basil Rathbone as SHERLOCK HOLMES).

Here then are fifty-two films along with their remakes. As the afore-mentioned Holmes would say, "the game is afoot."

TO THE HUNT.

★   ★   ★   ★   ★   ★   ★

▶ AND THEN THERE WERE NONE (1945)★AOV★   ▷ AND THEN THERE WERE NONE (1974)
Popular Pictures • Rene Clair   British/EMI • Peter Collinson
Barry Fitzgerald, Walter Huston, Louis Hayward,   Oliver Reed, Richard Attenborough, Elke Sommer
June Duprez

Plot: Ten people are systematically murdered one by one.

Notes: TEN LITTLE INDIANS, released in 1966, is also based upon the Agatha Christie novel. The film stars, among others, Hugh O'Brian and one time teen-aged singing idol, Fabian.

★ ★ ★

Don't look now, Ingrid, but your husband is out for blood—yours. Charles Boyer and Ingrid Bergman in GASLIGHT.

★ ★ ★

▶ ANGEL STREET (1939)   ▷ GASLIGHT (1944)★AOV★
British National • Thorold Dickinson   MGM • George Cukor
Anton Walbrook, Diana Wynyard, Robert Newton Ingrid Bergman, Charles Boyer, Joseph Cotten,
                                              Angela Lansbury

Plot: A man tries to drive his wife mad in order to conceal a theft and a murder that he has committed.

Notes: ANGEL STREET was a hit on both the Broadway and London stages. Irene Dunne and Hedy Lamarr were each offered the role which brought Ingrid Bergman her first Oscar.

★ ★ ★

☆   ☆   ☆   ☆   ☆   ☆   ☆

▶ BIG CLOCK, THE (1947)
Paramount • John Farrow
Charles Laughton, Ray Milland, Maureen O'Sullivan

▷ NO WAY OUT (1987)★AOV★
Robert Garland • Roger Donaldson
Kevin Kostner, Sean Young, Howard Duff, Gene Hackman

Plot: A man solves a murder only to find out that there has been a giant cover-up and that the crime was committed by his boss.

Notes: Maureen O'Sullivan was the wife of the late director John Farrow and is the mother of actress Mia Farrow. Howard Duff played Dashiell Hammett's Sam Spade on radio during the nineteen forties.

★ ★ ★

▶ BIG SLEEP, THE (1946)★AOV★
Warners • Howard Hawks
Humphrey Bogart, Lauren Bacall, Martha Vickers

▷ BIG SLEEP, THE (1977)★AOV★
British/ITC • Michael Winner
Robert Mitchum, Sarah Miles, Richard Boone

Plot: Philip Marlowe's involvement in the problems of a wealthy family leads him to discover love, intrigue and murder in one fell swoop.

Notes: Literary great William Faulkner was one of the writers who worked on the 1946 screenplay of this Raymond Chandler novel.

★ ★ ★

▶ BLIND ALLEY (1939)
Columbia • Charles Vidor
Chester Morris, Ralph Bellamy, Ann Dvorak

▷ DARK PAST, THE (1948)★AOV★
Columbia • Rudolph Maté
William Holden, Lee J. Cobb, Nina Foch

Plot: A psychiatrist, held hostage by a mad killer, tries analysis in order to get his captor to surrender to the police.

Notes: Two popular film detectives of the nineteen thirties and forties were "Boston Blackie" and "Ellery Queen." Who played them? Chester Morris and Ralph Bellamy.

★ ★ ★

▶ BREATHLESS (1959)★AOV★
French • Jean-Luc Godard
Jean Seberg, Jean-Paul Belmondo

▷ BREATHLESS (1983)★AOV★
Miko • James McBride
Richard Gere, Art Metrano, Valerie Kaprisky

Plot: A man, accompanied by a young woman, is being hunted by the law for stealing a car and killing a policeman in the process.

★ ★ ★

▶ CASTLE OF TERROR (1964)
Italian • Anthony Dawson
Barbara Steele, George Riviere

▷ WEB OF THE SPIDER (1970)★AOV★
Italian • Anthony Dawson
Anthony Franciosa, Michele Mercier

Plot: On a wager, a man spends the night in a supposedly haunted house.

Notes: Anthony Franciosa, once married to Shelley Winters, was one of the stars of TV's "Name of the Game" series (See below).

★ ★ ★

★   ★   ★   ★   ★   ★   ★

▶ CHICAGO DEADLINE (1949)
Paramount • Louis Allen

Alan Ladd, Donna Reed, June Havoc, Arthur
Kennedy

▷ FAME IS THE NAME OF THE GAME (1966)
MMTV • Stuart Rosenberg

Anthony Franciosa, Jill St. John, Susan St. James

Plot: A reporter investigates a murder and the trail leads to criminal conspiracy and corruption at
the highest political levels.

Notes: The 1966 movie first served as a pilot for "The Name of the Game" television series. It was
then released to the theaters.

Bogey and Baby, "Alone Together"—Humphrey Bogart and Lauren Bacall in THE BIG SLEEP.

★ ★ ★

▶ CORBEAU, LE (1943)★AOV★
(American Title: THE RAVEN)
French • Henri-Georges Clouzot

Pierre Fresnay, Ginette Leclerc

▷ THIRTEENTH LETTER, THE (1951)

TCF • Otto Preminger

Charles Boyer, Linda Darnell

Plot: A small provincial town suffers from an outbreak of poison pen letters.
Notes: The scene is shifted from France in the original to Canada in the remake.

★ ★ ★

▶ DEAR DETECTIVE (1977)
French • Philippe De Broca

Annie Giradot, Philippe Noirot

▷ DEAR DETECTIVE (1979)★AOV★
MMTV • Dean Hargrove

Brenda Vaccaro, Arlen Dean Snyder

Plot: A lady detective has a romance with a college professor while solving a murder.
Notes: The first film is also shown under the title of DEAR INSPECTOR.

▶ DIABOLIQUE (1954)★AOV★
French • Henri-Georges Clouzot
Simone Signoret, Vera Clouzot

▷ REFLECTIONS OF MURDER (1974)★AOV★
MMTV • John Badham
Tuesday Weld, Sam Waterston, Joan Hackett

Plot: The wife and mistress of a tyrannical schoolmaster conspire to kill the bane of their existence—his body then disappears—is he really dead?

Notes: The late Simone Signoret was the wife of French singer-actor Yves Montand.

★ ★ ★

▶ DIAL M FOR MURDER (1954)★AOV★
Warners • Alfred Hitchcock
Ray Milland, Grace Kelly, Robert Cummings, John Williams

▷ DIAL M FOR MURDER (1981)
MMTV • Boris Sagal
Angie Dickinson, Christopher Plummer, Anthony Quayle

Plot: A jealous husband plots the "perfect crime"—the killing of his wife.

Notes: John Williams, who plays a detective in the 1954 film, played the same role in the stage version.

★ ★ ★

▶ D.O.A. (1949)★AOV★
United Artists • Rudolph Maté
Edmond O'Brien, Luther Adler, Pamela Britton

▷ D.O.A. (1988)★AOV★
Touchstone • Rocky Morton, Annabelle Jankel
Dennis Quaid, Meg Ryan

Plot: A dying man tries to find out who has given him a slow-acting poison and why.

Notes: A third version of this "film noir" was filmed in 1970 as COLOR ME DEAD, with Tom Tryon and Carolyn Jones in leading roles.

★ ★ ★

▶ FATHER BROWN, DETECTIVE (1934)
Paramount • Edward Sedgwick
Walter Connolly, Paul Lukas

▷ DETECTIVE, THE (1954)★AOV★
Columbia • Robert Hammer
Alec Guinness, Peter Finch

Plot: A Catholic cleric turns detective and retrieves a priceless cross that a master criminal has stolen.

Notes: "Father Brown" is the creation of mystery writer G.K. Chesterton.

★ ★ ★

▶ FEAR IN THE NIGHT (1947)★AOV★
United Artists • Maxwell Shane
Paul Kelly, DeForrest Kelly

▷ NIGHTMARE (1956)
United Artists • Maxwell Shane
Edward G. Robinson, Kevin McCarthy, Virginia Christine

Plot: A man who has had a strange dream discovers that, while under hypnosis, he has committed a murder.

Notes: DeForrest Kelly (no relation to his co-star Paul) can be seen on both big screen and small as the doctor on "Star Trek."

★ ★ ★

☆   ☆   ☆   ☆   ☆   ☆   ☆

▶ FIVE STAR FINAL (1931)   ▷ TWO AGAINST THE WORLD (1936)
Warners • Mervyn Le Roy   Warners • William McGann
Edward G. Robinson, Ona Munson   Humphrey Bogart, Claire Dodd

Plot: A newspaper editor, seeking sensational stories, leaves tragedy in his wake.

Notes: Robinson also played a newspaper editor on radio's "Big Town."

★ ★ ★

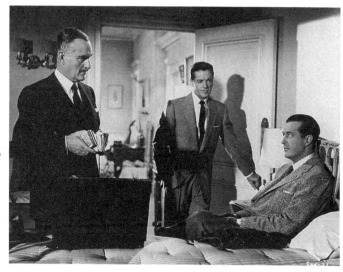

John Williams, Robert Cummings and Ray Milland (left to right). Which of the three is out to get Grace Kelly in DIAL M FOR MURDER?

★ ★ ★

▶ FRIGHTENED LADY, THE (1932)   ▷ CASE OF THE FRIGHTENED LADY, THE
                                            (1940)★AOV★
British/Gainsborough • T. Hayes Hunter   British/Pennant • George King
Emlyn Williams, Cathleen Nesbitt   Marius Goring, Felix Aylmer

Plot: A woman with a demented son tries to protect him from the law and from himself.

Notes: English-born Emlyn Williams was a noted playwright ("The Corn is Green") as well as a stage and screen actor.

★ ★ ★

▶ HOUND OF THE BASKERVILLES, THE   ▷ HOUND OF THE BASKERVILLES, THE
(1939)★AOV★   (1959)★AOV★
TCF • Sidney Lanfield   United Artists • Terence Fisher
Basil Rathbone, Nigel Bruce   Peter Cushing, Andre Morell

Plot: The life of an English baronet is threatened by a supernatural hound and the intrepid Sherlock Holmes is called in to investigate.

Notes: The quintessential Holmes/Watson team of Basil Rathbone and Nigel Bruce made their first appearance in the 1939 film. A spoof of the Arthur Conan Doyle novel was released in 1977 starring Dudley Moore as Watson and Peter Cook as Holmes.

★ ★ ★

▶ I THE JURY (1953)
Parklane • Harry Essex
Biff Elliott, Peggie Castle, Preston Foster

▷ I THE JURY (1982)★AOV★
American Cinema/Larco • Richard T. Heffron
Armond Assante, Barbara Carrera, Paul Sorvino

Plot: Mickey Spillane's Mike Hammer investigates the murder of his friend.
Notes: The victim in the updated second film is a Vietnam veteran.

★ ★ ★

Someone has killed Betty Grable's sister in I WAKE UP SCREAMING. Is it Victor Mature, seen here hat in hand?

★ ★ ★

▶ I WAKE UP SCREAMING (1941)★AOV★
TCF • H. Bruce Humberstone
Betty Grable, Victor Mature, Laird Cregar, Carole Landis

▷ VICKI (1953)
TCF • Harry Horner
Jeanne Crain, Jean Peters, Richard Boone, Elliott Reid

Plot: After the murder of her sister, a girl joins forces with the innocent prime suspect in the case to find the real killer.
Notes: Although the 1941 film stars the then popular team of Betty Grable and Victor Mature, it was Laird Cregar whom the critics singled out for praise. Cregar, a promising young actor, died in his late twenties, a victim of strenuous dieting.

★ ★ ★

▶ JUDGE AND JAKE WYLER, THE (1972)
MMTV • David Lowell Rich
Bette Davis, Doug McClure

▷ PARTNERS IN CRIME (1973)
MMTV • Jack Smight
Lee Grant, Lou Antonio

Plot: A lady judge takes an ex-con on as her partner in a detective agency.
Notes: Featured in the 1973 film are Gary Crosby, son of Bing, and Vic Tayback, proprietor of Mel's Diner on TV's "Alice" show.

★ ★ ★

★   ★   ★   ★   ★   ★   ★

▶ KENNEL MURDER CASE, THE (1933)★AOV★
Warners • Michael Curtiz
William Powell, Mary Astor, Eugene Pallette

▷ CALLING PHILO VANCE (1939)
Warners • William Clemens
James Stephenson, Margot Stevenson, Martin Kosleck

Plot: Philo Vance is called in to investigate an apparent suicide.

Notes: From 1929 through 1933, William Powell played detective Philo Vance in four films. In 1934, he teamed with Myrna Loy for the first of the highly successful "Thin Man" series.

A savage looking Richard Boone terrorizes Jeanne Crain in VICKI, the remake of I WAKE UP SCREAMING.

▶ KIND LADY (1935)
MGM • George B. Seitz
Basil Rathbone, Aline MacMahon, Mary Carlisle

▷ KIND LADY (1951)
MGM • John Sturgis
Maurice Evans, Ethel Barrymore, Angela Lansbury, Betsy Blair

Plot: A confidence man and his cronies keep a woman prisoner in her own home.

Notes: Betsy Blair, the first Mrs. Gene Kelly, made her mark in movies as the lonely girl who befriends MARTY (1955). Angela Lansbury's actress mother, Moyna MacGill, has a small role in the 1951 production.

★   ★   ★

☆   ☆   ☆   ☆   ☆   ☆   ☆

▶ LAST WARNING, THE (1928)
Universal • Paul Leni

Laura La Plante, Montague Love, John Boles

▷ HOUSE OF FEAR, THE (1939)
Universal • Joe May

William Gargan, Irene Hervey

Plot: A backstage murder takes place amid rehearsals for a new play.

Notes: The 1928 version was first filmed as a silent, but dialogue was tacked on and the film is considered a talkie. Irene Hervey is the ex-wife of singer Allan Jones and the mother of singer Jack Jones.

★ ★ ★

▶ LODGER, THE (1944)⋆AOV⋆
TCF • John Brahms

Laird Cregar, Merle Oberon, George Sanders

▷ MAN IN THE ATTIC (1953)
TCF • Hugo Fregonese

Jack Palance, Constance Smith

Plot: An attic lodger is thought to be the infamous "Jack the Ripper."

Notes: A silent (1927)⋆AOV⋆ and an early sound version (1932), both filmed in Great Britain, preceded the 1944 production. The silent was directed by Alfred Hitchcock, who also contributed to its screenplay.

★ ★ ★

▶ LOVE FROM A STRANGER (1936)⋆AOV⋆
Trafalgar • Rowland V. Lee

Ann Harding, Basil Rathbone

▷ LOVE FROM A STRANGER (1947)⋆AOV⋆
Eagle Lion • Richard Whorf

Sylvia Sidney, John Hodiak

Plot: Much to her horror, a woman discovers that the "charmer" she has married is, in reality, a murderer.

Notes: LOVE FROM A STRANGER is based upon "Philomel Cottage," a story by Agatha Christie. Before becoming a director, Richard Whorf was a contract player at MGM.

★ ★ ★

▶ MALTESE FALCON, THE (1931)
Warners • Roy Del Ruth

Ricardo Cortez, Bebe Daniels, Dudley Digges

▷ MALTESE FALCON, THE (1941)⋆AOV⋆
Warners • John Huston

Humphrey Bogart, Mary Astor, Sidney Greenstreet, Peter Lorre

Plot: After the death of his partner, detective Sam Spade is dragged into the search for a jewel-encrusted statuette.

Notes: George Raft was offered the starring role in the 1941 film. He declined, not wanting to work under neophyte director John Huston. The film, Huston and actor Sidney Greenstreet were Oscar-nominated—there were no winners, however. The Huston/Bogart version of the Dashiell Hammett novel was the third filmed. In between that production and the earlier one came SATAN WAS A LADY (1936), starring Warren William and Bette Davis.

▶ MAN WHO KNEW TOO MUCH, THE
(1934)★AOV★
British/GFD • Alfred Hitchcock
Leslie Banks, Edna Best, Peter Lorre

▷ MAN WHO KNEW TOO MUCH, THE
(1956)★AOV★
Paramount • Alfred Hitchcock
James Stewart, Doris Day

Plot: A child is kidnapped when his parents innocently become involved in an assassination plot.

Notes: Oscars went to Jay Livingston and Ray Evans for "Que Sera, Sera," the song they wrote for the 1956 production.

★ ★ ★

Bogie and "the stuff dreams are made of." Humphrey Bogart and THE MALTESE FALCON.

★ ★ ★

▶ MIDNIGHT LACE (1960)★AOV★
Universal • David Miller
Doris Day, Rex Harrison, Myrna Loy, John Gavin

▷ MIDNIGHT LACE (1980)
MMTV • Ivan Nagy
Mary Crosby, Gary Frank, Celeste Holm, Carolyn Jones

Plot: A wife doesn't realize that her husband is behind all the threats that she has been receiving.

Notes: Mary Crosby is the daughter of singer Bing Crosby and his second wife, Kathryn Grant.

★ ★ ★

▶ MIRAGE (1965)★AOV★
Universal • Edward Dmytryk
Gregory Peck, Walter Matthau, Diane Baker

▷ JIGSAW (1968)
Universal • James Goldstone
Bradford Dillman, Harry Guardino, Hope Lange

Plot: As a man falls to his death during a power blackout, another man who sees it happen loses his memory.

Notes: The pulsating score of the 1965 production was composed and arranged by Quincy Jones.

★ ★ ★

☆ ☆ ☆ ☆ ☆ ☆ ☆

▶ MURDER MY SWEET (1944)★AOV★
RKO • Edward Dmytryk

Dick Powell, Claire Trevor, Anne Shirley, Mike
Mazurki

▷ FAREWELL MY LOVELY (1975)★AOV★
AVCO Embassy • Dick Richards

Robert Mitchum, Charlotte Rampling, John Ireland

Plot: Detective Philip Marlowe searches for an ex-con's girlfriend and becomes involved in a web of
greed, intrigue and murder.

Notes: In a complete change of pace, movie favorite Dick Powell went from crooner to tough guy.
Besides Powell, Mitchum and Bogart, Philip Marlowe has been played by James Garner, Elliott
Gould and two Montgomerys, Robert and George. In 1942, RKO released a loosely adapted version
of the Raymond Chandler novel titled THE FALCON TAKES OVER, starring Tom Conway and
Lynn Bari.

★ ★ ★

▶ MURDERS IN THE RUE MORGUE (1932)
Universal • Robert Florey

Bela Lugosi, Sidney Fox, Leon Ames

▷ MURDERS IN THE RUE MORGUE (1986)
MMTV • Jeannot Szwarc

George C. Scott, Rebecca De Mornay, Ian
McShane

Plot: A particularly grisly double murder takes place in nineteenth century Paris.

Notes: John Huston collaborated on the screenplay of the 1932 film. A 1971 ★AOV★ version of the
Edgar Allan Poe story stars Lilli Palmer, Jason Robards Jr. and Herbert Lom.

★ ★ ★

▶ MYSTERY OF MR. X (1934)
MGM • Edgar Selwyn

Robert Montgomery, Elizabeth Allan, Lewis Stone

▷ HOUR OF THIRTEEN, THE (1952)
MGM • Harold French

Peter Lawford, Dawn Addams, Roland Culver

Plot: A jewel thief in Edwardian London, suspected in a series of murders, sets out to find the real
murderer.

Notes: The remake was shot in London. Its three stars are British.

★ ★ ★

▶ MYSTERY OF THE WAX MUSEUM
(1933)★AOV★
Warners • Michael Curtiz

Lionel Atwill, Fay Wray, Glenda Farrell, Frank
McHugh

▷ HOUSE OF WAX (1953)★AOV★

Warners • Andre de Toth

Vincent Price, Carolyn Jones, Phyllis Kirk, Frank
Lovejoy

Plot: A mad sculptor, disfigured in a fire, builds a museum and covers the dead bodies he exhibits
with wax.

Notes: The most famous of the "3-D" films, the 1953 production helped character actor Vincent
Price to become a horror superstar.

★ ★ ★

☆   ☆   ☆   ☆   ☆   ☆   ☆

▶ NIGHT MUST FALL (1937)
MGM • Richard Thorpe
Robert Montgomery, Rosalind Russell, May Whitty

▷ NIGHT MUST FALL (1964)
MGM • Karel Reisz
Albert Finney, Susan Hampshire, Mona Washbourne

Plot: A psychopathic axe murderer insinuates himself into the household of a rich old lady.

Notes: Robert Montgomery was Oscar-nominated for his role in NIGHT MUST FALL, but lost to Spencer Tracy in CAPTAINS COURAGEOUS. English character actress May Whitty became a Dame by royal proclamation and henceforth was billed as "Dame May Whitty."

★ ★ ★

A frightened Doris Day and James Stewart search for their abducted son in THE MAN WHO KNEW TOO MUCH.

★ ★ ★

▶ OUT OF THE PAST (1947)★AOV★
RKO • Jacques Tourneur
Robert Mitchum, Jane Greer, Kirk Douglas, Rhonda Fleming

▷ AGAINST ALL ODDS (1984)★AOV★
Columbia • Taylor Hackford
Jeff Bridges, Rachel Ward, Richard Widmark, Jane Greer

Plot: One man is hired to find another's girl-friend—when he does, the two fall in love.

Notes: Jane Greer appears in the second film, which was released thirty-seven years after the first one. She plays the mother of her original character.

★ ★ ★

▶ PICKUP ON SOUTH STREET (1953)
TCF • Samuel Fuller

Richard Widmark, Jean Peters, Thelma Ritter, Richard Kiley

▷ CAPETOWN AFFAIR, THE (1967)
TCF • Robert D. Webb

James Brolin, Jacqueline Bisset, Claire Trevor

Plot: A pickpocket steals a wallet which contains micro-film and finds himself involved in espionage.

Notes: The locale of CAPETOWN AFFAIR is South Africa. Thelma Ritter was Oscar-nominated for her role in the 1953 production. Several times thus honored, she never won the coveted award. Richard Kiley, the villain in the same version, possesses a fine singing voice and has put it to use on the Broadway stage ("No Strings," "Man of La Mancha").

★ ★ ★

Dick Powell and a detective's best friend—his gun—in MURDER MY SWEET. Powell, Warner's resident "boy crooner" made a sudden turnabout and launched a career as a tough guy.

★ ★ ★

▶ RIDE THE PINK HORSE (1947)
Universal-International • Robert Montgomery

Robert Montgomery, Wanda Hendrix

▷ HANGED MAN, THE (1974)
MMTV • Don Siegal

Robert Culp, Edmond O'Brien, Vera Miles

Plot: A man sets out to find the murderer of his friend.

Notes: As so often is the case in the movies, there is a locale switch from one version to another—the first takes place in New Mexico, the second in New Orleans.

★ ★ ★

▶ SECRET OF THE BLUE ROOM (1933)
Universal • Kurt Neumann

Lionel Atwill, Edward Arnold, Paul Lukas, Gloria Stuart

▷ MURDER IN THE BLUE ROOM (1944)
Universal • Leslie Goodwin

Anne Gwynne, Donald Cook, Regis Toomey

Plot: A murderer lurks in the "haunted house" of an heiress.

★ ★ ★

☆　　☆　　☆　　☆　　☆　　☆　　☆

▶ SEVEN KEYS TO BALDPATE (1935)
RKO • William Hamilton, Edward Killy
Gene Raymond, Margaret Callahan, Eric Blore

▷ SEVEN KEYS TO BALDPATE (1947)
RKO • Lew Landers
Philip Terry, Margaret Lindsay

Plot: A writer comes to Baldpate Inn to find a quiet atmosphere in which to work and finds anything but.

Notes: The films are based upon a novel by Earl Der Biggers, more familiarly known as the creator of Charlie Chan. Before it was bought by RKO, the story was a Broadway show starring George M. Cohan, who also appears in the first of two silent versions. A 1929 RKO sound production stars Richard Dix. Philip Terry was once married to Joan Crawford.

★ ★ ★

▶ SORRY WRONG NUMBER (1948)★AOV★
Paramount • Anatole Litvak
Barbara Stanwyck, Burt Lancaster, Wendell Corey

▷ SORRY WRONG NUMBER (1989)
MMTV • Tony Wharmby
Loni Anderson, Carl Weintraub, Hal Holbrook, Patrick McNee

Plot: A bedridden woman overhears her husband plotting her death and tries to prevent it from happening.

Notes: SORRY WRONG NUMBER had its beginnings as a radio play by Lucille Fletcher—it starred Agnes Moorehead.

★ ★ ★

▶ SPIRAL STAIRCASE, THE (1946)★AOV★
RKO • Robert Siodmak
Dorothy McGuire, George Brent, Ethel Barrymore

▷ SPIRAL STAIRCASE, THE (1975)★AOV★
Warners • Peter Collinson
Jacqueline Bisset, Mildred Dunnock, Christopher Plummer

Plot: A psychopathic killer stalks a mute servant girl working in his mother's home.

Notes: Christopher Plummer can be seen at least once a year on prime-time television as Baron Von Trapp in THE SOUND OF MUSIC.

★ ★ ★

▶ SUSPICION (1941)★AOV★
RKO • Alfred Hitchcock
Joan Fontaine, Cary Grant, Nigel Bruce

▷ SUSPICION (1988)★AOV★
MMTV • Andrew Grieve
Jane Curtin, Anthony Andrews, Betsy Blair

Plot: A girl marries a charming ne'er do well, and soon after, she begins to think that he wants to kill her.

Notes: One of the most popular films of the early nineteen forties, the ending was changed so that Cary Grant would not have to play a killer. A scoundrel and a wastrel, yes, but not a murderer.

★ ★ ★

★   ★   ★   ★   ★   ★   ★

▶ THEY WON'T FORGET (1937)★AOV★
Warners • Mervyn Le Roy

Claude Rains, Gloria Dickson, Otto Kruger, Lana Turner

▷ MURDER OF MARY PHAGAN (1988)
MMTV • Billy Hale

Jack Lemmon, Richard Jordan

Plot: The murder of a girl in a southern city results in a lynching.

Notes: Both films are based upon a 1913 incident in Atlanta, Georgia. Lana Turner is seen as the murdered girl, her first really important role.

Is it a bird? Is it a plane? No, it's actor Robert Donat escaping from a window in a scene from THE THIRTY-NINE STEPS.

★   ★   ★

▶ THIRTEENTH GUEST, THE (1932)★AOV★

Monogram • Albert Ray

Ginger Rogers, Lyle Talbot

▷ MYSTERY OF THE 13th GUEST, THE (1943)
Monogram • William Beaudine

Helen Parrish, Dick Purcell

Plot: A group of people are reassembled to solve a murder which had occurred several years previously.

Notes: Miss Rogers, on her way to stardom, stopped off at Monogram, one of the "Poverty Row" studios and made the 1932 film. Later that year, RKO released FLYING DOWN TO RIO with Fred Astaire, and the rest, as they say, is history.

★   ★   ★

☆   ☆   ☆   ☆   ☆   ☆   ☆

▶ THIRTY-NINE STEPS, THE (1935)★AOV★
Gaumont • Alfred Hitchcock
Robert Donat, Madeleine Carroll, Lucie Mannheim

▷ THIRTY-NINE STEPS, THE (1959)★AOV★
Rank • Ralph Thomas
Kenneth More, Taina Elg, Brenda de Banzie

Plot: A young man accidently becomes involved in murder and espionage. Along the way, he falls in love.

Notes: A third version was released in 1978★AOV★ starring Robert Powell, Karen Dotrice and John Mills.

★ ★ ★

▶ TIME TO KILL (1942)
TCF • Herbert I. Leeds
Lloyd Nolan, Heather Angel

▷ BRASHER DOUBLOON, THE (1947)
TCF • John Brahm
George Montgomery, Nancy Guild

Plot: A detective investigates a case involving the counterfeiting of rare coins.

Notes: There is a switch from film to film in detective characters, not unlike MURDER MY SWEET and THE FALCON TAKES OVER (see above). TIME TO KILL spotlights Brett Halliday's Michael Shayne, while THE BRASHER DOUBLOON puts Raymond Chandler's Philip Marlowe through his paces.

★ ★ ★

▶ TOWER OF LONDON (1939)
Universal • Rowland V. Lee
Basil Rathbone, Boris Karloff, Barbara O'Neil, Vincent Price

▷ TOWER OF LONDON (1962)★AOV★
AIP/Admiral • Roger Corman
Vincent Price, Joan Freeman

Plot: Richard III kills his way to the English throne with the help of a faithful executioner.

Notes: Vincent Price, featured in the first production, stars in the second. As his stock in Hollywood rose, his roles got better.

★ ★ ★

▶ TWO IN THE DARK (1936)
RKO • Ben Stoloff
Walter Abel, Margot Grahame, Gail Patrick, Wallace Ford

▷ TWO O'CLOCK COURAGE (1945)
RKO • Anthony Mann
Tom Conway, Ann Rutherford, Bettijane Greer

Plot: An amnesiac is suspected of having murdered a theatrical producer.

Notes: Shortly after this film, Bettijane Greer dropped the first part of her name and became the not so plain Jane Greer.

★ ★ ★

▶ WHISTLING IN THE DARK (1932)
MGM • Elliott Nugent
Ernest Truex, Una Merkel, Edward Arnold

▷ WHISTLING IN THE DARK (1941)
MGM • S. Sylvan Simon
Red Skelton, Conrad Veidt, Ann Rutherford

Plot: An actor, playing a radio detective, is caught up in a real murder plot and bumbles his way to a solution.

Notes: The 1941 production was a big hit for both Red Skelton and the studio. It spawned two comedy-mystery sequels, WHISTLING IN DIXIE (1942) and WHISTLING IN BROOKLYN (1943).

★ ★ ★

☆   ☆   ☆   ☆   ☆   ☆   ☆

▶ WINDOW, THE (1949)★AOV★
RKO • Ted Tetzlaff

Bobby Driscoll, Barbara Hale, Arthur Kennedy

▷ BOY CRIED MURDER, THE (1966)
Universal • George Breakston

Veronica Hurst, Phil Brown

Plot: A boy with a vivid imagination is not believed by anyone but the killer when he says that he has witnessed a murder.

Notes: Bobby Driscoll was a child star at Disney Studios when he was borrowed for THE WINDOW. The remake has an all-British cast.

★ ★ ★

▶ WITNESS FOR THE PROSECUTION (1957)★AOV★
United Artists • Billy Wilder

Charles Laughton, Tyrone Power, Marlene Dietrich, Elsa Lanchester

▷ WITNESS FOR THE PROSECUTION (1982)
MMTV • Alan Gibson

Ralph Richardson, Deborah Kerr, Beau Bridges

Plot: A London barrister defends a man accused of murdering a rich old woman.

Notes: Both Charles Laughton and his wife, Elsa Lanchester, were Oscar-nominated—neither, however, was a winner.

★ ★ ★

CHAPTER FIVE

CRIME DOES PAY AGAIN AND AGAIN—IN THE MOVIES

Crime does pay—and pay handsomely—in the movies. The Warner brothers knew this and as sound became a fact of life in the movie industry, their studio established itself as the leading maker of the crime (also read gangster) film. With Tommy guns blazing, their rat-tat-tat sounds and the screeching of get-away cars reverberating in theaters everywhere, the "shoot-em-up" genre was soon a staple in the movie bill of fare for a Depression-racked audience.

Throughout the nineteen thirties, some of the most famous and still remembered personalities of the Silver Screen "packed a rod" and wore prison stripes: Edward G. Robinson as LITTLE CAESAR, crying "Mother of Mercy, is this the end of Rico?;" Paul Muni as Tony Camonte in SCARFACE (the busy Hollywood Production Code enforcers made director Howard Hawks tack on "The Shame of a Nation" to the original title); Humphrey Bogart in two unforgettable characterizations, first as Duke Mantee in THE PETRIFIED FOREST and then as "Mad Dog" Earle in HIGH SIERRA; and finally the riveting Jimmy Cagney as Tom Powers shoving that grapefruit into leading lady Mae Clarke's face in PUBLIC ENEMY, while two decades later, as Cody Jarrett in WHITE HEAT, descending into an inferno of flame, screaming for his mother. These and a few others were and still are the prototypes of the crime film by which we measure the genre.

Through the years, many great and not so great crime films have been remade, with major roles going to such up-and-coming stars of the era as Jack Palance, Lee Marvin and Robert Ryan. Comparisons are inevitable. Changes have benefited certain screenplays—others have been re-filmed almost verbatim. Some "repeat performances" have been hits at the box-office while others have been resounding flops.

Several films in the genre have been remade more than once. Perhaps this is because since time immemorial, crime has held a strange fascination for us which has never abated and probably never will. From the highwaymen of Merry Olde England to the Godfathers of today, we've always enjoyed seeing a knock-down-drag-em out story of good versus evil and for the most part, the crime genre seems to have filled the bill.

▶ ASPHALT JUNGLE, THE (1950)★AOV★
MGM • John Huston

Sterling Hayden, Louis Calhern, Marilyn Monroe

▷ BADLANDERS, THE (1958)
MGM • Delmar Daves

Alan Ladd, Ernest Borgnine, Katy Jurado

Plot: A band of crooks plan a robbery.

Notes: THE BADLANDERS is a western wherein the bad guys are planning to rob a gold mine—yet another version of the game "Changing the Genre." A third, CAIRO, starring George Sanders, was released in 1962, and still one more variation on the theme, the all Black COOL BREEZE (1972), features Raymond St. Jacques.

★ ★ ★

*"Wither thou goest I will go."
Tony Curtis and Sidney Poitier
are THE DEFIANT ONES,
escaped convicts whose fates
are bound together by a pair
of manacles.*

★ ★ ★

▶ BLUEBEARD (1944)
PRC • Edgar G. Ulmer

John Carradine, Jean Parker

▷ BLUEBEARD (1972)★AOV★
Alexander Salkind • Edward Dmytryk

Richard Burton, Raquel Welch

Plot: A man cannot control his desire to kill the women he has married.

Notes: PRC stands for Producers Releasing Corporation, another of the so-called "Poverty Row" studios. BLUEBEARD was one of its few "prestige" films.

★ ★ ★

▶ CRIME AND PUNISHMENT (1935)★AOV★
Columbia • Josef von Sternberg

Peter Lorre, Edward Arnold

▷ CRIME AND PUNISHMENT, USA (1958)
Allied Artists • Denis Sanders

George Hamilton, Frank Silvera

Plot: A student is filled with remorse after killing an elderly pawnbroker.

Notes: A French version of the Dostoevski novel was released in 1958 starring Jean Gabin, and a Russian one was made in 1975★AOV★.

★ ★ ★

★ ★ ★ ★ ★ ★ ★

▶ CRIMINAL CODE, THE (1931)★AOV★
Columbia • Howard Hawks
Walter Huston, Phillips Holmes, Boris Karloff

▷ CONVICTED (1950)
Columbia • Henry Levin
Glenn Ford, Ernest Borgnine

Plot: A man is convicted of manslaughter and sent to prison—the warden tries to help him after he is innocently involved in a murder.

Notes: In between the two films listed came PENITENTIARY (1938), which stars Walter Connolly, John Howard and Jean Parker.

★ ★ ★

A blonde Barbara Stanwyck in DOUBLE INDEMNITY. Her performance as the murderous Phyllis Dietrichson remains a classic study of unparalleled greed.

★ ★ ★

▶ CROWD ROARS, THE (1938)
MGM • Richard Thorpe
Robert Taylor, Edward Arnold, Maureen O'Sullivan

▷ KILLER McCOY (1947)
MGM • Roy Rowland
Mickey Rooney, Ann Blyth, Brian Donlevy

Plot: A boxer becomes involved with a criminal element.

Notes: Three years after appearing in THE CROWD ROARS, Robert Taylor and Edward Arnold co-starred in another crime yarn titled JOHNNY EAGER. The 1938 film is not to be confused with a 1932 production with the same name, listed in Chapter Eleven.

★ ★ ★

▶ DEAD RINGER (1964)
Warners • Paul Henreid

Bette Davis, Karl Malden, Peter Lawford

▷ KILLER IN THE MIRROR (1986)
MMTV • Frank De Felitta

Ann Jillian, Len Cariou, Max Gail

   Plot: A woman kills her wealthy twin sister and assumes her identity.

   Notes: The director of the 1964 film, Paul Henreid, co-starred in two films with Bette Davis: NOW VOYAGER (1942) and DECEPTION (1946).

★ ★ ★

Humphrey Bogart and Ida Lupino, whose love for each other is doomed from the start, in HIGH SIERRA. When George Raft turned down the role of "Mad Dog" Earle, Bogart grabbed it and turned in a memorable performance.

★ ★ ★

▶ DEFIANT ONES, THE (1958)★AOV★
United Artists • Stanley Kramer

Tony Curtis, Sidney Poitier

▷ DEFIANT ONES, THE (1986)
MMTV • David Lowell Rich

Robert Urich, Carl Weathers

   Plot: Two convicts, one black and one white, escape from a chain gang—though they hate each other, they are shackled to each other and must stay together.

   Notes: Robert Urich is best known to television audiences as detectives Dan Tanna ("Vegas") and Spenser ("Spenser For Hire"). Carl Weathers became famous as Apollo Creed in the ROCKY films.

★ ★ ★

▶ DOUBLE INDEMNITY (1944)★AOV★
Paramount • Billy Wilder

Barbara Stanwyck, Fred MacMurray, Edward G. Robinson

▷ DOUBLE INDEMNITY (1973)
MMTV • Jack Smight

Richard Crenna, Lee J. Cobb, Samantha Eggar

   Plot: A conniving wife and a weak insurance salesman plot to kill her husband and collect on his insurance.

   Notes: The writing credits of the 1949 film are quite formidable: Novel by James M. Cain, Screenplay by Raymond Chandler and Billy Wilder. Barbara Stanwyck's Oscar-nominated performance remains one of the screen's most incisive portrayals of greed.

★ ★ ★

★   ☆   ☆   ☆   ☆   ☆   ☆

▶ DR. SOCRATES (1935)
Warners • William Dieterle
Paul Muni, Ann Dvorak, Mayo Methot

▷ KING OF THE UNDERWORLD (1938)
Warners • Louis Seiler
Kay Francis, Humphrey Bogart

Plot: A doctor becomes involved with gangsters.

Notes: Paul Muni and Kay Francis play the same character—he is a male medic in the original, she is his female counterpart in the remake. Mayo Methot, featured in DR. SOCRATES, was the third Mrs. Humphrey Bogart.

★ ★ ★

Jack Palance, Shelley Winters and a cute canine in a quiet scene from I DIED A THOUSAND TIMES. This remake of HIGH SIERRA had Palance in the Bogart role and Winters reprising Ida Lupino's.

★ ★ ★

▶ ESCAPE (1930)
British/ATP • Basil Dean
Gerald du Maurier, Madeleine Carroll

▷ ESCAPE (1948)
TCF • Joseph L. Mankiewicz
Rex Harrison, Peggy Cummins

Plot: A man who feels he has been sent to prison unjustly, attempts an escape.

Notes: Madeleine Carroll, who appears in the 1930 film, later emigrated to America and became an important Paramount Studios star. Neither of the above movies should be confused with ESCAPE (1940), an anti-Nazi film starring Robert Taylor and Norma Shearer.

★ ★ ★

▶ EVELYN PRENTICE (1934)
MGM • William K. Howard
William Powell, Myrna Loy, Rosalind Russell

▷ STRONGER THAN DESIRE (1939)
MGM • Leslie Fenton
Walter Pidgeon, Virginia Bruce, Ann Dvorak

Plot: A wife, who thinks she has killed the man blackmailing her, finds her husband defending another woman for the crime.

Notes: Ann Dvorak was married to director Leslie Fenton when STRONGER THAN DESIRE was being filmed.

★ ★ ★

▶ GLASS KEY, THE (1935)
Paramount • Frank Tuttle

George Raft, Edward Arnold, Claire Dodd, Ray Milland

▷ GLASS KEY, THE (1942)★ᴬᴼⱽ★
Paramount • Stuart Heisler

Alan Ladd, Veronica Lake, Brian Donlevy, William Bendix

Plot: The aide to a politician tries to save his boss from being implicated in a murder.

Notes: Veronica Lake and Alan Ladd proved such a potent pair in THIS GUN FOR HIRE (see below) that they were quickly re-teamed in THE GLASS KEY.

★ ★ ★

Burt Lancaster looks at a sultry Ava Gardner in Ernest Hemingway's THE KILLERS, but at whom is she gazing?

★ ★ ★

▶ GUILTY AS HELL (1932)
Paramount • Erle C. Kenton

Edmund Lowe, Victor McLaglen, Richard Arlen

▷ NIGHT CLUB SCANDAL (1937)
Paramount • Ralph Murphy

John Barrymore, Lynne Overman, Charles Bickford

Plot: A prominent doctor kills his wife and tries to incriminate her lover.

Notes: In both films, the audience knows who the guilty party is right from the start. The story revolves around the process by which he is found out.

★ ★ ★

▶ HIDEOUT (1934)
MGM • W.S. Van Dyke

Robert Montgomery, Maureen O'Sullivan, Mickey Rooney

▷ I'LL WAIT FOR YOU (1941)
MGM • Robert B. Sinclair

Robert Sterling, Marsha Hunt

Plot: A racketeer, hiding out in the country, learns to like his new life and the girl he has met.

Notes: Robert Sterling was an MGM contract player when he made I'LL WAIT FOR YOU. During the nineteen forties, he married and divorced MGM star Ann Sothern. He later wed Anne Jeffreys (they are still together) and co-starred with her on the "Topper" TV series.

★ ★ ★

▶ HIGH SIERRA (1941)★AOV★
Warners • Raoul Walsh
Humphrey Bogart, Ida Lupino, Joan Leslie

▷ I DIED A THOUSAND TIMES (1955)
Warners • Stuart Heisler
Jack Palance, Shelley Winters, Lori Nelson

Plot: An escaped killer is involved with two women before he meets his maker.

Notes: John Huston co-wrote the 1941 screenplay. George Raft turned down the lead—Bogart grabbed the role and made Roy Earle an immortal character of the Silver Screen. In between 1941 and 1955 came COLORADO TERRITORY, a Western variation on the theme. The 1949 film was directed by Raoul Walsh and stars Joel McCrea, Virginia Mayo and Dorothy Malone.

★ ★ ★

Ronald Reagan in the 1966 remake of THE KILLERS— probably the only film in which our former President played a real meanie.

★ ★ ★

▶ I SAW WHAT YOU DID (1965)
Universal • William Castle
John Ireland, Joan Crawford, Leif Ericson

▷ I SAW WHAT YOU DID (1988)
MMTV • Fred Walton
Robert Carradine, David Carradine, Shawnee Smith

Plot: A murderer plans to kill the two teenagers who say they saw him commit a crime—they've really seen nothing.

★ ★ ★

▶ I WANT TO LIVE (1958)★AOV★
United Artists • Robert Wise
Susan Hayward, Simon Oakland, Theodore Bikel

▷ I WANT TO LIVE (1983)
MMTV • David Lowell Rich
Lindsay Wagner, Martin Balsam, Don Stroud

Plot: A woman is convicted of murder and dies in the gas chamber at San Quentin.

Notes: The real Barbara Graham died in 1955. Susan Hayward won an Academy Award for her gutsy portrayal of the condemned woman.

★ ★ ★

⋆   ⋆   ⋆   ⋆   ⋆   ⋆   ⋆

▶ INFERNO (1953)
TCF • Roy Baker
Robert Ryan, Rhonda Fleming, William Lundigan

▷ ORDEAL (1953)
MMTV • Lee H. Katzin
Arthur Hill, Diana Muldaur, MacDonald Carey

Plot: A millionaire plots revenge upon his wife, who, along with her lover, has left him to die in the desert.

Notes: After a Hollywood career spent starring in B films, MacDonald Carey went into television as a principal player on the popular soap opera, "Days of our Lives."

★ ★ ★

▶ KILLERS, THE (1946)
Universal-International • Robert Siodmak
Burt Lancaster, Ava Gardner, Edmond O'Brien

▷ KILLERS, THE (1964)⋆AOV⋆
Universal-International • Don Siegal
Ronald Reagan, Lee Marvin, Angie Dickinson, John Cassavetes

Plot: A detective investigates the killing of an ex-boxer who has double-crossed a crime boss.

Notes: The 1964 production was Ronald Reagan's last commercial vehicle to date and probably the only film in which he plays an out-and-out villain.

★ ★ ★

▶ KISS BEFORE THE MIRROR, A (1933)
Universal • James Whale
Frank Morgan, Nancy Carroll, Paul Lukas

▷ WIVES UNDER SUSPICION (1938)⋆AOV⋆
Universal • James Whale
Warren William, Gail Patrick, Ralph Morgan

Plot: A lawyer, defending a jealous man who has killed his wife, finds himself in an identical situation.

Notes: Frank Morgan, star of the 1933 film and Ralph Morgan, who is featured in the remake, were brothers.

★ ★ ★

▶ LADIES OF THE BIG HOUSE (1931)
Paramount • Marion Gering
Sylvia Sidney, Gene Raymond

▷ WOMEN WITHOUT NAMES (1940)
Paramount • Robert Florey
Ellen Drew, Robert Paige

Plot: A couple is framed on a murder charge—while in prison, the wife finds an eye witness to the actual crime.

Notes: Sylvia Sidney was a New York-trained stage actress. Signed by Paramount, she remained at that studio from 1930 to 1936. In 1938, Sidney married actor Luther Adler, but divorced him nine years later.

★ ★ ★

▶ LAST MILE, THE (1932)⋆AOV⋆
World-Wide • Sam Bischoff
Preston Foster, George E. Stone

▷ LAST MILE, THE (1958)⋆AOV⋆
United Artists • Howard W. Koch
Mickey Rooney, Frank Conroy

Plot: A vicious killer is slated for execution as tensions in the prison mount.

Notes: The central character in THE LAST MILE, "Killer" Mears, was played by Spencer Tracy on Broadway and by Clark Gable on the Los Angeles stage. Both actors won movie contracts as a result of their appearances in the play.

★ ★ ★

▶ LAST OF MRS. CHENEY, THE (1929)
MGM • Sidney Franklin
Norma Shearer, Basil Rathbone, Hedda Hopper

▷ LAST OF MRS. CHENEY, THE (1937)
MGM • Richard Boleslawski
Joan Crawford, Robert Montgomery, William Powell

Plot: A female con-artist, operating in British society, falls in love.

Notes: A third version of this old chestnut was released on 1951. Titled THE LAW AND THE LADY, it stars Greer Garson, Michael Wilding and Fernando Lamas. Hedda Hopper appeared in many films before becoming a gossip columnist.

★ ★ ★

Leslie Howard expounding on life and love to a blonde Bette Davis in THE PETRIFIED FOREST.

★ ★ ★

▶ LIFE OF JIMMY DOLAN, THE (1933)
Warners • Archie Mayo
Douglas Fairbanks Jr., Loretta Young

▷ THEY MADE ME A CRIMINAL (1939)★AOV★
Warners • Busby Berkeley
John Garfield, Ann Sheridan, Claude Rains

Plot: A boxer, thinking that he has killed a man, becomes a fugitive on the run.

Notes: The same Busby Berkeley was responsible for the delightful dance numbers in the landmark Warner Brothers musicals of the nineteen thirties.

★ ★ ★

▶ M (1930)★AOV★
Nero Films • Fritz Lang
Peter Lorre

▷ M (1951)
Columbia • Joseph Losey
David Wayne, Luther Adler

Plot: A psychopathic killer of children is hunted down by underworld criminals not wanting police investigations into their activities.

Notes: The Lorre/Lang version is a German language production. Both actor and director were part of the exodus from Germany which occurred before the beginning of World War II.

★ ★ ★

★ ★ ★ ★ ★ ★ ★

▶ MAN WHO LIVED TWICE, THE (1936)
Columbia • Harry Lachman
Ralph Bellamy, Marian Marsh

▷ MAN IN THE DARK, THE (1953)
Columbia • Lew Landers
Edmond O'Brien, Audrey Totter

Plot: A man goes through an operation to remove his criminal tendencies.

Notes: Edmond O'Brien had a varied career in films. He won a Best Supporting Actor Award for his work in THE BAREFOOT CONTESSA.

★ ★ ★

▶ MAYOR OF HELL, THE (1933)
Warners • Archie Mayo
James Cagney, Madge Evans, Frankie Darro

▷ CRIME SCHOOL (1938)
Warners • Louis Seiler
Humphrey Bogart, Gale Page, Dead End Kids

Plot: A racketeer becomes superintendent of a reform school and in this capacity, changes his outlook on life and tries to better conditions there.

Notes: A similar plot is used in HELL'S KITCHEN (1939), which stars Ronald Reagan and The Dead End Kids.

★ ★ ★

▶ MOUTHPIECE, THE (1932)
Warners • James Flood, Elliott Nugent
Warren William, Sidney Fox

▷ ILLEGAL (1955) ★AOV★
Warners • Lewis Allen
Edward G. Robinson, Nina Foch

Plot: A District Attorney becomes a criminal lawyer.

Notes: Sidney Fox, a young Warner Bothers contract player, started out in films at about the same time as Bette Davis. After a few years, unlike that of Miss Davis, her career petered out.

★ ★ ★

▶ NARROW CORNER, THE (1933)
Warners • Alfred E. Green
Douglas Fairbanks Jr., Ralph Bellamy, Patricia Ellis

▷ ISLE OF FURY (1936)
Warners • Frank McDonald
Humphrey Bogart, Margaret Lindsay, Donald Woods

Plot: A man on the run finds temporary peace on a South Sea island.

Notes: The story was adapted from a Somerset Maugham novel.

★ ★ ★

▶ NO ORCHIDS FOR MISS BLANDISH (1948)
British/Renown • St. John L. Clowes
Jack La Rue, Linden Travers

▷ GRISSOM GANG, THE (1971) ★AOV★
ABC • Robert Aldrich
Scott Wilson, Connie Stevens, Kim Darby

Plot: An heiress is kidnapped and falls in love with one of her captors.

Notes: Singer-actress Connie Stevens, once married to Eddie Fisher, starred in the nineteen fifties television series, "Hawaiian Eye."

★ ★ ★

▶ PAID (1930)
MGM • Sam Wood

Joan Crawford, Kent Douglass, Robert Armstrong

▷ WITHIN THE LAW (1939)
MGM • Gustav Machaty

Ruth Hussey, Tom Neal, Paul Kelly

Plot: A woman, unjustly sent to prison, plots revenge on those responsible.

Notes: The 1939 version was filmed by MGM's "B" unit which provided second features for the double bill policy of the era.

★ ★ ★

Femme fatale Lana Turner and John Garfield are contemplating the murder of her elderly and unloved husband in THE POSTMAN ALWAYS RINGS TWICE.

★ ★ ★

▶ PETRIFIED FOREST, THE (1936)★AOV★
Warners • Archie Mayo

Leslie Howard, Bette Davis, Humphrey Bogart

▷ ESCAPE IN THE DESERT (1945)
Warners • Edward A. Blatt

Philip Dorn, Jean Sullivan, Helmut Dantine

Plot: An escaped prisoner holds a group of people captive in the Arizona desert.

Notes: Bogart's Duke Mantee, is an escaped convict. As with many remakes filmed during the war years, the villain of ESCAPE IN THE DESERT is an unrepentant Nazi. Helmut Dantine made a career out of playing both Nazis and anti-Nazis.

★ ★ ★

★   ★   ★   ★   ★   ★   ★

▶ PICTURE SNATCHER, THE (1933)
Warners • Lloyd Bacon
James Cagney, Ralph Bellamy

▷ ESCAPE FROM CRIME (1942)
Warners • D. Ross Lederman
Richard Travis, Julie Bishop

Plot: A parolee becomes a newspaper photographer.

Notes: Jackie Gleason has a small role in the 1942 film. His billing reads Jackie C. Gleason.

★ ★ ★

▶ POSTMAN ALWAYS RINGS TWICE, THE
(1946)★AOV★
MGM • Tay Garnett
Lana Turner, John Garfield, Cecil Kellaway

▷ POSTMAN ALWAYS RINGS TWICE, THE
(1981)★AOV★
Northstar/Lorimar • Bob Rafelson
Jack Nicholson, Jessica Lange, John Colicos

Plot: A woman and her lover plot the murder of her elderly husband.

Notes: The films are based upon a best seller of the same name by James M. Cain.

★ ★ ★

▶ PUBLIC ENEMY'S WIFE (1936)
Warners • Nick Grinde
Pat O'Brien, Margaret Lindsay, Cesar Romero

▷ BULLETS FOR O'HARA (1942)
Warners • William K. Howard
Roger Pryor, Anthony Quinn, Joan Perry

Plot: The wife of an escaped gangster helps an FBI man to trap her husband.

Notes: One of the writers of the 1936 film was David O. Selznick. Anthony Quinn, featured in the 1942 production, has won two Best Supporting Actor awards thus far, in 1952 (VIVA ZAPATA) and in 1956 (LUST FOR LIFE).

★ ★ ★

▶ PUBLIC HERO NUMBER ONE (1935)
MGM • J. Walter Ruben
Chester Morris, Jean Arthur, Lionel Barrymore

▷ GETAWAY, THE (1941)
MGM • Edward Buzzell
Robert Sterling, Donna Reed, Charles Winninger,
Dan Dailey

Plot: A lawman goes undercover to trap a gang and its leader.

Notes: At the start of his movie career, Dan Dailey, featured in THE GETAWAY, played small roles in several MGM dramas. In 1947, he co-starred with Betty Grable in the Twentieth Century-Fox film, MOTHER WORE TIGHTS and became a musical comedy star.

★ ★ ★

▶ RAFFLES (1930)
Samuel Goldwyn • George Fitzmaurice
Ronald Colman, Kay Francis

▷ RAFFLES (1939)
Samuel Goldwyn • Sam Wood
David Niven, Olivia de Havilland

Plot: A British cricket player is also a daring gentleman thief.

Notes: A silent version of the E.W. Hornung novel (The character was used in several short stories and novels) was released in 1917 with John Barrymore in the title role. A later silent (1925) features House Peters.

★ ★ ★

▶ SCARFACE (1932)★AOV★
Howard Hughes • Howard Hawks
Paul Muni, George Raft, Ann Dvorak

▷ SCARFACE (1983)★AOV★
Universal • Brian De Palma
Al Pacino, Steven Bauer, Michelle Pfeiffer

Plot: The life and times of a mobster.

Notes: Noted in the introduction to this chapter is the 1932 title addition. The script was based upon the life of Al Capone, a notorious gangster of the nineteen twenties. The Pacino version has been updated to modern times—the actor plays a drug runner operating out of Miami.

★ ★ ★

SCARFACE and Constant Companion—
Paul Muni and a machine gun. The versatile
Muni played criminals, scientists and
statesmen with equal skill.

★ ★ ★

▶ SHADOW OF A DOUBT (1943)★AOV★
Universal • Alfred Hitchcock
Joseph Cotten, Teresa Wright, MacDonald Carey

▷ STEP DOWN TO TERROR (1959)
Universal-International • Harry Keller
Charles Drake, Coleen Miller, Rod Taylor

Plot: A psychopathic killer returns to his home town and unsuspecting family after a long absence.

Notes: Joseph Cotten was a member of Orson Welles' Mercury Theater Group. He made his screen debut in CITIZEN KANE (1941). Alma Reville, Mrs. Alfred Hitchcock, was a scriptwriter on the 1943 film.

★ ★ ★

▶ SPHINX, THE (1933)★AOV★
Monogram • Phil Rosen
Lionel Atwill, Sheila Terry

▷ PHANTOM KILLER, THE (1942)
Monogram • William Beaudine
Dick Purcell, Joan Woodbury

Plot: A murderer uses his deaf mute twin as an alibi.

★ ★ ★

★   ★   ★   ★   ★   ★   ★

▶ STATE'S ATTORNEY (1933)
RKO • George Archainbaud

John Barrymore, Helen Twelvetrees

▷ CRIMINAL LAWYER (1937)
RKO • Christy Cabanne

Lee Tracy, Margot Grahame, Eduardo Ciannelli

Plot: A lawyer, whose underworld connections have been carefully hidden, becomes a district attorney.

Notes: Lee Tracy was a leading man during the nineteen thirties and forties. His was a fast-talking breezy style of acting. Featured along with Tracy is Eduardo Ciannelli, one of those "men you love to hate." He can be seen in many crime films of the era.

★ ★ ★

▶ STRANGERS ON A TRAIN (1951)★AOV★
Warners • Alfred Hitchcock

Robert Walker, Farley Granger

▷ ONCE YOU KISS A STRANGER (1970)
Warners • Robert Sparr

Carole Lynley, Paul Burke

Plot: A psychopath, meeting a golf pro on a train, outlines a bizarre murder plan—they will swap killings.

Notes: In the remake, Carol Lynley plays the role of the psychopath, enacted by Robert Walker in the original. In 1987, a parody, THROW MOMMA FROM THE TRAIN★AOV★, was released. It stars Danny De Vito (who also directed) and Billy Crystal.

★ ★ ★

▶ STREET OF CHANCE (1930)
Paramount • John Cromwell

William Powell, Kay Francis, Jean Arthur, Regis Toomey

▷ HER HUSBAND LIES (1937)
Paramount • Edward Ludwig

Ricardo Cortez, Gail Patrick, Akim Tamiroff

Plot: A gambler tries to prevent his younger brother from emulating his life style.

Notes: Twenty years after HER HUSBAND LIES was released, its leading lady was the executive producer of the Perry Mason TV series.

★ ★ ★

▶ STREET WITH NO NAME, THE (1948)
TCF • William Keighley

Richard Widmark, Mark Stevens, Lloyd Nolan

▷ HOUSE OF BAMBOO (1955)
TCF • Samuel Fuller

Robert Stack, Robert Ryan, Cameron Mitchell, Sessue Hayakawa

Plot: Government agents risk their lives by going undercover to fight crime.

Notes: HOUSE OF BAMBOO is set in Tokyo. Japan's Sessue Hayakawa is best known to film fans for his role in BRIDGE ON THE RIVER KWAI.

★ ★ ★

▶ THEY LIVE BY NIGHT (1948)⋆AOV⋆
RKO • Nicholas Ray
Farley Granger, Cathy O'Donnell, Howard da Silva

▷ THIEVES LIKE US (1974)
United Artists • Robert Altman
Keith Carradine, Shelley Duval

Plot: Young lovers are fugitives from the law.

Notes: John Houseman agreed to produce THEY LIVE BY NIGHT only if Nicholas Ray was signed to direct. Keith Carradine follows in the footprints of his actor-father John. Keith's brothers, David and Robert, are also "in the business."

★ ★ ★

Alan Ladd and Veronica Lake in THIS GUN FOR HIRE. Ladd's portrayal of an enigmatic killer was his breakthrough role. His career, masterminded by his agent-wife, silent screen star Sue Carol, lasted for over three decades.

★ ★ ★

▶ THIS GUN FOR HIRE (1942)⋆AOV⋆
Paramount • Frank Tuttle
Alan Ladd, Veronica Lake, Robert Preston

▷ SHORT CUT TO HELL (1957)
Paramount • James Cagney
Robert Ivers, Georgeann Johnson, William Bishop

Plot: A racketeer hires a gunman to commit a murder and then double crosses him.

Notes: SHORT CUT TO HELL was one of Cagney's few ventures into directing. The films were adapted from a novel by famed suspense writer Graham Greene.

★ ★ ★

▶ TO HAVE AND HAVE NOT (1944)⋆AOV⋆
Warners • Howard Hawks
Humphrey Bogart, Lauren Bacall, Hoagy Carmichael, Walter Brennan

▷ BREAKING POINT, THE (1950)
Warners • Michael Curtiz
John Garfield, Patricia Neal, Juano Hernandez

Plot: A charter boat captain becomes involved in smuggling.

Notes: Ernest Hemingway's original novel, TO HAVE AND HAVE NOT, was re-written to include an involvement with World War II. Bogart and Bacall first met on the set of the 1944 film. A third version, THE GUN RUNNERS, starring Audie Murphy, Eddie Albert and Patricia Owens, was released in 1958.

★ ★ ★

☆   ☆   ☆   ☆   ☆   ☆   ☆

▶ TRIAL OF MARY DUGAN, THE (1929)
MGM • Bayard Veiller
Norma Shearer, H.B. Warner

▷ TRIAL OF MARY DUGAN, THE (1940)
MGM • Norman Z. McLeod
Laraine Day, Robert Young

Plot: A courtroom drama, wherein a young girl is defended by her lawyer-brother.

Notes: The 1929 film was Norma Shearer's first talkie. At the time of filming, the actress was the undisputed queen of the MGM lot—her husband, Irving Thalberg, was its production head.

★ ★ ★

▶ TWENTY THOUSAND YEARS IN SING SING (1932)
Warners • Michael Curtiz
Spencer Tracy, Bette Davis, Lyle Talbot

▷ CASTLE ON THE HUDSON (1940)

Warners • Anatole Litvak
John Garfield, Pat O'Brien, Ann Sheridan

Plot: "Castle on the Hudson" is, of course, a euphemism for Sing Sing prison—the story is about a hardened criminal and the girl who loves him.

Notes: The 1932 production was based upon a book by the warden at Sing Sing, Lewis E. Lawes. It established Broadway actor Spencer Tracy as a bona fide Hollywood star. The role had originally been intended for another New York performer, James Cagney.

★ ★ ★

▶ UP THE RIVER (1930)
Fox • John Ford
Spencer Tracy, Humphrey Bogart

▷ UP THE RIVER (1938)
TCF • Alfred Werker
Preston Foster, Tony Martin

Plot: An ex-convict tries to hide his past—two pals break out of jail to help him.

Notes: The original film is noted for the casting of the two future superstars and the direction of John Ford. In the early nineteen thirties, Fox and Twentieth Century were separate production companies. By 1935, the two had merged and become Twentieth Century-Fox.

★ ★ ★

▶ VALIANT, THE (1929)
Fox • William K. Howard
Paul Muni

▷ MAN WHO WOULDN'T TALK, THE (1940)
TCF • David Burton
Lloyd Nolan, Jean Rogers, Eric Blore

Plot: A man on trial for murder refuses to testify in his own behalf.

Notes: Eric Blore, whose forte was playing "gentlemen's gentlemen," played that kind of character in the Astaire/Rogers films.

★ ★ ★

▶ WOMAN'S FACE, A (1938)
Swedish • Gustave Molander
Ingrid Bergman

▷ WOMAN'S FACE, A (1941)★AOV★
MGM • George Cukor
Joan Crawford, Melvyn Douglas

Plot: A woman with a scarred face turns to crime.

Notes: Though the original star, Ingrid Bergman, was in Hollywood in 1941, Joan Crawford was signed for the role.

★ ★ ★

★   ★   ★   ★   ★   ★   ★

CHAPTER SIX

TWO STEPS INTO THE UNKNOWN: FANTASY REDOS

For we who love movies, the word fantasy connotes a voyage into the unknown where the unbridled imagination of a storyteller and the resources of a filmmaker combine to spin a yarn replete with special effects and plotlines which test our credulity.

Wonder what Heaven is all about?

Like to relive a year in your life?

Let Hollywood be your guide. Step into the world of fantasy: Robert Montgomery in HERE COMES MR. JORDAN (1941) dies, finds himself among the angels and comes back down to earth—he wasn't supposed to die in the first place; Joan Leslie in REPEAT PERFORMANCE (1947) kills her husband as the chimes ring in the new year. She tearfully wishes that she could go back in time and lo and behold, she does.

HERE COMES MR. JORDAN and REPEAT PERFORMANCE are only two of the several fantasy genre films which have been remade. In the chapter which follows, we enter a world in which almost anything goes. I have included a few science fiction films within its pages because even though some of the scenarios put forth in these journeys into the unknown have come to pass, they contain enough of the fantastic to warrant inclusion in any discussion of the genre.

★ ★ ★ ★ ★ ★ ★

▶ ALICE IN WONDERLAND (1933)
Paramount • Norman Z. McLeod

Charlotte Henry, Cary Grant, Gary Cooper, W.C.
Fields

▷ ALICE IN WONDERLAND (1986)
MMTV • Harry Harris

Telly Savalas, Red Buttons, Imogene Coca, Martha
Raye

Plot: A little girl dreams about White Rabbits, Chesire Cats, Mock Turtles, a Queen of Hearts and
other odd things.

Notes: The ever popular Lewis Carroll fantasy was filmed combining puppets and live action in
1950 ★AOV★ and by Walt Disney in animated form, circa 1951 ★AOV★. A British live action version
titled ALICE'S ADVENTURES IN WONDERLAND ★AOV★ came out in 1972. It features, among
others, Dudley Moore, Peter Sellers and Ralph Richardson.

▶ ANGEL ON MY SHOULDER (1946) ★AOV★
United Artists • Archie Mayo

Paul Muni, Claude Rains, Anne Baxter

▷ ANGEL ON MY SHOULDER (1980) ★AOV★
MMTV • John Berry

Peter Strauss, Richard Kiley, Barbara Hershey

Plot: A murdered gangster is sent back to Earth by the Devil to take over the body of an upright
judge.

Notes: The same author, Harry Segall, wrote ANGEL ON MY SHOULDER and HERE COMES MR.
JORDAN. Claude Rains stars in both, as the Devil in the first film and the angel, Mr. Jordan, in the
second.

▶ BERKELEY SQUARE (1933)
Fox • Frank Lloyd

Leslie Howard, Heather Angel

▷ I'LL NEVER FORGET YOU (1951)
TCF • Roy Baker

Tyrone Power, Ann Blyth, Michael Rennie

Plot: A man is transported back in time to the eighteenth century and falls in love.

Notes: The 1951 film starts out in black and white but switches to color as the story unfolds. Ann
Blyth is married to the brother of the late singer-actor Dennis Day.

▶ BLOB, THE (1958) ★AOV★
Tonylyn • Irvin S. Yeaworth Jr.

Steve McQueen, Aneta Corseaut

▷ BLOB, THE (1988) ★AOV★
Tri-Star • Chuck Russell

Kevin Dillon, Shawnee Smith

Plot: A small town is invaded by a blob-like substance from outer space.

Notes: Burt Bacharach wrote a title tune for the first production. A 1971 film sequel was aptly
titled BEWARE! THE BLOB.

★   ★   ★   ★   ★   ★   ★

▶ BLUE BIRD, THE (1940)★AOV★
TCF • Walter Lang

Shirley Temple, Gale Sondergaard

▷ BLUE BIRD, THE (1976)
TCF • George Cukor

Elizabeth Taylor, Ava Gardner, Jane Fonda, Cicely Tyson

Plot: Two children search for the Blue Bird of Happiness, only to find it in their own back yard.

Notes: The 1976 version of the Maurice Maeterlinck fairy tale was the first ever Russian-American co-production.

★ ★ ★

Fredric March in his Academy Award-winning dual role as Dr. Jekyll and his demonic alter ego, Mr. Hyde.

★ ★ ★

▶ CANTERVILLE GHOST, THE (1943)
MGM • Jules Dassin

Charles Laughton, Robert Young, Margaret O'Brien

▷ CANTERVILLE GHOST, THE (1986)★AOV★
Peter Scott Productions • Paul Bogart

John Gielgud, Alyssa Milano, Andrea Marcovicci, Ted Wass

Plot: An ancient castle is home to a seventeenth century ghost.

Notes: In the mid nineteen seventies, a television version of THE CANTERVILLE GHOST was filmed starring David Niven.

★ ★ ★

▶ CAT PEOPLE, THE (1942)★AOV★
RKO • Jacques Tourneur

Simone Simon, Kent Smith, Tom Conway

▷ CAT PEOPLE, THE (1982)★AOV★
Universal • Paul Schraeder

Nastassia Kinski, Malcolm McDowell

Plot: A girl believes that she will turn into a panther when her passion is aroused.

Notes: THE CAT PEOPLE (1942) was the first in a series of horror films produced at RKO by Val Lewton. Another film, CURSE OF THE CAT PEOPLE, released in 1944, features Simone Simon and Kent Taylor, stars of the original film.

★ ★ ★

★ ★ ★ ★ ★ ★ ★

▶ CHRISTMAS CAROL, A (1938)★AOV★
MGM • Edward L. Marin

Reginald Owen, Gene Lockhart, Leo G. Carroll,
Ann Rutherford

▷ CHRISTMAS CAROL, A (1984)
MMTV • Clive Donner

George C. Scott, Edward Woodward

Plot: A rich miser discovers the joys and blessings of Christmas.

Notes: Three other variations of the Charles Dickens story were made in England: A CHRISTMAS CAROL★AOV★ starring Alastair Sim in 1951 and two films titled SCROOGE—a 1935★AOV★ drama and a 1970★AOV★ musical featuring Albert Finney.

★ ★ ★

Edward Everett Horton (left) and Claude Rains (right) welcome Robert Montgomery to Heaven in HERE COMES MR. JORDAN. There is one problem however— Montgomery's character is not scheduled to die.

★ ★ ★

▶ DEATH TAKES A HOLIDAY (1934)
Paramount • Mitchell Leisen

Fredric March, Evelyn Venable

▷ DEATH TAKES A HOLIDAY (1974)
MMTV • Michael Butler

Monte Markham, Myrna Loy, Melvyn Douglas

Plot: Death assumes mortal form in order to better understand why he is so feared.

Notes: The films are based upon a popular play of the nineteen twenties by Maxwell Anderson, a noted playwright of the era.

★ ★ ★

▶ DR. JEKYLL AND MR. HYDE (1932)★AOV★
Paramount • Rouben Mamoulian

Fredric March, Miriam Hopkins, Rose Hobart

▷ DR. JEKYLL AND MR. HYDE (1941)★AOV★
MGM • Victor Fleming

Spencer Tracy, Lana Turner, Ingrid Bergman

Plot: A research chemist discovers a formula which turns him into a murderous monster.

Notes: John Barrymore stars in a 1921★AOV★ silent version of the Robert Louis Stevenson novel. For his performance in the 1932 production, Fredric March won the first of his two Academy Awards. In a British variation on the theme, DR. JEKYLL AND SISTER HYDE (1971)★AOV★, the scientist is a beautiful woman.

★ ★ ★

★ ★ ★ ★ ★ ★ ★

► DRACULA (1931)★AOV★   ▷ DRACULA (1958)
Universal • Tod Browning   Hammer • Terence Fisher
Bela Lugosi, Helen Chandler, David Manners   Peter Cushing, Christopher Lee

Plot: A vampire from Transylvania works his evil ways upon those around him.

Notes: Bela Lugosi became a superstar in horror films as a result of his performance as Count Dracula. The Bram Stoker novel has been remade on two other occasions thus far (1973★AOV★ and 1979★AOV★).

James Mason, Warren Beatty and Buck Henry (left to right) in HEAVEN CAN WAIT, the remake of HERE COMES MR. JORDAN. Imagining Warren Beatty in Heaven was worth the price of admission for many movie goers.

★ ★ ★

► FLY, THE (1958)★AOV★   ▷ FLY, THE (1986)★AOV★
TCF • Kurt Neumann   TCF • David Cronenberg
David Hedison, Patricia Owens, Vincent Price,   Jeff Goldblum, Geena Davis
Herbert Marshall

Plot: Through a miscalculation in a scientific experiment, a scientist turns himself into a fly.

Notes: Two sequels were made after the first version was released: RETURN OF THE FLY (1959) and CURSE OF THE FLY (1965).

★ ★ ★

► FRANKENSTEIN (1931)★AOV★   ▷ FRANKENSTEIN, THE TRUE STORY (1973)
Universal • James Whale   MMTV • Jack Smight
Boris Karloff, Colin Clive, Mae Clarke   James Mason, David McCallum

Plot: A research scientist creates a living monster and gives him a criminal brain.

Notes: Boris Karloff, a gentle man in real life, achieved screen immortality in the role of the monster. Several versions and sequels of the Mary Shelley novel have been filmed, including one during the nineteen eighties. It is not inconceivable that there will be others for future generations to enjoy.

★ ★ ★

▶ GUY NAMED JOE, A (1943)★AOV★
MGM • Victor Fleming
Spencer Tracy, Irene Dunne, Van Johnson

▷ ALWAYS (1989)
Universal • Steven Spielberg
Richard Dreyfuss, Holly Hunter, Brad Johnson, John Goodman

Plot: A dead flyer comes back to help the new man in his former girl friend's life.

Notes: During the filming of A GUY NAMED JOE, Van Johnson was seriously injured in a motorcycle accident. Spencer Tracy insisted that production be halted until Johnson could return to the set. The song "Smoke Gets in Your Eyes" is played throughout ALWAYS. It was Irene Dunne, the star of the 1943 film, who introduced the lovely Jerome Kern melody in the film ROBERTA (1935).

★ ★ ★

▶ HERE COMES MR. JORDAN (1941)★AOV★
Columbia • Alexander Hall
Robert Montgomery, Evelyn Keyes, Claude Rains

▷ HEAVEN CAN WAIT (1978)★AOV★
Paramount • Warren Beatty
Warren Beatty, Julie Christie, James Mason

Plot: A boxer, not scheduled to die, is given another chance at life on Earth.

Notes: Robert Montgomery, a matinee idol during the Golden Age of Hollywood, is probably best known to today's generation as Elizabeth ("Bewitched") Montgomery's father. Her syndicated show is still being seen on regular and cable television. Warren Beatty also produced and helped write the screenplay of HEAVEN CAN WAIT.

★ ★ ★

▶ INVADERS FROM MARS (1953)★AOV★
Alperson • William Cameron Menzies
Leif Ericson, Arthur Franz, Helena Carter

▷ INVADERS FROM MARS (1986)★AOV★
Cannon • Tobe Hooper
Louise Fletcher, Karen Black, Bud Court

Plot: Aliens land in a boy's back yard.

Notes: Louise Fletcher won an Academy Award for ONE FLEW OVER THE CUCKOO'S NEST which she made nine years before appearing in the remake of "Invaders."

★ ★ ★

▶ INVASION OF THE BODY SNATCHERS (1956)★AOV★
Allied Artists • Don Siegal
Kevin McCarthy, Dana Wynter, Carolyn Jones

▷ INVASION OF THE BODY SNATCHERS (1978)★AOV★
United Artists-Philip Kaufman
Donald Sutherland, Kevin McCarthy, Leonard Nimoy

Plot: An alien force tries to gain control of an American city.

Notes: For the remake, Kevin McCarthy reprises his role in a cameo appearance. Originally set in a small town, the second version takes place in San Francisco.

★ ★ ★

☆   ☆   ☆   ☆   ☆   ☆   ☆

▶ INVISIBLE MAN, THE (1933)★AOV★   ▷ INVISIBLE MAN, THE (1975)
Universal • James Whale   MMTV • Robert Michael Lewis
Claude Rains, Henry Travers, Gloria Stuart   David McCallum, Jackie Cooper, Henry Darrow

Plot: A scientist develops a formula which can render him invisible.

Notes: Claude Rains made his film debut in the 1933 production. Though seen only briefly in the film, he became a star because of the role.

★ ★ ★

Now you see him, now you don't. Claude Rains became a star after his portrayal of THE INVISIBLE MAN.

★ ★ ★

▶ ISLAND OF LOST SOULS (1932)   ▷ ISLAND OF DR. MOREAU (1977)★AOV★
Paramount • Erle C. Kenton   AIP/Cinema 77 • Don Taylor
Charles Laughton, Bela Lugosi   Burt Lancaster, Michael York

Plot: A mad doctor tries to speed up the process of evolution by turning animals into humans—instead he creates half-human, half-animal creatures.

Notes: Don Taylor, director of the remake, was an MGM contract player in the nineteen forties.

★ ★ ★

⋆   ⋆   ⋆   ⋆   ⋆   ⋆   ⋆

▶ IT'S A WONDERFUL LIFE (1946)⋆AOV⋆   ▷ IT HAPPENED ONE CHRISTMAS (1977)
Liberty Films • Frank Capra   MMTV • Donald Wrye
James Stewart, Donna Reed, Henry Travers,   Marlo Thomas, Wayne Rogers, Orson Welles
Lionel Barrymore

   Plot: A guardian angel shows a would be suicide the true value of living.
   Notes: Marlo Thomas plays the role originally done by James Stewart. She is the daughter of
   Danny Thomas and the wife of talk show host Phil Donahue.

★ ★ ★

▶ JOURNEY TO THE CENTER OF THE EARTH   ▷ WHERE TIME BEGAN (1978)⋆AOV⋆
(1959)⋆AOV⋆
TCF • Henry Levin   Spanish • Piquer Simon
James Mason, Pat Boone, Arlene Dahl   Kenneth More, Jack Taylor

   Plot: A professor and his colleagues follow a trail which leads them to the center of the earth.
   Notes: The films are based upon the works of author Jules Verne. Pat Boone, better known as a
   singer and Arlene Dahl (mother of Lorenzo Lamas), best known for glamour and fashion, are
   interesting cast choices for a film of this type.

★ ★ ★

▶ KING KONG (1933)⋆AOV⋆   ▷ KING KONG (1976)⋆AOV⋆
RKO • Merian C. Cooper   Dino de Laurentis • John Guillermin
Fay Wray, Bruce Cabot, Robert Armstrong   Jeff Bridges, Jessica Lange, Charles Grodin

   Plot: A giant ape, brought to the United States by a film producer, leaves terror and destruction
   in his wake.
   Notes: The final sequence takes place atop New York City's famous Empire State Building.
   Somewhat similar to KING KONG in plot is MIGHTY JOE YOUNG, a 1949 release featuring Terry
   Moore.

★ ★ ★

▶ LAST MAN ON EARTH, THE (1964)   ▷ OMEGA MAN, THE (1971)⋆AOV⋆
Italian • Sidney Salkow   Warners • Boris Sagal
Vincent Price, Franca Bettoia   Charlton Heston, Rosalind Cash

   Plot: A man wages war against the germs that are plaguing the earth.
★ ★ ★

▶ MAN IN HALF MOON STREET, THE (1944)   ▷ MAN WHO COULD CHEAT DEATH, THE
                                            (1959)
Paramount • Ralph Murphy   Paramount • Terence Fisher
Nils Asther, Helen Walker   Christopher Lee, Hazel Court, Anton Diffring

   Plot: A young-looking scientist, actually an old man, kills for the glandular extract he needs to
   retain his youth.
   Notes: The remake of the Barre Lyndon story was filmed in England.

★ ★ ★

▶ MIRACLE ON 34th STREET (1947)★AOV★
TCF • George Seaton

Maureen O'Hara, Natalie Wood, John Payne,
Edmund Gwenn

▷ MIRACLE ON 34th STREET (1973)
MMTV • Fielder Cook

Sebastian Cabot, David Hartman, Jane Alexander

Plot: A department store Santa Claus claims to be the real thing.

Notes: Edmund Gwenn, playing Kris Kringle in the original film, won Best Supporting Actor Award while director George Seaton, who also wrote the screen play, received his Oscar for the latter effort.

★ ★ ★

Wide-eyed Robert Armstrong points to something as a frightened Bruce Cabot and Fay Wray look on. Can that "something" be KING KONG?

★ ★ ★

▶ 1984 (1955)
Holiday • Michael Anderson

Edmond O'Brien, Michael Redgrave, Jan Sterling

▷ 1984 (1984)★AOV★
Umbrella/Rosenblum/Virgin • Michael Radford

Richard Burton, John Hurt

Plot: A man's life is controlled by the head of the totalitarian state in which he lives.

Notes: Both films are based on the chilling futuristic novel by George Orwell.

★ ★ ★

★   ★   ★   ★   ★   ★   ★

▶ NOT OF THIS EARTH (1957)
Allied Artists • Roger Corman

Paul Birch, Beverly Garland

▷ NOT OF THIS EARTH (1988)★AOV★
Jim Wynorski

Traci Lords, Arthur Roberts

Plot: An alien comes to earth to get blood in order to save his planet.

Notes: Beverly Garland can be seen in television reruns of "My Three Sons" as Fred MacMurray's wife.

★   ★   ★

▶ OUTWARD BOUND (1930)
Warners • Robert Milton

Leslie Howard, Douglas Fairbanks Jr., Helen Chandler

▷ BETWEEN TWO WORLDS (1944)
Warners • Edward A. Blatt

John Garfield, Eleanor Parker, Paul Henreid

Plot: Passengers on a mysterious liner are all dead and on their way to "the next world."

Notes: The remake was updated to World War II. Featured in the cast of this 1944 film is Faye Emerson, once married to Elliott Roosevelt, son of Franklin Delano Roosevelt.

★   ★   ★

▶ PICTURE OF DORIAN GRAY, THE (1945)★AOV★
MGM • Albert Lewin

Hurd Hatfield, George Sanders, Angela Lansbury

▷ PICTURE OF DORIAN GRAY, THE (1973)
MMTV • Glenn Jordan

Shane Briant, Charles Aidman, Nigel Davenport

Plot: Oscar Wilde's Dorian Gray maintains a youthful image—a hidden picture is the true indication of his age.

Notes: THE SINS OF DORIAN GRAY★AOV★, a 1983 MMTV, stars Belinda Bauer as a female Dorian Gray.

★   ★   ★

▶ PINOCCHIO (1940)★AOV★
Disney • Ben Sharpsteen, Hamilton Luske

Voices of Dickie Jones, Cliff Edwards

▷ PINOCCHIO (1976)
Rothman/Wohl • Ron Field, Sid Smith

Danny Kaye, Sandy Duncan, Flip Wilson

Plot: A puppet, wanting to become a real boy, has many adventures before reaching his goal.

Notes: "When You Wish Upon a Star," sung by Cliff Edwards in the original film, won the 1940 Best Song Academy Award.

★   ★   ★

▶ REPEAT PERFORMANCE (1947)
Eagle-Lion • Alfred L. Werker

Joan Leslie, Louis Hayward, Richard Basehart

▷ TURN BACK THE CLOCK (1989)
MMTV • Larry Elikann

Connie Sellecca, David Dukes, Gene Barry

Plot: A woman, who kills her husband on New Year's Eve, gets a chance to relive the previous twelve months.

Notes: Joan Leslie, who stars in the original production, makes a cameo appearance in the remake. She is seen as one of the guests at a New Year's Eve party.

★   ★   ★

▶ SVENGALI (1931)★AOV★
Warners • Archie Mayo
John Barrymore, Marian Marsh, Donald Crisp

▷ SVENGALI (1954)★AOV★
British/Renown • Noel Langley
Donald Wolfit, Hildegarde Neff

Plot: A hypnotist turns a girl into a great singer, but she does not reciprocate his love.

Notes: The latest version of the Svengali/Trilby story was released in 1983★AOV★. This MMTV stars Peter O'Toole, Jodie Foster and Elizabeth Ashley. O'Toole plays a music teacher who takes a rock singer under his wing.

★ ★ ★

Hurd Hatfield, the youthful looking title-rolist, is at the piano in this scene from THE PICTURE OF DORIAN GRAY. Flanking him are Lowell Gilmore (left) and George Sanders (right). But where has Dorian Gray hidden his tell-tale portrait?

★ ★ ★

▶ THING, THE (1951)★AOV★
RKO • Christian Nyby
James Arness, Kenneth Tobey

▷ THING, THE (1982)★AOV★
Universal • John Carpenter
Kurt Russell, A. Wilford Brimley

Plot: A United States scientific expedition at an Antarctic outpost is threatened by an alien organism.

Notes: James Arness, the star of the 1951 production, is most familiar to fans as Marshal Matt Dillon on the long running "Gunsmoke" television series (see RED RIVER, Chapter Ten).

★ ★ ★

▶ THINGS TO COME (1936)★AOV★
British/London films • William Cameron Menzies
Raymond Massey, Ralph Richardson, Cedric Hardwicke

▷ SHAPE OF THING TO COME, THE (1979)
Canadian • George McCowan
Jack Palance, Carol Lynley, John Ireland

Plot: War is followed by plague, rebellion and a new kind of society.

Notes: The films are based upon H.G. Wells' science fiction novel, "Things To Come." A fascinating aspect of the writer's work is that many of his fantastic predictions, made over a half century ago, have come to pass—like a rocket ship to the moon.

☆   ☆   ☆   ☆   ☆   ☆   ☆

▶ TIME MACHINE, THE (1960)★AOV★
MGM • George Pal
Rod Taylor, Alan Young, Yvette Mimieux

▷ TIME MACHINE, THE (1978)★AOV★
MMTV • Henry Schellerup
John Beck, Priscilla Barnes, Andrew Duggan

Plot: A scientist invents a machine which transports him into an unknown future.

Notes: Alan Young is known to several generations as the owner, but never master, of television's talking horse, "Mr. Ed."

★ ★ ★

▶ TOPPER (1937)★AOV★
MGM/Hal Roach • Norman Z. McLeod
Cary Grant, Constance Bennett, Roland Young

▷ TOPPER (1979)
MMTV • Charles S. Dubin
Kate Jackson, Andrew Stevens, Jack Warden

Plot: A stuffy banker has the starch taken out of him by a pair of fun-seeking ghosts visible only to him.

Notes: Two sequels followed the 1937 film: TOPPER TAKES A TRIP (1938) and TOPPER RETURNS (1941). Although Cary Grant appears in neither, Constance Bennett stars in the first sequel, again with Roland Young—title-rolist in every production except the one made in 1979.

★ ★ ★

▶ WEIRD WOMAN (1944)
Universal • Reginald LeBorg
Anne Gwynne, Evelyn Ankers, Ralph Morgan, Lon Chaney Jr.

▷ BURN, WITCH, BURN! (1962)
British • Sidney Hayers
Janet Blair, Peter Wyngarde, Margaret Johnston

Plot: A woman, hating both her former sweetheart and his new wife, plots a deathly revenge on both of them.

Notes: Janet Blair, the star of the 1962 film, was a top performer during the nineteen forties. Her forte was musical comedy—she had been a band singer before coming to Hollywood. Lon Chaney Jr. was born Creighton Chaney, but changed his name to Lon Jr. early on in his movie career.

★ ★ ★

★   ★   ★   ★   ★   ★   ★

CHAPTER SEVEN

MUSIC, MUSIC, MUSIC: REMAKING THE MUSICAL

It was a time of depression—the nineteen thirties—bread lines and headlines, a time of changes—and the film industry reflected these changes.

At first hesitantly, then full speed ahead, Hollywood plunged into the age of the talkies. With the Stock Market Crash on that bleak October day in 1929 reverberating throughout the nation, people needed to escape into a world of make believe where, for a couple of hours, they could forget their troubles.

The movie musical provided some relief for the shell-shocked generation. The earliest "all-singing, all-dancing" motion pictures became so popular with their audiences that each studio hastened to find suitable plots and stars for what promised to put millions into its respective coffer.

That promise was so well realized that, as time went by, many of these film musicals were remade. The stars appearing in the originals and their remakes were some of the brightest in film history and the composers and choreographers working on the sound stages of these projects form a veritable Who's Who of Show Business.

In these days of astronomical production costs, it is highly improbable that we will see a resurrection of the movie musical as we once knew it—what we do have left are a heritage and some mighty fond memories.

★ ★ ★ ★ ★ ★ ★

▶ BABES IN TOYLAND (1934)
Hal Roach • Gus Meine
Stan Laurel, Oliver Hardy, Charlotte Henry

▷ BABES IN TOYLAND (1961)★AOV★
Disney • Jack Donohue
Ray Bolger, Tommy Kirk, Annette Funicello

Plot: A villain tries to take over Toyland, but giant toy soldiers, which have accidently been constructed, prevent this.

Notes: Annette Funicello spent much of her youth at the Disney studios as a Television Mouseketeer. In the program's theme song were such immortal lyrics as M-I-C-K-E-Y M-O-U-S-E. A third film version of the Victor Herbert operetta, starring Drew Barrymore, was released in 1986.

★ ★ ★

▶ BITTER SWEET (1933)★AOV★
British and Dominion • Herbert Wilcox
Anna Neagle, Fernand Gravet

▷ BITTER SWEET (1940)★AOV★
MGM • W.S. Van Dyke
Jeanette MacDonald, Nelson Eddy

Plot: The films are based upon a Noel Coward operetta.

Notes: Anna Neagle and producer-director Herbert Wilcox were husband and wife in real life.

★ ★ ★

▶ BROADWAY MELODY (1929)★AOV★
MGM • Harry Beaumont
Anita Page, Bessie Love, Charles King

▷ TWO GIRLS ON BROADWAY (1940)
MGM • S. Sylvan Simon
Joan Blondell, George Murphy, Lana Turner

Plot: Chorus girls seek fame and fortune on Broadway.

Notes: BROADWAY MELODY was the first screen musical ever produced. It won a Best Picture Academy Award.

★ ★ ★

▶ DESERT SONG, THE (1929)
Warners • Roy Del Ruth
John Boles, Carlotta King

▷ DESERT SONG, THE (1953)
Warners • H. Bruce Humberstone
Gordon MacRae, Kathryn Grayson

Plot: A mysterious romantic hero leads his North African comrades against their enemies.

Notes: In between the 1929 and 1953 versions of the Sigmund Romberg operetta was a 1943 release starring Dennis Morgan and Irene Manning. Filmed during World War II, with an updated script, it had the Nazis replacing the Arabs of the original story.

★ ★ ★

▶ FARMER'S DAUGHTER, THE (1940)
Paramount • James Hogan
Martha Raye, Charles Ruggles, Richard Denning

▷ SUMMER STOCK (1950)★AOV★
MGM • Charles Walters
Judy Garland, Gene Kelly, Gloria De Haven

Plot: A country girl becomes involved with show business characters.

Notes: Gene Kelly made his movie debut opposite Judy Garland in FOR ME AND MY GAL in 1942.

★ ★ ★

★　　★　　★　　★　　★　　★　　★

► FLEET'S IN, THE (1942)
Paramount • Victor Schertzinger

Dorothy Lamour, William Holden, Betty Hutton,
Eddie Bracken

▷ SAILOR BEWARE (1951)
Paramount • Hal Walker

Dean Martin, Jerry Lewis, Corinne Calvet

Plot: A sailor meets and falls in love with a glamorous cafe singer.

Notes: The 1928 version of the story stars Clara Bow. Director Schertzinger teamed with lyricist Johnny Mercer and composed the songs for the 1942 film. Betty Hutton makes her screen debut in this version, which also features the music of the Jimmy Dorsey orchestra.

 ★　★　★

Jeanette MacDonald and Nelson Eddy (leading the band) in BITTER SWEET. The popular singing duo co-starred in eight films.

 ★　★　★

► GIRL CRAZY (1943)★AOV★
MGM • Norman Taurog

Judy Garland, Mickey Rooney, June Allyson,
Tommy Dorsey

▷ WHEN THE BOYS MEET THE GIRLS (1965)
MGM • Alvin Ganzer

Connie Francis, Harve Presnell, Louis Armstrong

Plot: A brash young playboy, sent to a small college out west, finds friendship and romance there.

Notes: The earliest version of GIRL CRAZY was released in 1932. It stars the then popular comedy team of Bert Wheeler and Robert Woolsey.

★　★　★

☆   ☆   ☆   ☆   ☆   ☆   ☆

▶ GOLD DIGGERS OF BROADWAY (1929)   ▷ GOLD DIGGERS OF 1933 (1933)★AOV★
Warners • Roy Del Ruth   Warners • Mervyn Le Roy
Conway Tearle, Winnie Lightner, Nick Lucas   Joan Blondell, Dick Powell, Ruby Keeler

Plot: Three chorus girls are on the prowl for rich husbands.

Notes: Nick Lucas was a popular singer of the nineteen twenties and thirties. Busby Berkeley choreographed the 1933 production.

★ ★ ★

Mickey Rooney and Judy Garland in GIRL CRAZY. With songs by the Gershwins including "I Got Rhythm," who could ask for anything more?

★ ★ ★

▶ GOOD NEWS (1930)   ▷ GOOD NEWS (1947)★AOV★
MGM • Nick Grinde, Edgar McGregor   MGM • Charles Walters
Bessie Love, Stanley Smith, Cliff Edwards,   June Allyson, Mel Torme, Peter Lawford
Dorothy McNulty

Plot: The big game is approaching at Tate College and the football hero has to pass an exam in order to play.

Notes: Dorothy McNulty later changed her name to Penny Singleton and starred in a series of films based upon Chic Young's cartoon character, "Blondie." Cliff Edwards is most famous as the voice of Disney's beloved Jiminy Cricket.

★ ★ ★

▶ GREAT WALTZ, THE (1938)
MGM • Julien Duvivier
Fernand Gravet, Luise Rainer

▷ GREAT WALTZ, THE (1972)
MGM • Andrew L. Stone
Horst Bucholtz, Rossano Brazzi, Mary Costa

Plot: The biography of composer Johann Strauss.

Notes: The original production was shot on the MGM lot, the remake in Vienna, birthplace of the composer.

★ ★ ★

The GOOD NEWS is that by the final reel, June Allyson rescues football hero Peter Lawford from the clutches of conniving campus cutie Patricia Marshal.

★ ★ ★

▶ HIT THE DECK (1930)
RKO • Luther Reed
Jack Oakie, Polly Walker

▷ HIT THE DECK (1954)★AOV★
MGM • Roy Rowland
Tony Martin, Jane Powell, Debbie Reynolds, Vic Damone, Ann Miller

Plot: Three sailors experience love and laughter while on shore leave.

Notes: Singers Tony Martin and Vic Damone are married to performers Cyd Charisse and Diahann Carroll respectively. Music for the 1954 film comes from the pen of Vincent Youmans.

★ ★ ★

▶ IT'S A DATE (1940)
Universal • William Seiter
Deanna Durbin, Walter Pidgeon, Kay Francis

▷ NANCY GOES TO RIO (1950)
MGM • Robert Z. Leonard
Jane Powell, Ann Sothern, Barry Sullivan, Carmen Miranda

Plot: Two actresses, a mother and a daughter, are both unknowingly up for the same part—they also fall in love with the same man.

Notes: Carmen Miranda, a popular star of Twentieth Century-Fox musicals, was known as "The Brazilian Bombshell." Her trademarks were platform shoes and unusual headgear.

★ ★ ★

▶ JAZZ SINGER, THE (1927)★AOV★   ▷ JAZZ SINGER, THE (1980)★AOV★
Warners • Alan Crosland   EMI • Richard Fleischer
Al Jolson, Warner Oland   Neil Diamond, Laurence Olivier, Lucie Arnaz

Plot: A cantor's son becomes a Broadway star.

Notes: Sandwiched in between the 1927 and 1980 productions was one released by Warners in 1953. It stars Danny Thomas and Peggy Lee.

★ ★ ★

May McAvoy is persuading Al Jolson as THE JAZZ SINGER to heed the siren song of Show Business.

★ ★ ★

▶ LOVES OF CARMEN, THE (1948)★AOV★   ▷ CARMEN JONES (1954)★AOV★
Columbia • Charles Vidor   TCF • Otto Preminger
Rita Hayworth, Glenn Ford   Harry Belafonte, Dorothy Dandridge, Pearl Bailey

Plot: A soldier falls desperately in love with a femme fatale.

Notes: Rita Hayworth's father, Eduardo Cansino, was an assistant choreographer on the 1948 film—her brother and uncle are seen in bit roles. Much of the singing in the all-Black 1954 version of the Bizet opera is dubbed even though the major stars are singers. There were two foreign productions of "Carmen" filmed, one in 1983★AOV★, the other in 1984★AOV★.

★ ★ ★

▶ NEW MOON (1930)   ▷ NEW MOON (1940)★AOV★
MGM • Jack Conway   MGM • Robert Z. Leonard
Grace Moore, Lawrence Tibbett, Adolphe Menjou   Jeanette MacDonald, Nelson Eddy

Plot: Life, love and music in old French Louisiana.

Notes: The noted composer Sigmund Romberg set to music the lovely lyrics of Oscar Hammerstein II.

★ ★ ★

▶ NO NO NANETTE (1930)
Warners • Clarence Badger
Bernice Claire, ZaSu Pitts, Lucien Littlefield

▷ NO NO NANETTE (1940) ★AOV★
RKO • Herbert Wilcox
Anna Neagle, Victor Mature, Richard Carlson, Eve Arden

Plot: A girl helps her uncle out of a financial jam.

Notes: The first film contains some color sequences, not a common practice during the early nineteen thirties.

★ ★ ★

Ginger Rogers on the bandstand in ROBERTA. Can Fred Astaire be far away?

★ ★ ★

▶ RHYTHM ON THE RANGE (1936)
Paramount • Norman Taurog
Bing Crosby, Frances Farmer, Martha Raye, Bob Burns

▷ PARDNERS (1956)
Paramount • Norman Taurog
Dean Martin, Jerry Lewis, Lori Nelson

Plot: A hired hand on a ranch rounds up some local bad men.

Notes: The music in PARDNERS comes from the prolific pens of the Academy Award-winning team of Sammy Cahn and James Van Heusen.

★ ★ ★

★   ★   ★   ★   ★   ★   ★

▶ RIO RITA (1929)
RKO • Luther Reed

Bebe Daniels, John Boles, Bert Wheeler, Robert
Woolsey

▷ RIO RITA (1942)
MGM • S. Sylvan Simon

Kathryn Grayson, John Carroll, Bud Abbott, Lou
Costello

Plot: Ranchers near the Mexican border hunt down those who would disturb the peace.

Notes: The 1942 film is an updated version of the original with Nazi spies as the villains. Wheeler
and Woolsey were the nineteen twenties and thirties equivalents of Abbott and Costello.

★   ★   ★

*A timeless story of love played
out against the backdrop of
the mighty Mississippi. Irene
Dunne and Allan Jones in
SHOW BOAT.*

★   ★   ★

▶ ROBERTA (1935)★AOV★
RKO • William Seiter

Irene Dunne, Randolph Scott, Fred Astaire,
Ginger Rogers

▷ LOVELY TO LOOK AT (1952)
MGM • Mervyn Le Roy

Kathryn Grayson, Howard Keel, Red Skelton, Ann
Miller

Plot: An American inherits a Paris fashion shop.

Notes: ROBERTA is the screen version of a popular stage hit of the nineteen thirties. Featured in
the Broadway show was an up-and-coming young comic named Bob Hope.

★   ★   ★

▶ ROSE MARIE (1936)★AOV★
MGM • W.S. Van Dyke

Jeanette MacDonald, Nelson Eddy, James
Stewart

▷ ROSE MARIE (1954)
MGM • Mervyn Le Roy

Howard Keel, Ann Blyth, Fernando Lamas

Plot: A Canadian Mountie searches for a fugitive and falls in love with the sister of the wanted man.

Notes: MGM also filmed a silent version of the operetta in 1927 starring Joan Crawford.

★   ★   ★

★   ★   ★   ★   ★   ★   ★

▶ SHE LOVES ME NOT (1934)
Paramount • Elliott Nugent
Bing Crosby, Miriam Hopkins, Kitty Carlisle

▷ HOW TO BE VERY, VERY POPULAR (1955)
TCF • Nunally Johnson
Betty Grable, Sheree North, Robert Cummings

Plot: Showgirl witnesses to a murder take refuge in a men's college dorm.

Notes: The hit song from the 1934 film, "Love in Bloom," later became comedian Jack Benny's theme.

★   ★   ★

*A 1951 voyage for SHOW BOAT.
Kathryn Grayson as Magnolia Hawks and
Howard Keel as Gaylord Ravenal.*

★   ★   ★

▶ SHOW BOAT (1936)
Universal • James Whale
Irene Dunne, Allan Jones, Helen Morgan

▷ SHOW BOAT (1951)★AOV★
MGM • George Sidney
Kathryn Grayson, Ava Gardner, Howard Keel

Plot: A young show boat entertainer lives life and falls in love along the Mississippi.

Notes: SHOW BOAT had been a huge Broadway hit, adapted for the stage by Oscar Hammerstein II from Edna Ferber's sprawling novel, with music and lyrics by Hammerstein and Jerome Kern. The first production of the story was filmed as a silent in 1929. A prologue was added, featuring the Broadway cast performing the play's best known songs.

★   ★   ★

★   ★   ★   ★   ★   ★   ★

▶ THANKS A MILLION (1935)★ᴬᴼⱽ★
TCF • Roy Del Ruth

Dick Powell, Fred Allen, Ann Dvorak, Paul Whiteman

▷ IF I'M LUCKY (1945)
TCF • Lewis Seiler

Perry Como, Vivian Blaine, Phil Silvers, Harry James

Plot: A singer runs for governor with the help of his wise-cracking manager.

Notes: Perry Como is a "graduate" of the Big Band Era. He sang with bands led by Freddy Carlone and Ted Weems, leaving the latter in the early nineteen forties to become a solo performer.

★ ★ ★

Danny Kaye is surrounded by the enemy in UP IN ARMS. Have no fear. In true Hollywood fashion, the intrepid Danny will prevail.

★ ★ ★

▶ THAT NIGHT IN RIO (1940)
TCF • Irving Cummings

Alice Faye, Don Ameche, Carmen Miranda

▷ ON THE RIVIERA (1951)
TCF • Walter Lang

Danny Kaye, Gene Tierney, Corinne Calvet

Plot: A night club performer impersonates a look-a-like aristocrat.

Notes: The same plotline was first used by Twentieth Century-Fox in FOLIES BERGERE (1935), starring Maurice Chevalier, Merle Oberon and Ann Sothern.

★ ★ ★

▶ THAT GIRL FROM PARIS (1936)
RKO • Leigh Jason

Lily Pons, Gene Raymond, Jack Oakie, Lucille Ball

▷ FOUR JACKS AND A JILL (1941)
RKO • Jack Hively

Anne Shirley, Ray Bolger, Desi Arnaz

Plot: A girl falls in love with a band leader and complications set in, but things work out and the two live happily ever after.

Notes: Lily Pons enjoyed a long career as a Metropolitan Opera star. Lucille Ball did not know Desi Arnaz when the original film was being shot, but by the time the remake featuring the Cuban band leader went into production, she was Mrs. Arnaz.

★ ★ ★

★ ★ ★ ★ ★ ★ ★

▶ TIN PAN ALLEY (1940)
TCF • Walter Lang
Alice Faye, Betty Grable, John Payne, Jack Oakie

▷ I'LL GET BY (1950)
TCF • Richard Sale
June Haver, Gloria DeHaven, William Lundigan, Dennis Day

Plot: Two struggling song "pluggers" meet up with a sister act.

Notes: TIN PAN ALLEY is the only pairing of the studio's two top blondes of the nineteen forties, although they did separate cameos in FOUR JILLS IN A JEEP (1944).

★ ★ ★

Jack Haley as The Tin Man in THE WIZARD OF OZ. Haley's son was once married to Liza Minnelli, daughter of Judy Garland, his father's fellow traveler along the Yellow Brick Road.

★ ★ ★

▶ TWENTY MILLION SWEETHEARTS (1934)
Warners • Ray Enright
Dick Powell, Ginger Rogers, Pat O'Brien

▷ MY DREAM IS YOURS (1949)
Warners • Michael Curtiz
Doris Day, Jack Carson, Lee Bowman

Plot: A radio story wherein an agent promotes a singer into a star.

Notes: Doris Day sang with the bands of Bob Crosby and Les Brown before being signed by Warner Brothers. In MY DREAM IS YOURS she reprises the role played by Dick Powell in the original film.

★ ★ ★

★   ★   ★   ★   ★   ★   ★

▶ WHERE THE BOYS ARE (1960)★AOV★
MGM • Henry Levin

George Hamilton, Paula Prentiss, Jim Hutton, Connie Francis

▷ WHERE THE BOYS ARE (1984)★AOV★
ITC • Hy Averback

Lorna Luft, Lisa Hartman, Wendy Schall, Russell Todd

Plot: College hijinks during Spring Break in Fort Lauderdale.

Notes: The two most interesting facts about the 1984 production are that it stars Lorna Luft, daughter of Judy Garland, and that it was directed by Hy Averback, a former radio announcer.

★   ★   ★

▶ WHOOPEE (1930)★AOV★
Samuel Goldwyn • Thornton Freeland

Eddie Cantor, Ethel Shutta

▷ UP IN ARMS (1944)★AOV★
Samuel Goldwyn • Elliott Nugent

Danny Kaye, Dinah Shore, Dana Andrews

Plot: A musical about a hypochondriac and the scrapes he gets into.

Notes: A small part in WHOOPEE is played by thirteen year old Betty Grable. UP IN ARMS introduced Danny Kaye to movie audiences. The inimitable Danny had scored a tremendous hit in the stage version of "Lady in the Dark."

★   ★   ★

▶ WIZARD OF OZ, THE (1939)★AOV★
MGM • Victor Fleming

Judy Garland, Jack Haley, Bert Lahr, Ray Bolger

▷ WIZ, THE (1978)★AOV★
Universal/Motown • Sidney Lumet

Diana Ross, Michael Jackson, Nipsey Russell, Lena Horne

Plot: During a tornado, a girl dreams about a yellow brick road and a place called Oz.

Notes: A rarely seen version of THE WIZARD OF OZ was released in 1925★AOV★ with an actress named Dorothy Dawn as Dorothy and Oliver Hardy (sans Stan Laurel) as The Tin Woodsman. MGM had wanted Shirley Temple to play the lead in the 1939 production, but Twentieth Century-Fox refused to loan her out. Scarecrow Ray Bolger was to have played The Tin Man in the same production, but switched roles with Buddy Ebsen. The latter became ill due to the metal paint in his make-up and was replaced by Jack Haley.

★   ★   ★

★   ★   ★   ★   ★   ★   ★

CHAPTER EIGHT

A MUSICAL METAMORPHOSIS: A CHANGE IN GENRE

One of the most fascinating aspects of the film remake involves a change in genre. All but one of the following comedy or dramatic productions underwent a metamorphosis and resurfaced as a movie musical (The opposite occurred in the case of MAD ABOUT MUSIC) and for the most part, as the film changed, so did the casts.

And what changes they were. Only by an imaginative filmmaker's decree could Margaret Sullavan and Judy Garland play the same role, June Allyson step into Norma Shearer's shoes, Danny Kaye play a part originally enacted by Gary Cooper and Dennis Morgan substitute for the feisty Jimmy Cagney. In many cases, there are several changes in the plotline, in others, very few. Sometimes the name is different, sometimes it remains the same.

Several of the fifty-four film pairings listed below show Hollywood at its tuneful best, utilizing some of our favorite musical comedy stars. It is said that comedians long to play Shakespeare. I wonder, however, how many of the performers in the original productions would like to have tried their hand at singing and dancing in the revised roles.

An interesting thought indeed.

▶ AH, WILDERNESS (1955)
MGM • Clarence Brown
Wallace Beery, Lionel Barrymore, Mickey Rooney

▷ SUMMER HOLIDAY (1948)
MGM • Rouben Mamoulian
Walter Houston, Frank Morgan, Mickey Rooney,
Jackie "Butch" Jenkins

Plot: A bit of Americana, as a small-town family copes with life's problems at the turn of the century.

Notes: Jackie "Butch" Jenkins reprises the part originally played by Mickey Rooney in the earlier version, while Rooney assumes a a more mature role.

★ ★ ★

Small town Americana, Hollywood style. Rosemary Lane, Gale Page, Priscilla Lane and Lola Lane (left to right) in FOUR DAUGHTERS. There were only three Lane sisters so Gale Page was signed to play the fourth daughter.

★ ★ ★

▶ ALGIERS (1938)★AOV★
Walter Wanger • John Cromwell
Charles Boyer, Hedy Lamarr, Sigrid Gurie

▷ CASBAH (1948)
Universal • John Berry
Tony Martin, Marta Toren, Yvonne De Carlo

Plot: All for love, a wanted thief leaves the relative safety of the Casbah and is captured by the police.

Notes: Both films are derived from PEPE LE MOKO, a 1936 French release starring Jean Gabin in the title role.

★ ★ ★

▶ ANNA AND THE KING OF SIAM (1946)★AOV★
TCF • John Cromwell
Irene Dunne, Rex Harrison, Linda Darnell

▷ KING AND I, THE (1956)★AOV★
TCF • Walter Lang
Deborah Kerr, Yul Brynner, Rita Moreno

Plot: An English governess comes to Siam to tutor the king's many children and, in the process, teaches His Royal Highness a few things.

Notes: Yul Brynner played "The King" on Broadway. His stage co-star was English performer Gertrude Lawrence.

★ ★ ★

▶ **AUNTIE MAME (1958)**★AOV★
Warners • Morton Da Costa
Rosalind Russell, Forrest Tucker, Coral Browne

▷ **MAME (1974)**★AOV★
Warners/ABC • Gene Saks
Lucille Ball, Robert Preston, Bea Arthur

Plot: A young boy comes to live with his larger than life aunt.

Notes: In the 1974 version of the Patrick Dennis novel, which was based upon the life of his real aunt, Bea "Golden Girls" Arthur reprises her Broadway role as Mame's best friend.

★ ★ ★

Frank Sinatra in YOUNG AT HEART. In this musical version of FOUR DAUGHTERS, Sinatra is seen in the role originally played by John Garfield.

★ ★ ★

▶ **BACHELOR MOTHER (1939)**★AOV★
RKO • Garson Kanin
Ginger Rogers, David Niven, Charles Coburn

▷ **BUNDLE OF JOY (1956)**★AOV★
RKO • Norman Taurog
Debbie Reynolds, Eddie Fisher, Adolphe Menjou

Plot: A girl who works at a department store finds an abandoned baby—everyone thinks the son of the store owner is the child's father, including the boss himself.

Notes: Debbie Reynolds and Eddie Fisher were America's favorite "young marrieds" when they filmed BUNDLE OF JOY. It was long before Fisher's affair and subsequent marriage to Elizabeth Taylor.

★ ★ ★

★　　★　　★　　★　　★　　★　　★

▶ BALL OF FIRE (1942)★AOV★
Samuel Goldwyn • Howard Hawks

Gary Cooper, Barbara Stanwyck, Dana Andrews

▷ SONG IS BORN, A (1948)
Samuel Goldwyn • Howard Hawks

Danny Kaye, Virginia Mayo

Plot: A stripper moves in with a group of professors compiling a dictionary—*they* learn a thing or two from *her*.

Notes: In 1942 Ginger Rogers was first choice for the role, but Barbara Stanwyck played the part and received an Oscar nomination for her efforts. Such star musicians as Louis Armstrong, Benny Goodman, Tommy Dorsey and Lionel Hampden appear in the 1948 film.

★　★　★

▶ BROADWAY BILL (1934)
Columbia • Frank Capra

Warner Baxter, Myrna Loy

▷ RIDING HIGH (1950)
Paramount • Frank Capra

Bing Crosby, Coleen Gray. Oliver Hardy

Plot: A horse owner keeps the faith and his animal comes through by winning a crucial race.

Notes: Oliver Hardy appears in the film without partner Stan Laurel.

★　★　★

▶ BROTHER RAT (1938)
Warners • William Keighley

Eddie Albert, Jane Wyman, Ronald Reagan, Priscilla Lane, Wayne Morris

▷ ABOUT FACE (1952)
Warners • Ray Del Ruth

Eddie Bracken, Gordon MacRae, Phyllis Kirk, Joel Grey

Plot: Cadets at a military academy get in and out of scrapes before graduation.

Notes: Jane Wyman and Ronald Reagan met during the filming of BROTHER RAT. They were married from 1940 to 1948.

★　★　★

▶ CHARLEY'S AUNT (1941)
TCF • Archie Mayo

Jack Benny, Kay Francis

▷ WHERE'S CHARLEY? (1952)
Warners • David Butler

Ray Bolger, Allyn McLerie, Mary Germaine

Plot: An Oxford undergrad impersonates his wealthy aunt from Brazil.

Notes: A silent version of CHARLEY'S AUNT, starring Sidney Chaplin (brother of Charlie), was filmed in 1925 and an early talkie, starring Charles Ruggles, came out in 1930. Ray Bolger, appearing in the Broadway version, also titled "Where's Charley?," stopped the show nightly when he sang "Once in Love with Amy."

★　★　★

▶ CONNECTICUT YANKEE, A (1931)

Fox • David Butler

Will Rogers, Maureen O'Sullivan, Myrna Loy

▷ CONNECTICUT YANKEE IN KING ARTHUR'S COURT, A (1948)★AOV★
Paramount • Tay Garnett

Bing Crosby, Rhonda Fleming, William Bendix

Plot: A man, living in the twentieth century, dreams that he has been transported back to the days of King Arthur and the Knights of the Round Table.

Notes: The first version of the Mark Twain novel was filmed by Fox in 1921 starring Harry Myers.

★　★　★

☆ ☆ ☆ ☆ ☆ ☆ ☆

▶ DADDY LONGLEGS (1931)
Fox • Alfred Santell
Janet Gaynor, Warner Baxter

▷ DADDY LONGLEGS (1955)
TCF • Jean Negulesco
Fred Astaire, Leslie Caron

Plot: An orphan falls in love with her mysterious benefactor.

Notes: A silent version was filmed in 1919 starring Canadian-born Mary Pickford, ever billed as "America's Sweetheart."

★ ★ ★

Has Virginia Mayo invited THE KID FROM BROOKLYN, Danny Kaye, to her boudoir for purposes other than bringing her a bottle of milk?

★ ★ ★

▶ FARMER TAKES A WIFE, THE (1935)
TCF • Victor Fleming
Janet Gaynor, Henry Fonda

▷ FARMER TAKES A WIFE, THE (1953)★ᴀᴏᵛ★
TCF • Harry Levin
Betty Grable, Dale Robertson

Plot: A young farmer and his wife live and love along the Erie Canal during the eighteen twenties.

Notes: THE FARMER TAKES A WIFE was Henry Fonda's first film. He had appeared in the role on the Broadway stage.

★ ★ ★

▶ FOUR DAUGHTERS (1938)
Warners • Michael Curtiz
The Lane Sisters, Claude Rains, John Garfield

▷ YOUNG AT HEART (1954)★ᴀᴏᵛ★
Warners • Gordon Douglas
Frank Sinatra, Doris Day, Gig Young, Ethel Barrymore

Plot: Small town Americana, in which four sisters find love, marriage and tragedy.

Notes: John Garfield had been a member of the "Group Theater" in New York when he was signed by Warners. FOUR DAUGHTERS was his first film. In the original, Garfield dies. Sinatra, playing the same role in the remake, lives.

★ ★ ★

▶ GIGI (1948)
French/Code Cinema • Jacqueline Audry
Danielle Delorme, Gaby Morlay

▷ GIGI (1958)★AOV★
MGM • Vincente Minnelli
Leslie Caron, Maurice Chevalier, Louis Jordan

Plot: A young girl, raised to be a courtesan, marries the worldly man she loves and domesticates him.

Notes: The 1958 production won nine Academy Awards including Best Film, Best Director, Best Song and a special career Oscar for Maurice Chevalier.

★ ★ ★

Mr. and Mrs. Douglas Fairbanks Sr. (Mary Pickford) in THE TAMING OF THE SHREW. A generation later, Mr. and Mrs. Richard Burton (Elizabeth Taylor) filmed a rousing version of this comedy by Shakespeare.

★ ★ ★

▶ GIRL OF THE GOLDEN WEST, THE (1930)

Warners • John F. Dillon
Ann Harding, James Rennie

▷ GIRL OF THE GOLDEN WEST, THE (1938)★AOV★
MGM • Robert Z. Leonard
Jeanette MacDonald, Nelson Eddy, Walter Pidgeon

Plot: A lady saloon owner reforms a bandit.

Notes: A silent version of the story, starring Sylvia Breamer and J. Warren Kerrigan, was filmed in 1923 by First National. Featured in the cast of the 1938 film is Buddy Ebsen, more familiarly known to television audiences as Jed Clampett on "The Beverly Hillbillies" and as detective "Barnaby Jones."

★ ★ ★

▶ GOODBYE MR. CHIPS (1939)★AOV★
MGM • Sam Wood
Robert Donat, Greer Garson

▷ GOODBYE MR. CHIPS (1969)
MGM/APJAC • Herbert Ross
Peter O'Toole, Petula Clark

Plot: The life and times of an English schoolmaster.

Notes: Robert Donat won an Oscar for his performance in the 1939 film which also marked the American film debut of Greer Garson.

★ ★ ★

Howard Keel takes a fuming Kathryn Grayson over his knee in KISS ME KATE, Cole Porter's musical version of THE TAMING OF THE SHREW.

★ ★ ★

▶ GUARDSMAN, THE (1931)
MGM • Sidney Franklin
Alfred Lunt, Lynn Fontanne

▷ CHOCOLATE SOLDIER, THE (1941)★AOV★
MGM • Roy Del Ruth
Nelson Eddy, Rise Stevens

Plot: A jealous actor puts his wife's fidelity to the test.

Notes: THE GUARDSMAN was the only film made by the Broadway legends Lunt and Fontanne as a team. Both were Oscar-nominated. Fontanne lost to another Broadway actress, Helen Hayes, while Lunt lost to Fredric March and Wallace Beery, who tied for the award.

★ ★ ★

▶ HOME IN INDIANA (1944)
TCF • Henry Hathaway

Lon McCallister, Jeanne Crain, June Haver, Walter Brennan

▷ APRIL LOVE (1957)
TCF • Henry Levin

Pat Boone, Shirley Jones, Arthur O'Connell

Plot: A farm boy competes in a harness race and has two pretty young ladies cheering him on.

Notes: June Haver is the wife of actor Fred MacMurray. Walter Brennan won three Oscars during his long career.

★ ★ ★

Greta Garbo, Melvyn Douglas and director Ernst Lubitsch (left to right) plot out a scene from NINOTCHKA.

★ ★ ★

▶ HOOPLA (1933)
Fox • Frank Lloyd

Clara Bow, Richard Cromwell

▷ DIAMOND HORSESHOE (1945)
TCF • George Seaton

Betty Grable, Dick Haymes

Plot: A showgirl agrees to make the son of the show's manager fall in love with her. She then intends to leave him, but the opposite occurs and the two marry.

Notes: The 1933 film was the last one for the "It" girl, Clara Bow. Betty Grable married bandleader Harry James in 1943. Singer Dick Haymes had worked for James a few years earlier.

★ ★ ★

▶ I AM A CAMERA (1945)★AOV★
British/Romulus • Henry Cornelius
Julie Harris, Laurence Harvey, Shelley Winters

▷ CABARET (1972)★AOV★
ABC/Allied Artists • Bob Fosse
Liza Minnelli, Michael York, Joel Grey

Plot: An English writer observes the rise of National Socialism in pre-World War II Berlin.

Notes: The films are based upon the stories of Christopher Isherwood, who lived in Germany during the late nineteen twenties and thirties. Liza Minnelli, Joel Grey and Bob Fosse won Oscars for CABARET.

★ ★ ★

Capitalist Fred Astaire is trying to thaw out communist Cyd Charisse in SILK STOCKINGS, Cole Porter's musical version of NINOTCHKA. Can Cyd hold out for long?

★ ★ ★

▶ IF I WERE KING (1938)
Paramount • Frank Lloyd
Ronald Colman, Frances Dee, Basil Rathbone

▷ VAGABOND KING, THE (1956)
Paramount • Michael Curtiz
Kathryn Grayson, Oreste, Rita Moreno

Plot: A fourteenth century poet tangles with Louis XI and leads a popular uprising against the monarch.

Notes: Basil Rathbone was Oscar-nominated for his role in IF I WERE KING. John Barrymore stars in a silent version of the story titled BELOVED ROGUE.

★ ★ ★

▶ JEANNIE (1941)
British • GFD/Tansa • Harold French
Barbara Mullen, Michael Redgrave

▷ LET'S BE HAPPY (1957)
ABP/Marcel Hellman • Henry Levin
Vera-Ellen, Tony Martin

Plot: A girl inherits some money and goes on an extended European vacation.

Notes: Michael Redgrave is the father of actresses Lynn and Vanessa.

★ ★ ★

▶ KID GALAHAD (1937)
Warners • Michael Curtiz
Edward G. Robinson, Bette Davis, Wayne Morris

▷ KID GALAHAD (1962)★AOV★
United Artists/Mirsch • Phil Karlson
Elvis Presley, Gig Young, Lola Albright

Plot: A bellhop becomes a fighter and falls in love with his promoter's girlfriend.

Notes: THE WAGONS ROLL AT NIGHT (1941) is similar in plot to KID GALAHAD, but its setting is a circus big top.

★ ★ ★

Lifestyles of the rich and famous—James Stewart, Ruth Hussey, John Howard, Katharine Hepburn and Cary Grant (left to right) in THE PHILADELPHIA STORY.

★ ★ ★

▶ KISMET (1944)
MGM • William Dieterle
Ronald Colman, Marlene Dietrich, James Craig, Joy Page

▷ KISMET (1956)★AOV★
MGM • Vincente Minnelli
Howard Keel, Ann Blyth, Vic Damone, Dolores Gray

Plot: The daughter of a beggarly magician is wooed by the son of a caliph.

Notes: Two earlier versions were filmed, a 1920 silent and a 1930 talkie. Otis Skinner appears in both and also starred in the Broadway play. Skinner's leading lady in the 1930 film is Loretta Young.

★ ★ ★

▶ KISS ME KATE (1953)★AOV★
MGM • George Sidney
Kathryn Grayson, Howard Keel, Ann Miller

▷ TAMING OF THE SHREW, THE (1967)★AOV★
Columbia/Royal/FAI • Franco Zeffirelli
Elizabeth Taylor, Richard Burton, Michael York

Plot: Shakespeare's tale of a shrewish girl and the bridegroom who tames her.

Notes: An early version of the Bard's comedy was released in 1929★AOV★. It stars Douglas Fairbanks Sr. and Mary Pickford, then Mr. and Mrs., as were Taylor and Burton in the 1967 production.

★ ★ ★

★   ★   ★   ★   ★   ★   ★

▶ LILIOM (1930)★AOV★
Fox • Frank Borzage
Charles Farrell, Rose Hobart

▷ CAROUSEL (1956)
TCF • Henry King
Gordon MacRae, Shirley Jones

Plot: A carnival barker dies in a brawl and returns to earth to look in on his family.
Notes: A French version of LILIOM was released in 1935. Directed by Fritz Lang, it stars Charles Boyer.
CAROUSEL was also a hit Broadway musical by the legendary team of Richard Rodgers and Oscar
Hammerstein II.

★ ★ ★

*"Well Did You Evah?" This Cole Porter
song has Frank and Bing cavorting in a
scene from HIGH SOCIETY, the musical
remake of THE PHILADELPHIA STORY.*

★ ★ ★

▶ LITTLE SHOP OF HORRORS, THE
(1960)★AOV★
Vestron • Roger Corman
Jonathan Haze, Jackie Joseph, Jack Nicholson

▷ LITTLE SHOP OF HORRORS, THE
(1986)★AOV★
Geffen Company • Frank Oz
Rick Moranis, Ellen Greene, Steve Martin

Plot: A man develops a bloodthirsty plant and has to kill in order to feed it.

Notes: The 1960 production was shot in two days. The story was done on Broadway as a musical
and became the basis of the 1986 film.

★ ★ ★

★   ★   ★   ★   ★   ★   ★

▶ LOST HORIZON (1937)★AOV★
Columbia • Frank Capra

Ronald Colman, Jane Wyatt, Margo, Thomas
Mitchell, Sam Jaffe

▷ LOST HORIZON (1972)
Columbia • Charles Jarrett

Peter Finch, Liv Ullmann, Olivia Hussey, Charles
Boyer

Plot: A group of men stumble upon an idyllic civilization in the mountains of Tibet.

Notes: Oscar-nominated, the 1937 film lost to THE GREAT ZIEGFELD. The late actress Margo
was the wife of actor Eddie Albert.

★ ★ ★

▶ MAD ABOUT MUSIC (1938)
Universal • Norman Taurog

Deanna Durbin, Herbert Marshall, Gail Patrick

▷ TOY TIGER (1956)
Universal-International • Jerry Hopper

Jeff Chandler, Laraine Day, Tim Hovey

Plot: An imaginative child "adopts" a businessman as a father.

Notes: Felix Jackson, co-author of the screenplay for MAD ABOUT MUSIC, was the second of
Deanna Durbin's three husbands.

★ ★ ★

▶ MALE ANIMAL, THE (1942)

Warners • Elliott Nugent

Henry Fonda, Olivia de Havilland, Jack Carson,
Joan Leslie

▷ SHE'S WORKING HER WAY THROUGH
COLLEGE (1952)
Warners • H. Bruce Humberstone

Ronald Reagan, Virginia Mayo, Gene Nelson

Plot: A hitherto soft-spoken college professor asserts himself when an old college classmate come
to town.

Notes: Jack Carson was an actor equally at home in drama, comedy and musicals. Among his co-
stars were such diverse performers as Doris Day, Ann Sothern, Rosalind Russell and Joan
Crawford.

★ ★ ★

▶ MATCHMAKER, THE (1958)
Paramount • Joseph Anthony

Shirley Booth, Paul Ford, Shirley MacLaine

▷ HELLO DOLLY (1969)★AOV★
TCF • Gene Kelly

Barbra Streisand, Walter Matthau, Tommy Tune

Plot: A lady matchmaker meets her own "match" in a wealthy Yonkers merchant.

Notes: Carol Channing played Dolly Levi on the Broadway stage. Ginger Rogers, Betty Grable,
Dorothy Lamour and Ethel Merman were others who did the role both on Broadway and on the road.
An all-Black stage version starred Pearl Bailey and singing band leader Cab Calloway.

★ ★ ★

▶ MERRY WIDOW, THE (1934)★AOV★
MGM • Ernst Lubitsch

Jeanette MacDonald, Maurice Chevalier

▷ MERRY WIDOW, THE (1952)
MGM • Curtis Bernhardt

Lana Turner, Fernando Lamas

Plot: An impoverished king orders a nobleman to court a wealthy widow.

Notes: John Gilbert and Mae Marsh star in a 1925 version of the Franz Lehar operetta (No
Dialogue! No Music!) directed by Erich von Stroheim.

☆   ☆   ☆   ☆   ☆   ☆   ☆

▶ MIDNIGHT (1939)
Paramount • Mitchell Leisen

Claudette Colbert, Don Ameche, John Barrymore,
Mary Astor

▷ MASQUERADE IN MEXICO (1945)
Paramount • Mitchell Leisen

Dorothy Lamour, Patric Knowles, Arturo de
Cordova

Plot: A penniless girl is hired by a businessman to entice another man away from his wife.

Notes: In December of 1989, Claudette Colbert was honored at the Kennedy Center for the Performing Arts. Among those paying tribute to her was Don Ameche, co-star of MIDNIGHT.

★   ★   ★

"The Voice" again, this time with Anne Jeffreys in one of his earliest films, STEP LIVELY.

★   ★   ★

▶ MILKY WAY, THE (1936)＊AOV＊
Paramount • Leo McCarey

Harold Lloyd, Adolphe Menjou, Veree Teasdale

▷ KID FROM BROOKLYN, THE (1946)＊AOV＊
Samuel Goldwyn • Norman Z. McLeod

Danny Kaye, Virginia Mayo, Vera-Ellen

Plot: A timid milkman becomes a prize fighter.

Notes: Off screen, Adolphe Menjou and Veree Teasdale were husband and wife. A married couple was also involved in THE KID FROM BROOKLYN. Sylvia Fine, Mrs. Danny Kaye in private life, wrote much of her husband's special material.

★   ★   ★

☆   ☆   ☆   ☆   ☆   ☆   ☆

▶ MY SISTER EILEEN (1942)
Columbia • Alexander Hall
Rosalind Russell, Brian Aherne, Janet Blair

▷ MY SISTER EILEEN (1955)
Columbia • Richard Quine
Betty Garrett, Jack Lemmon, Janet Leigh

Plot: Two sisters from Ohio arrive in New York City and live in a Greenwich Village basement apartment. In their search for fame and fortune they meet "kooky" people.

Notes: In 1953, Rosalind Russell appeared in "Wonderful Town," the Broadway Musical version of MY SISTER EILEEN.

★ ★ ★

The luminous Margaret Sullavan, circa 1940, in one of her biggest hits, THE SHOP AROUND THE CORNER.

★ ★ ★

▶ NINOTCHKA (1939)★AOV★
MGM • Ernst Lubitsch
Greta Garbo, Melvyn Douglas, Ina Claire

▷ SILK STOCKINGS (1957)★AOV★
MGM • Rouben Mamoulian
Fred Astaire, Cyd Charisse, Janis Paige

Plot: Capitalism (Melvyn Douglas) meets Communism (Greta Garbo) head on and Love conquers all.

Notes: Ads for Ninotchka read "Garbo Laughs." Both she and the film were Oscar-nominated. A similar plot of a lady Communist and a male capitalist is used in COMRADE X, which stars Clark Gable and Hedy Lamarr. A 1940 variation, HE STAYED FOR BREAKFAST, stars Melvyn Douglas as a Russian in love with American lovely Loretta Young.

★ ★ ★

★   ★   ★   ★   ★   ★   ★

▶ OLIVER TWIST (1948)★AOV★
GFD/Cineguild • David Lean

Alec Guinness, Robert Newton, Anthony Newly,
John Howard Davies

▷ OLIVER! (1968)★AOV★
Columbia/Warwick/Romulus • Carol Reed

Ron Moody, Oliver Reed, Mark Lester

Plot: A mistreated orphan boy in Victorian England joins a gang of youthful thieves.

Notes: A silent filming of the Dickens novel, starring Lon Chaney Sr. as Fagin and Jackie Coogan as Oliver, was released in 1922★AOV★. An early talkie, featuring Dickie Moore in the title role, came out in 1933★AOV★. The latest version is a 1982★AOV★ MMTV with George C. Scott as Fagin.

★   ★   ★

We know something they don't know. Judy Garland and Van Johnson are secret pen pals IN THE GOOD OLD SUMMERTIME, a musical remake of THE SHOP AROUND THE CORNER.

★   ★   ★

▶ PHILADELPHIA STORY, THE (1940)★AOV★
MGM • George Cukor

Katharine Hepburn, Cary Grant, James Stewart,
Ruth Hussey

▷ HIGH SOCIETY (1956)★AOV★
MGM • Charles Walters

Bing Crosby, Frank Sinatra, Grace Kelly, Celeste
Holm

Plot: A society heiress, about to marry for the second time, has a fling with a magazine writer and returns to her first husband.

Notes: Katharine Hepburn had played the role on Broadway and owned the screen rights. The stage cast included Joseph Cotten, Van Heflin and Shirley Booth. Cary Grant donated much of his film salary to the British War Relief and Jimmy Stewart won the 1940 Academy Award. HIGH SOCIETY was the last commercial film made by Grace Kelly before her marriage to The Prince of Monaco.

★   ★   ★

▶ PYGMALION (1938)★AOV★
Gabriel Pascal • Anthony Asquith
Leslie Howard, Wendy Hiller

▷ MY FAIR LADY (1964)★AOV★
CBS/Jack L. Warner • George Cukor
Rex Harrison, Audrey Hepburn

Plot: A professor of linguistics wagers that he can make a "lady" out of a Cockney flower seller.

Notes: The films are based upon a famous play by George Bernard Shaw. Cary Grant, upon being offered the role of Henry Higgins in the movie version of the hit Broadway musical, turned it down saying that if Rex Harrison did not get the part, he (Grant) would not see the movie. Harrison played the egotistical professor and was voted Best Actor of 1964. Other Oscars went to the film itself and to director George Cukor. Julie Andrews played Eliza Doolittle on Broadway, but was not considered a big enough name for the movie.

★ ★ ★

▶ RIVER OF ROMANCE (1929)
Paramount • Richard Wallace
Charles "Buddy" Rogers, Mary Brian, Wallace Beery

▷ MISSISSIPPI (1935)
Paramount • Edward Sutherland
Bing Crosby, Joan Bennett, W.C. Fields

Plot: A peace-loving man, who avoids duels, joins a riverboat crew and proves that he is not a coward.

Notes: The first filming of the Booth Tarkington novel took place in 1924 under the title of THE FIGHTING COWARD. "Buddy" Rogers followed in the footsteps of Douglas Fairbanks Sr. as Mary Pickford's husband.

★ ★ ★

▶ ROOM SERVICE (1938)★AOV★
RKO • William Seiter
The Marx Brothers, Lucille Ball, Ann Miller

▷ STEP LIVELY (1944)★AOV★
RKO • Tim Whelan
Frank Sinatra, George Murphy, Gloria De Haven, Anne Jeffreys

Plot: A penniless producer does everything he can to avoid being evicted from his hotel room while he tries to find a backer for his show.

Notes: Like his friend and co-star Ronald Reagan (THIS IS THE ARMY), veteran actor and Republican George Murphy went into politics and served a term in the United States Senate.

★ ★ ★

▶ SHOP AROUND THE CORNER, THE (1940)★AOV★
MGM • Ernst Lubitsch
Margaret Sullavan, James Stewart, Frank Morgan

▷ IN THE GOOD OLD SUMMERTIME (1949)★AOV★
MGM • Robert Z. Leonard
Judy Garland, Van Johnson, S.Z. Sakall

Plot: A floorwalker and a shopgirl, who dislike each other, don't know it, but they are secret pen pals.

Notes: It was in the 1949 production that a little girl named Liza (Minnelli) made her film "debut."

★ ★ ★

▶ SMALL TOWN GIRL (1938)
MGM • William Wellman

Janet Gaynor, Robert Taylor, James Stewart,
Binnie Barnes

▷ SMALL TOWN GIRL (1953)
MGM • Leslie Kardos

Jane Powell, Ann Miller, Farley Granger, Bobby
Van

Plot: A girl traps a young man, who is drunk, into a proposal of marriage, and then sets about winning his love when he is sober.

Notes: Choreography for the 1953 film was under the direction of Busby Berkeley.

★ ★ ★

Paulette Goddard, Mary Boland and Norma Shearer (left to right) are only three of THE WOMEN in an all-star cast. To what or to whom are they drinking?

★ ★ ★

▶ SMILES OF A SUMMER NIGHT (1955)★AOV★
Swedish • Ingmar Bergman

Gunnar Bjornstrand, Eva Dahlbeck, Ulla Jacobsson

▷ LITTLE NIGHT MUSIC, A (1977)★AOV★
Sascha Film • Harold Prince

Elizabeth Taylor, Diana Rigg, Len Cariou

Plot: A worldly lawyer and his young wife spend a weekend at the home of his former mistress.

Notes: The Broadway version of the Bergman story starred Glynis Johns. Both the show and the 1977 film feature a song which has become a standard, "Send in the Clowns."

★ ★ ★

▶ STAR IS BORN, A (1937)★AOV★
David O. Selznick • William Wellman

Janet Gaynor, Fredric March, Adolphe Menjou

▷ STAR IS BORN, A (1954)★AOV★
Warners/Transcona • George Cukor

Judy Garland, James Mason, Charles Bickford, Jack Carson

Plot: An aspiring actress meets and marries a Hollywood leading man—as her star waxes bright, his wanes.

Notes: A STAR IS BORN is based, in part, upon WHAT PRICE HOLLYWOOD?, a 1932 movie directed by George Cukor and starring Constance Bennett and Lowell Sherman. A third production, released in 1976★AOV★, stars Barbra Streisand and Kris Kristofferson.

★ ★ ★

★   ★   ★   ★   ★   ★   ★

▶ STATE FAIR (1933)
Fox • Henry King

Will Rogers, Janet Gaynor, Lew Ayres, Sally Eilers

▷ STATE FAIR (1945)
TCF • Walter Lang

Jeanne Crain, Dana Andrews, Dick Haymes, Vivian Blaine

Plot: A family goes to the Iowa State Fair and gets much more than its members bargained for.

Notes: The songs in the 1945 film were written by Richard Rodgers and Oscar Hammerstein II, both of whom received Oscars for "It Might As Well be Spring." A third version was filmed in 1962★AOV★ starring Alice Faye, Pat Boone, Ann-Margret, Tom Ewell and Bobby Darin.

★   ★   ★

▶ STRAWBERRY BLONDE, THE (1941)★AOV★
Warners • Raoul Walsh

James Cagney, Rita Hayworth, Olivia de Havilland, Alan Hale

▷ ONE SUNDAY AFTERNOON (1948)
Warners • Raoul Walsh

Dennis Morgan, Janis Paige, Dorothy Malone, Don Defore

Plot: A turn-of-the-century dentist is attracted to one woman but marries another more suited to him.

Notes: The first version of the story (original title: ONE SUNDAY AFTERNOON) was filmed in 1932, with Gary Cooper starred.

★   ★   ★

▶ SWING HIGH, SWING LOW (1937)★AOV★
Paramount • Mitchell Leisen

Carole Lombard, Fred MacMurray, Dorothy Lamour

▷ WHEN MY BABY SMILES AT ME (1948)
TCF • Walter Lang

Betty Grable, Dan Dailey, June Havoc

Plot: An entertainer becomes successful and while coping with fame, loses his wife. When he falls on hard times, she is there to pick up the pieces.

Notes: The same plot is used in THE DANCE OF LIFE★AOV★, a 1929 release starring Nancy Carroll. All three films are based upon a Broadway play titled "Burlesque," which starred a very young Barbara Stanwyck.

★   ★   ★

▶ THREE BLIND MICE (1938)
TCF • William Seiter

Loretta Young, Joel McCrea, David Niven, Marjorie Weaver

▷ MOON OVER MIAMI (1941)★AOV★
TCF • Walter Lang

Betty Grable, Don Ameche, Robert Cummings, Carole Landis

Plot: Three sisters leave their small town to seek wealthy husbands—only one of them succeeds.

Notes: A third version of a popular theme, THREE LITTLE GIRLS IN BLUE, was released in 1946. Set in Atlantic City at the turn-of-the-century, the film stars June Haver, George Montgomery, Vivian Blaine and Vera-Ellen.

★   ★   ★

☆ ☆ ☆ ☆ ☆ ☆ ☆

▶ TOM, DICK AND HARRY (1941)★AOV★
RKO • Garson Kanin
Ginger Rogers, Burgess Meredith, George Murphy

▷ GIRL MOST LIKELY, THE (1956)★AOV★
RKO • Mitchell Leisen
Jane Powell, Keith Andes, Cliff Robertson

Plot: A girl must choose between three suitors and daydreams about life with each.

Notes: TOM, DICK AND HARRY was Ginger Rogers' last film as a contract player for RKO.

★ ★ ★

▶ TOM JONES (1963)★AOV★

United Artists/Woodfall • Tony Richardson
Albert Finney, Susannah York

▷ BAWDY ADVENTURES OF TOM JONES, THE (1976)★AOV★
Universal • Cliff Owens
Trevor Howard, Nicky Henson

Plot: A foundling grows up to marry a squire's daughter.

Notes: The 1963 film and its director won Oscars.

★ ★ ★

▶ TOM SAWYER (1930)
Paramount • John Cromwell
Jackie Coogan, Mitzi Green

▷ TOM SAWYER (1973)★AOV★
United Artists • Don Taylor
Johnnie Whitaker, Celeste Holm, Jodie Foster

Plot: Tom Sawyer and assorted friends have many adventures in their home town of Hannibal, Missouri.

Notes: A silent version of the Mark Twain classic starring Jack Pickford was released by Paramount in 1917. David Selznick filmed THE ADVENTURES OF TOM SAWYER in 1938. A Movie Made for Television (MMTV) featuring Jane Wyatt and Buddy Ebsen was shown in 1973.

★ ★ ★

▶ TOO MANY HUSBANDS (1940)
Columbia • Wesley Ruggles
Jean Arthur, Melvyn Douglas, Fred MacMurray

▷ THREE FOR THE SHOW (1955)
Columbia • W.C. Potter
Betty Grable, Jack Lemmon, Marge and Gower Champion

Plot: Supposedly drowned, a man returns to find that his wife has remarried. After dangling both husbands on a string, she goes back to the first one.

Notes: The films are based upon a play by Somerset Maugham and are somewhat similar in plot to MY FAVORITE WIFE (see Chapter Three).

★ ★ ★

▶ WOMEN, THE (1939) ★AOV★
MGM • George Cukor
Norma Shearer, Joan Crawford, Rosalind Russell,
Paulette Goddard, Joan Fontaine

▷ OPPOSITE SEX, THE (1956)
MGM • David Miller
June Allyson, Joan Collins, Ann Sheridan, Joan
Blondell

Plot: There is bitchiness, competition and divorce within a group of women who are supposedly friends.

Notes: The films are based upon a Broadway smash hit by Clare Boothe who later married publisher Henry Luce and went on to become a popular Washington Congresswoman. THE WOMEN is a black and white production but contains a lavish Technicolor fashion show.

★ ★ ★

★   ★   ★   ★   ★   ★   ★

CHAPTER NINE

A NEVER-ENDING FANTASY: THE WAR FILM REVISITED

From the beginning of time, man has more often than not settled his grievances by pitting himself against his fellow man. Even though there is much talk of "trying to keep the peace," several attempts at this have not succeeded. War is seen as a valid means to an end and all the implements of waging war, from clubs and spears to the sophistication of computer-controlled missiles, have either been close at hand or on the drawing board.

Since the Stone Age, warfare has been the stuff of story-telling, entertainment and mythology. With the beginnings of the motion picture industry, there has been a body of film made devoted to the "celebration" of war. Several of these productions have gone the remake route with varying degrees of success. Battle front dramas, biographies of leaders, good and evil, accounts of victims and villains—many of these scenarios, original and repeat performances, have made for some fascinating film fare. The Crusades, The American Revolution, The Crimean War, The Civil War, two World Wars, Korea, Vietnam—filmmakers have had much from which to fashion their screen plays and they have given us Hollywood's version of each conflict. Often glamorized, in most cases fictionalized—but stripped of the glamour and the fiction, the reality and the essence of war does come through and man's inhumanity towards man is bared for all to see.

A sub-genre in this body of film is the spy or espionage thriller. Much of war is concerned with the gathering of data—often great battles are won or lost on the basis of correct intelligence. On our side, the information obtained is the work of "courageous agents," the enemy, of course, uses "scurrilous spies" for this task. Excitement is the key in the telling of these stories. An espionage film should be filled with thrills, chills and furtive action, providing the ticket buyer with a couple of hours of good entertainment. A well-produced film will accomplish its "mission."

★   ★   ★   ★   ★   ★   ★

Twenty-four film pairs are listed in this chapter.* A few have been updated to make a more current frame of reference for the movie goer—the rest are virtual replicas of the originals. As has been mentioned, some of the remakes have been successful while others have not.

In the case of such all-time greats as ALL QUIET ON THE WESTERN FRONT, THE LADY VANISHES and THE BEST YEARS OF OUR LIVES, however, one might well ponder the question of why there has been a remake. Perhaps the filmmakers involved should have heeded the old adage, "Why mess with success?"

---

* BREAKOUT (1958) and THE GREAT ESCAPE (1963)★ᴬᴼⱽ★ have the same plot but are based upon two different novels. The first, a British-made film, takes place in an Italian prisoner of war camp and stars Richard Todd, Michael Wilding and Richard Attenborough. The second, an American production, is set in a German P.O.W. camp and stars James Garner, Steve McQueen and again Richard Attenborough.

A similar plot can be discerned in both FOXHOLE IN CAIRO, a 1961 British release, and the 1985 MMTV production of THE KEY TO REBECCA. Each contains a Nazi spy in Cairo, who is reporting to Field Marshal Erwin Rommel. Based on different novels, the earlier film stars Peter Van Eyck, James Robertson Justice and Albert Lieven as Rommel, while the other features Cliff Robertson, David Soul and Robert Culp as Rommel.

☆   ☆   ☆   ☆   ☆   ☆   ☆

▶ ALL QUIET ON THE WESTERN FRONT   ▷ ALL QUIET ON THE WESTERN FRONT
(1930)★AOV★   (1979)
Universal • Lewis Milestone   MMTV • Delbert Mann
Lew Ayres, Louis Wolheim, Ben Alexander   Richard Thomas, Ernest Borgnine, Donald
                                          Pleasence

Plot: World War I, as seen from the German side.

Notes: One of the finest anti-war films ever made, the 1930 production, based upon a novel by famed German author Erich Maria Remarque, earned an Academy Award as Best Picture. Lewis Milestone was also honored. Ben Alexander co-starred with Jack Webb in an early television version of "Dragnet."

★   ★   ★

▶ ARCH OF TRIUMPH (1948)★AOV★   ▷ ARCH OF TRIUMPH (1985)
Enterprise • Lewis Milestone   MMTV • Waris Hussein
Ingrid Bergman, Charles Boyer, Charles Laughton   Anthony Hopkins, Lesley-Anne Down

Plot: While finding love and romance in the Paris of 1940 just before the Occupation, a refugee doctor meets and kills a Nazi tormentor from his own land.

Notes: As in the case of ALL QUIET ON THE WESTERN FRONT, ARCH OF TRIUMPH is based upon a novel by Erich Maria Remarque.

★   ★   ★

▶ BEST YEARS OF OUR LIVES, THE (1946)★AOV★ ▷ RETURNING HOME (1975)
Samuel Goldwyn • William Wyler   MMTV • Daniel Petrie
Fredric March, Myrna Loy, Dana Andrews, Teresa   Dabney Coleman, Tom Selleck, Whitney Blake
Wright, Virginia Mayo, Harold Russell

Plot: Three World War II veterans return to their hometown with mixed emotions and varying problems.

Notes: A landmark production, THE BEST YEARS OF OUR LIVES received a Best Film Oscar. Other awards went to director Wyler and actors March and Russell. The latter lost both hands during the fighting. His plight mirrored that of many returning vets.

★   ★   ★

▶ CAINE MUTINY, THE (1954)★AOV★   ▷ CAINE MUTINY COURT-MARTIAL, THE
                                          (1988)
Columbia • Stanley Kramer   MMTV • Robert Altman
Humphrey Bogart, José Ferrer, Van Johnson, Eric Bogosian, Jeff Daniels
Fred MacMurray

Plot: Naval officers mutiny against their captain.

Notes: The films are based upon Herman Wouk's prize-winning novel.

★   ★   ★

☆   ☆   ☆   ☆   ☆   ☆   ☆

▶ CEILING ZERO (1935)
Warners • Howard Hawks
James Cagney, Pat O'Brien

▷ INTERNATIONAL SQUADRON (1941)
Warners • Lothar Mendes
Ronald Reagan, James Stephenson

Plot: An irresponsible man becomes an ace pilot.

Notes: Ronald Reagan plays the Jimmy Cagney role in the remake, which has been updated to a World War II setting.

★ ★ ★

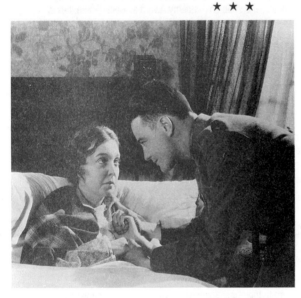

World War I as seen from the German side—ZaSu Pitts and Lew Ayres in a tender scene from ALL QUIET ON THE WESTERN FRONT. Miss Pitts was replaced by Beryl Mercer in the film when preview audiences, remembering her as a comedienne, could not take her seriously.

★ ★ ★

▶ DAWN PATROL, THE (1930)
Warners • Howard Hawks
Richard Barthelmess, Douglas Fairbanks Jr.

▷ DAWN PATROL, THE (1938)★AOV★
Warners • Edmund Goulding
Errol Flynn, David Niven, Basil Rathbone

Plot: During World War I, an aerial officer is forced to send some green recruits on dangerous missions.

★ ★ ★

▶ DIARY OF ANNE FRANK, THE (1959)★AOV★
TCF • George Stevens
Millie Perkins, Joseph Schildkraut, Shelley Winters, Ed Wynn

▷ DIARY OF ANNE FRANK, THE (1980)
MMTV • Boris Segal
Maximilian Schell, Melissa Gilbert, Joan Plowright, James Coco

Plot: A young Dutch Jew, hiding from the Nazis in an attic with her family, keeps a diary of her thoughts and feelings.

Notes: Anne Frank was captured by the Germans and died at Auschwitz. Her diary was used in the writing of the 1959 film's screen-play. A photo unit under director George Stevens went into that dreaded concentration camp at the end of the war and, for the first time, its horrors were documented on film for all to see. Shelley Winters was chosen Best Supporting Actress of 1959.

★ ★ ★

⋆　⋆　⋆　⋆　⋆　⋆　⋆

▶ GREAT IMPERSONATION, THE (1935)
Universal • Alan Crosland
Edmund Lowe, Valerie Hobson, Spring Byington

▷ GREAT IMPERSONATION, THE (1942)
Universal • John Rawlins
Ralph Bellamy, Evelyn Ankers, Karen Verne

Plot: A German spy murders his English double and assumes the duties of the latter.

Notes: The screenplay of the earlier film was updated one war to accommodate the times.

★ ★ ★

Three veterans in search of a future. Harold Russell, Dana Andrews and Fredric March (left to right) in THE BEST YEARS OF OUR LIVES. Both Russell and March won Oscars.

★ ★ ★

▶ GREEN GODDESS, THE (1930)
Warners • Alfred E. Green
George Arliss, H.B. Warner

▷ ADVENTURE IN IRAQ (1943)
Warners • D. Ross Lederman
Paul Cavanough, John Loder

Plot: A group of men fall into the hands of their enemies and are held hostage.

Notes: Another case of a screenplay being updated to World War II. John Loder, a British actor well-known during the nineteen thirties and forties, was one of actress Hedy Lamarr's many husbands.

★ ★ ★

▶ HASTY HEART, THE (1949)
British/ABP • Vincent Sherman
Ronald Reagan, Patricia Neal, Richard Todd

▷ HASTY HEART, THE (1983)⋆AOV⋆
MMTV • Martin Speer
Gregory Harrison, Cheryl Ladd, Perry King

Plot: A Scottish soldier discovers he has only a short time to live and tries to make the friendships he has previously shunned.

Notes: Each star of the 1983 production was featured in a popular television series. Perry King appeared in "Riptide," Cheryl Ladd (once Alan Ladd's daughter-in law) was one of "Charlie's Angels" and Gregory Harrison played a leading role in "Trapper John" and as of this writing, is being seen in prime-time on "Falcon Crest."

★   ★   ★   ★   ★   ★   ★

▶ JOURNEY INTO FEAR (1942)★AOV★
RKO • Norman Foster

Joseph Cotten, Dolores Del Rio, Ruth Warrick,
Orson Welles, Agnes Moorehead

▷ JOURNEY INTO FEAR (1976)★AOV★
MMTV • Daniel Mann

Shelley Winters, Zero Mostel, Vincent Price, Sam
Waterston

Plot: An industrialist finds himself enmeshed in a web of international intrigue.

Notes: JOURNEY INTO FEAR is based upon a novel by suspense writer Eric Ambler. The 1942
screenplay is credited to Joseph Cotten and Orson Welles. The latter started the project as its
director, but Norman Foster took over soon after filming began. The earlier production is set
during World War II Turkey, while the 1976 MMTV locale is the same country, circa the nineteen
seventies.

*Michael Redgrave,
Margaret Lockwood and
Paul Lukas (left to right)
in THE LADY
VANISHES. Redgrave
and Lockwood do not know
as yet that Lukas is the
arch villain in the piece.*

★   ★   ★

▶ JOURNEY'S END (1930)
British/Gainsborough • James Whale

Colin Clive, David Manners

▷ ACES HIGH (1976)
British/EMI • Jack Gold

Malcolm McDowell, Christopher Plummer

Plot: Tensions rise in combat during World War I.

Notes: JOURNEY'S END describes trench warfare in France at the time of World War I. ACES
HIGH, based on the same story, is about aerial combat during the same era. In the latter production
are cameos by Trevor Howard, Ray Milland and John Gielgud.

☆   ☆   ☆   ☆   ☆   ☆   ☆

▶ LADY VANISHES, THE (1938)★AOV★
Gaumont British/Gainsborough • Alfred
Hitchcock

Margaret Lockwood, Michael Redgrave, Dame May
Whitty, Paul Lukas

▷ LADY VANISHES, THE (1979)★AOV★
Rank/Hammer • Anthony Page

Cybill Shepherd, Elliott Gould, Angela Lansbury,
Herbert Lom

Plot: While en route to England by train, a young couple investigates the mysterious disappearance of an elderly lady spy.

Notes: It is a little known fact that when another director was unavailable, Alfred Hitchcock stepped into the breach and made THE LADY VANISHES a classic of the genre. Naughton Wayne and Basil Radford play two English gentlemen named Caldicott and Charters in the 1938 film. They proved such a hit that two years later, the actors reprised their roles in NIGHT TRAIN.

★ ★ ★

Eva Marie Saint and James Garner look to German soldier John Banner as their only of escape in THIRTY-SIX HOURS.

★ ★ ★

▶ MADEMOISELLE DOCTEUR (1937)
Grafton/Trafalgar • Edmond Greville

Dita Parlo, John Loder

▷ FRAULEIN DOKTOR (1968)
Paramount • Alberto Lattuada

Suzy Kendall, Kenneth More

Plot: The career of a double-agent during World War I, supposedly based on fact.

★ ★ ★

▶ MAN HUNT (1941)
TCF • Fritz Lang

Walter Pidgeon, Joan Bennett, George Sanders

▷ ROGUE MALE (1976)
MMTV • Clive Donner

Peter O'Toole, Alastair Sim

Plot: An Englishman's attempt to assassinate Hitler results in his being hunted by Gestapo agents upon his return to London.

Notes: "Rouge Male" is the title of the novel upon which both films are based. The 1976 version was produced by the British Broadcasting Company (the famed BBC).

★ ★ ★

★   ★   ★   ★   ★   ★   ★

▶ OPERATION PETTICOAT (1959)★AOV★
Universal • Blake Edwards
Cary Grant, Tony Curtis, Dina Merrill

▷ OPERATION PETTICOAT (1977)
MMTV • John Astin
John Astin, Jackie Cooper, Jamie Lee Curtis

Plot: The captain of a submarine, crippled during World War II, tries to reactivate his ship, with comical results.

Notes: Jamie Lee Curtis, daughter of Tony Curtis, star of the original film, plays a nurse in the 1977 production.

★ ★ ★

Bogie and his best girl, "Lullubelle." A close-up from the World War II film SAHARA. Its next incarnation was as a Western.

★ ★ ★

▶ PIED PIPER, THE (1942)
TCF • Irving Pichel
Monty Woolley, Anne Baxter, Roddy McDowall

▷ CROSSING TO FREEDOM (1990)
Grenada/MMTV • Norman Stone
Peter O'Toole, Mare Winningham, Alastair Haley

Plot: A feisty old Englishman leads a group of diverse refugee children across Nazi-occupied France.

Notes: The films are based upon a best-selling novel by Nevil Shute. Both the 1942 film and Monty Woolley were Oscar-nominated.

★ ★ ★

★   ★   ★   ★   ★   ★   ★

▶ RED BADGE OF COURAGE, THE (1951)★AOV★   ▷ RED BADGE OF COURAGE, THE (1974)
MGM • John Huston   MMTV • Lee Philips
Audie Murphy, Douglas Dick   Richard Thomas, Charles Aidman

Plot: During the Civil War, a young man gets his first taste of battle and runs away. He then
returns to duty and distinguishes himself.

Notes: Audie Murphy, who stars in the 1951 film version of the Civil War saga by Steven Crane,
was designated the most decorated infantryman of World War II.

★ ★ ★

▶ RENDEZVOUS (1935)   ▷ PACIFIC RENDEZVOUS (1942)
MGM • William K. Howard   MGM • George Sidney
William Powell, Rosalind Russell, Binnie Barnes   Lee Bowman, Jean Rogers, Mona Maris

Plot: A decoding expert breaks up an enemy spy ring.

Notes: Another case where the screenplay has been updated from World War I to World War II.
Rosalind Russell plays the role originally intended for Myrna Loy.

★ ★ ★

▶ SAHARA (1943)★AOV★   ▷ LAST OF THE COMANCHES, THE (1953)
Columbia • Zoltan Korda   Columbia • Andre de Toth
Humphrey Bogart, Bruce Bennett, Lloyd Bridges   Broderick Crawford, Lloyd Bridges, Martin
                                              Milner

Plot: A group, surviving an enemy attack, tries to hold out until help arrives.

Notes: Another genre change—the first film is set in the African desert of World War II, the
second in the American west. Lloyd Bridges plays different parts in each production.

★ ★ ★

▶ STRANGE DEATH OF ADOLPH HITLER,   ▷ MAGIC FACE, THE (1951)
THE (1943)
Universal • James Hogan   Columbia • Frank Tuttle
Ludwig Donath, Gale Sondergaard   Luther Adler, Patricia Knight

Plot: A stage impressionist kills Hitler, takes his place and causes Germany to lose the war.

Notes: The most interesting aspect of THE MAGIC FACE is that the noted war correspondent,
William L. Shirer, introduces this most improbable story. At the time the 1951 film was being shot,
Patricia Knight was married to film star Cornel Wilde.

★ ★ ★

★   ★   ★   ★   ★   ★   ★

▶ THIRTY-SIX HOURS (1964)
MGM • George Seaton

James Garner, Rod Taylor, Eva Marie Saint, John Banner

▷ BREAKING POINT, THE (1989)
Avnet/Kerner • Peter Markle

Corbin Bernsen, Joanna Pacula, John Glover

Plot: In 1944, an American officer is drugged by a German doctor and told that the war is over in order to obtain military intelligence from him.

Notes: Corbin Bernsen is, as of this writing, one of the stars of the television hit, "L.A. Law." John Banner, who appears in the 1964 production, can be seen in reruns of the television series, "Hogan's Heroes." THE BREAKING POINT was premiered on Turner Network Television (TNT) during the summer of 1989.

★   ★   ★

▶ THREE FACES EAST (1930)
Warners • Roy Del Ruth

Constance Bennett, Erich von Stroheim

▷ BRITISH INTELLIGENCE (1940) ★ AOV ★
Warners • Terry Morse

Boris Karloff, Margaret Lindsay

Plot: During World War I, a woman double-agent ferrets out a master spy who has become butler to a member of the British War Office Staff.

Notes: Production on the 1930 staff was headed by Darryl F. Zanuck, who, by 1935, had become the boss at Twentieth Century-Fox.

★   ★   ★

▶ WAR AND PEACE (1956) ★ AOV ★
Ponti/De Laurentis • King Vidor

Henry Fonda, Audrey Hepburn, Mel Ferrer, Vittorio Gassman

▷ WAR AND PEACE (1967)
Russian/Mosfilm • Sergei Bondarchuk

Ludmila Savelyeva, Sergei Bondarchuk

Plot: Life in Russia for an aristocratic family at the time of Napoleon's invasion.

Notes: King Vidor had a hand in writing the screenplay for the 1956 version of Leo Tolstoy's epic novel. Audrey Hepburn was Mel Ferrer's wife as well as co-star in 1956.

★   ★   ★

★ ★ ★ ★ ★ ★ ★

CHAPTER TEN

THEY WENT THAT-A-WAY AGAIN: THE WESTERN REVIVAL

The Western—an American phenomenon—stories by Zane Grey, Bret Harte and Max Brand. Ten gallon hats, six-shooters and smart horses. Serials, Saturday afternoons at the Bijou and feature films.

Early Western scenarios were stories of good versus evil: Straight shooters like Tom Mix and "Bronco Billy" Anderson outwitting stagecoach robbers, ridding a town of the bad guys, saving miners from the greedy and the unscrupulous. Heroes wore white, outlaws were dressed in black.

With the advent of sound came the singing cowboy. Strumming "sagebrush" guitars, riding the range and exercising their tonsils were such stalwarts as Gene Autry and Roy Rogers—Gene's horse was Champion and Roy rode Trigger. The singing cowboy proved so popular that even John Wayne did a stint as a character named "Singin' Sandy" very early in his career—he wisely stuck to straight westerns as his fame grew.

The Western was a real winner at the box-office and many of Hollywood's best known stars donned chaps and spurs, climbed on horses and brandished shooting irons. Historical and fictional characters such as Billy the Kid, Jesse James, Wyatt Earp and "The Westerner," came to life via performances by the likes of motion picture legends Robert Taylor, Tyrone Power, Henry Fonda and Gary Cooper, among others. All a part of Western lore, they galloped (and still do, via the magic of movies and television) across the silver screen in romanticized tales of the settling of the West and the beginnings of our nation as we now know it.

As America matured, so did the Western. The post-World War II era brought to the film industry several sub-genres, one of the most popular being the thinking man's or "adult" western, which boasted scripts involving a bit more than stagecoach robberies and cattle rustlers. Complex characterizations, more sophisticated conflicts and psychological nuances became part of the

★   ★   ★   ★   ★   ★   ★

Western's make-up.[*] Quite a few of these "new wave" films were money-makers—the adult western was here to stay.

A number of "horse operas," like other films thus far mentioned in our odyssey, have been remade—a few of these have gone through the process more than once. The romance of the wide open spaces, the lone cowboy on his horse, a full moon shining down on the prairie, the lowing of wandering cattle. This is the panorama of the West and Hollywood has brought us its version of this truly American phenomenon. Both original and remake, black and white, or in living color, the western is still with us for all to cherish and enjoy.

---

[*] A preview of this trend could be seen in John Ford's 1939 production of STAGECOACH.

▶ APACHE TRAIL (1942)
MGM • Richard Thorpe
Lloyd Nolan, Donna Reed, Chill Wills, William Lundigan

▷ APACHE WAR SMOKE (1952)
MGM • Harold Kress
Gilbert Roland, Robert Hutton, Glenda Farrell, Henry Morgan

Plot: A group of Apaches attack a stage coach.

Notes: The Henry Morgan who appears in the 1952 production later changed his name to Harry and went on to a long career in both films and on television.

★ ★ ★

A sprawling saga of the American West. Anne Baxter and Glenn Ford in a quiet scene from the second version of Edna Ferber's CIMARRON.

★ ★ ★

▶ BELLE STARR (1941)
TCF • Irving Cummings
Gene Tierney, Randolph Scott, Dana Andrews

▷ BELLE STARR (1980)
MMTV • John A. Alonzo
Elizabeth Montgomery, Cliff Potts

Plot: The life and times of the notorious female outlaw.

Notes: A sequel to the 1941 film, BELLE STARR'S DAUGHTER, starring Ruth Roman, George Montgomery and Rod Cameron, was released by Twentieth Century-Fox in 1948.

★ ★ ★

★   ★   ★   ★   ★   ★   ★

▶ BILLY THE KID (1930)
MGM • King Vidor

Johnny Mack Brown, Wallace Beery, Kay Johnson

▷ BILLY THE KID (1941)
MGM • David Miller

Robert Taylor, Brian Donlevy, Gene Lockhart

Plot: Outlaw Billy the Kid is relentlessly pursued by Sheriff Pat Garrett.

Notes: Johnny Mack Brown, who made his mark in films as a Western star, was one of Joan Crawford's early leading men. He appears opposite her in a 1928 silent titled OUR DANCING DAUGHTERS. Gene Lockhart was the father of actress June, whose great claim to fame is a stint as Lassie's owner in the nineteen fifties television series.

★ ★ ★

▶ CIMARRON (1930)★AOV★
RKO • Wesley Ruggles

Richard Dix, Irene Dunne

▷ CIMARRON (1961)
MGM • Anthony Mann

Glenn Ford, Maria Schell, Anne Baxter

Plot: Saga of a family settling in Oklahoma during the eighteen nineties.

Notes: Based on the novel by Edna Ferber, the 1930 production was chosen Best Picture of the year. Both stars were Oscar-nominated, but neither won.

★ ★ ★

▶ DEERSLAYER, THE (1957)
TCF • Kurt Neumann

Lex Barker, Forrest Tucker, Rita Moreno

▷ DEERSLAYER, THE (1978)★AOV★
MMTV • Dick Friedenberg

Steve Forrest, Ned Romero

Plot: A man, raised by a Mohican tribe, becomes involved with two white women whom he saves from a Huron attack.

Notes: Two silent productions of the James Fennimore Cooper novel were released in 1913 and 1923. A third version, made at Republic Studios, came out in 1943. Steve Forrest is the brother of actor Dana Andrews. During her lengthy career, Rita Moreno has won four major entertainment awards: an Oscar, an Emmy, a Tony and a Grammy.

★ ★ ★

▶ DESTRY RIDES AGAIN (1939)★AOV★
Universal • George Marshall

James Stewart, Marlene Dietrich, Brian Donlevy

▷ DESTRY (1954)
Universal-International • George Marshall

Audie Murphy, Thomas Mitchell, Mari Blanchard

Plot: A newly appointed, mild-mannered sheriff goes after the bad men in a wide open town.

Notes: The Max Brand story also served as a vehicle for cowboy star Tom Mix.

★ ★ ★

▶ FORBIDDEN VALLEY (1938)
Universal • Wyndham Gittens

Noah Beery Jr.

▷ SIERRA (1950)
Universal • Alfred E. Green

Audie Murphy, Wanda Hendrix, Dean Jagger, Burl Ives

Plot: A man, wrongly accused of a crime, comes out of hiding when the guilty party is revealed.

Notes: At the time SIERRA was being filmed, Audie Murphy and Wanda Hendrix were married. They divorced after a few years. James Arness and Tony Curtis play small roles in the 1950 movie.

▶ FRONTIER MARSHAL (1939)
TCF • Allan Dwan
Randolph Scott, Nancy Kelly, Cesar Romero

▷ MY DARLING CLEMENTINE (1946)⋆ᴬᴼⱽ⋆
TCF • John Ford
Henry Fonda, Linda Darnell, Victor Mature, Walter Brennan

Plot: Wyatt Earp and "Doc" Holliday clean up Tombstone and meet the feared Clampett gang at the OK Corral.

Notes: In an interesting bit of casting, Cesar Romero, a New Yorker of Latin extraction, was signed to play Westerner "Doc" Holliday. An earlier version of FRONTIER MARSHAL, starring cowboy actor George O'Brien, was released in 1933.

★ ★ ★

Hero vs. Varmint—Sheriff James Stewart shakes hands with badman Brian Donlevy in DESTRY RIDES AGAIN as some saloon regulars look on. Jimmy and Brian are not going to be friendly for long.

★ ★ ★

▶ HOME ON THE RANGE (1934)
Paramount • Arthur Jacobson
Randolph Scott, Evelyn Brent, Jackie Coogan

▷ CODE OF THE WEST (1947)
RKO • William Berke
James Warren, Raymond Burr, Debra Alden

Plot: A group of settlers wage war on the gang which has taken control of the town.

Notes: A silent version of the Zane Grey story, starring Owen Moore and Constance Bennett, was released by Paramount in 1925.

★ ★ ★

▶ JESSE JAMES (1938)⋆ᴬᴼⱽ⋆

TCF • Henry King
Tyrone Power, Henry Fonda, Nancy Kelly, Jane Darwell

▷ TRUE STORY OF JESSE JAMES, THE (1956)
TCF • Nicholas Ray
Robert Wagner, Jeffrey Hunter, Hope Lange, Agnes Moorehead

Plot: The life and times of the notorious outlaw.

Notes: A sequel to the 1938 film, THE RETURN OF FRANK JAMES, was released by Twentieth Century-Fox two years later, with Henry Fonda reprising his role of Frank James, Jesse's brother.

★ ★ ★

☆   ☆   ☆   ☆   ☆   ☆   ☆

▶ LAST OF THE BADMEN (1957)
Allied Artists • Paul Landres
George Montgomery, Meg Randall, Michael Ansara

▷ GUNFIGHT AT COMANCHE CREEK (1964)
Allied Artists • Frank McDonald
Audie Murphy, Coleen Miller, Ben Cooper

Plot: A western detective goes underground to unmask the leader of a gang of robbers.

Notes: George Montgomery was once married to singer Dinah Shore.

★ ★ ★

▶ LAST OF THE MOHICANS, THE (1936)∗AOV∗
United Artists • George B. Seitz
Randolph Scott, Binnie Barnes, Bruce Cabot

▷ LAST OF THE REDMEN (1947)
Republic • George Sherman
Jon Hall, Michael O'Shea, Evelyn Ankers

Plot: British soldiers escort a general's daughters through Indian territory.

Notes: Another version of the James Fennimore Cooper story under the original title was released in 1977∗AOV∗ featuring Steve Forrest. The three stars of the 1947 film were married to fellow performers: Jon Hall to singer Frances Langford, Michael O'Shea to actress Virginia Mayo and Evelyn Ankers to actor Richard Denning. Only the Langford-Hall marriage ended in divorce.

★ ★ ★

▶ LAST ROUND-UP, THE (1934)
Paramount • Henry Hathaway
Randolph Scott, Fred Kohler

▷ BORDER LEGION, THE (1940)∗AOV∗
Republic • Joseph Kane
Roy Rogers

Plot: Cattle rustling in the old west.

Notes: There were two silent versions of Zane Grey's "Border Legion" and an early sound version starred Richard Arlen, Jack Holt and Fay Wray. Henry Hathaway graduated to the big time and directed such films as THE TRAIL OF THE LONESOME PINE, JOHNNY APOLLO, THE HOUSE ON 92nd STREET and KISS OF DEATH.

★ ★ ★

▶ LAW AND ORDER (1932)
Universal • Edward L. Cahn
Walter Huston, Harry Carey

▷ LAW AND ORDER (1953)
Universal-International • Nathan Juran
Ronald Reagan, Dorothy Malone

Plot: Another variation on the taming of Tombstone.

Notes: The screenplay of the 1932 film is credited to John Huston, son of its star.

★ ★ ★

▶ LIGHT OF THE WESTERN STARS, THE
(1930)
Paramount • Otto Brower, Edwin H. Knopf
Richard Arlen, Mary Brian, Regis Toomey

▷ LIGHT OF THE WESTERN STARS, THE
(1940)∗AOV∗
Paramount • Leslie Selander
Victor Jory, Russell Hayden

Plot: Another ranchers vs. cattle thieves scenario.

Notes: This Zane Grey story was first filmed starring Dustin Farnum in 1918 and then again in 1925, by Paramount, with cowboy actor Jack Holt in the lead.

★ ★ ★

▶ MAN WITHOUT A STAR, THE (1955)★AOV★
Universal-International • King Vidor
Kirk Douglas, Jeanne Crain, Claire Trevor

▷ MAN CALLED GANNON, A (1969)
Universal • James Goldstone
Anthony Franciosa, Michael Sarrazin, Susan Oliver

Plot: A cowboy helps settlers in their fight against an encroaching band of cattlemen.

Notes: Featured in the 1955 production is Richard Boone, who later starred in the television western, "Have Gun, Will Travel." His character was known as Palladin.

★ ★ ★

Tyrone Power in the title role of JESSE JAMES, Nancy Kelly as his wife and Henry Fonda in the role of his brother Frank (left to right). A highly romanticized telling of the notorious bandit's life and times.

★ ★ ★

▶ NEVADA (1936)
Paramount • Charles Barton
Buster Crabbe, Kathleen Burke

▷ NEVADA (1944)
RKO • Edward Killy
Robert Mitchum, Nancy Gates, Anne Jeffreys

Plot: A cowboy, accused of murder during the Gold Rush, hunts for the real killer.

Notes: Paramount made a silent version of the Zane Grey story in 1927 starring Gary Cooper and Thelma Todd.

★ ★ ★

▶ NEVADA SMITH (1966)★AOV★
AVCO/Solar • Henry Hathaway
Steve McQueen, Karl Malden, Brian Keith

▷ NEVADA SMITH (1975)
MMTV • Gordon Douglas
Cliff Potts, Lorne Greene

Plot: A half-breed cowboy swears revenge for the murder of his parents.

Notes: Nevada Smith is a character in "The Carpetbaggers." In the movie version of the best-selling novel by Harold Robbins, he is played by Alan Ladd. The film was Ladd's last.

★ ★ ★

★   ★   ★   ★   ★   ★   ★

▶ OUTCASTS OF POKER FLAT, THE (1937)
RKO • Christy Cabanne

Preston Foster, Jean Muir, Van Heflin

▷ OUTCASTS OF POKER FLAT, THE (1952)
TCF • Joseph M. Newman

Dale Robertson, Anne Baxter, Cameron Mitchell

Plot: Four social rejects are trapped in a cabin during a snowstorm.

The story upon which the films are based was written by famed author of westerns, Bret Harte.
Anne Baxter is the grand-daughter of the well-known architect Frank Lloyd Wright.

★ ★ ★

▶ PLAINSMAN, THE (1936)★AOV★
Paramount • Cecil B. De Mille

Gary Cooper, Jean Arthur, James Ellison

▷ PLAINSMAN, THE (1966)
Universal • David Lowell Rich

Don Murray, Guy Stockwell, Bradford Dillman

Plot: The life and times of "Wild Bill" Hickok and other legendary characters such as "Calamity
Jane" and "Buffalo Bill" Cody.

Notes: Guy Stockwell is the brother of actor Dean. Their father Harry Stockwell was, at one time,
a performer on the Broadway musical stage.

★ ★ ★

▶ RED RIVER (1948)★AOV★
United Artists • Howard Hawks

John Wayne, Montgomery Clift, Joanne Dru

▷ RED RIVER (1988)
MMTV • Richard Michaels

James Arness, Bruce Boxleitner,Gregory
Harrison

Plot: A young cowboy rebels against his guardian, the leader of a cattle drive along the Chisholm
Trail.

Notes: RED RIVER was Montgomery Clift's first film. John Wayne proved a good friend to James
Arness. With Wayne's help, the young actor got the plum role of Matt Dillon in "Gunsmoke." He also
plays the Wayne role in the remake.

★ ★ ★

▶ RIDERS OF THE PURPLE SAGE (1931)
Fox • Hamilton MacFadden

George O'Brien, Marguerite Churchill, Noah
Beery Sr.

▷ RIDERS OF THE PURPLE SAGE (1941)
TCF • James Tinling

George Montgomery, Robert Barrat, Lynne
Roberts

Plot: A cowboy unmasks a judge who is, in reality, leading a gang of outlaws.

Notes: Two silent versions of the Zane Grey novel were filmed, one in 1918 starring William Farnum
and the other in 1925 with the legendary cowboy star Tom Mix portraying the hero.

★ ★ ★

▶ ROMANCE OF THE RIO GRANDE (1929)
Fox • Alfred Santell

Warner Baxter, Mary Duncan, Anthony Moreno

▷ ROMANCE OF THE RIO GRANDE (1941)
TCF • Herbert I. Leeds

Cesar Romero, Patricia Morison, Ricardo Cortez

Plot: Someone is trying to take over a ranch by violence and The Cisco Kid investigates.

Notes: The Cisco Kid is the hero of several novels by O. Henry. Warner Baxter, as Cisco, won an
Oscar in 1929 for IN OLD ARIZONA.

★ ★ ★

▶ SHOWDOWN AT ABILENE (1956)
Universal-International • Charles Haas

Jock Mahoney, David Janssen, Martha Hyer

▷ GUNFIGHT IN ABILENE (1967)
Universal • Joseph Kenny

Bobby Darin, Leslie Nielson, Don Galloway, Emily Banks

Plot: A returning Civil War veteran becomes sheriff and cleans up his home town.

Notes: Before his untimely death, Bobby Darin was a popular singer, making films, night club appearances and recordings. Don Galloway, who appears in "Gunfight," can still be seen on television screens whenever reruns of "Ironsides" are shown.

★ ★ ★

This time Henry Fonda (left) is on the side of the law. As Wyatt Earp in MY DARLING CLEMENTINE, he and Victor Mature (right) in the role of "Doc" Holliday are out to rid Tombstone of the Clanton gang. Linda Darnell plays Mature's girlfriend.

★ ★ ★

▶ SMOKY (1946)
TCF • Louis King

Fred MacMurray, Anne Baxter, Burl Ives

▷ SMOKY (1966)
TCF • George Sherman

Fess Parker, Diana Hyland, Katy Jurado

Plot: A spirited horse is stolen and has many adventures before being reunited with his master.

Notes: The first filming of this story, starring Victor Jory, was released by Fox in 1933. Burl Ives, folk singer-cum character actor, won a Best Supporting Actor Oscar for his work in another western, THE BIG COUNTRY (1958). Fess Parker played Davy Crockett in a Disney-produced television series.

★ ★ ★

★   ★   ★   ★   ★   ★   ★

▶ SPOILERS, THE (1930)
Paramount • Edward Carewe

Gary Cooper, William "Stage" Boyd, Betty
Compson

▷ SPOILERS, THE (1942)★AOV★
Universal • Ray Enright

John Wayne, Marlene Dietrich, Randolph Scott

Plot: Two men in the gold rush days of the Yukon fight over land rights and also over a saloon
entertainer.

Notes: A third version of the Rex Beach story, starring Anne Baxter, Jeff Chandler and Rory
Calhoun, was released by Universal-International in 1955. William "Stage" Boyd is not to be
confused with the actor of the same name who played "Hop-a-long Cassidy" in films and on
television.

★   ★   ★

▶ STAGECOACH (1939)★AOV★
United Artists • John Ford

John Wayne, Claire Trevor, Thomas Mitchell, Andy
Devine, John Carradine

▷ STAGECOACH (1966)
TCF • Gordon Douglas

Bing Crosby, Ann-Margret, Van Heflin, Alex
Cord, Robert Cummings

Plot: A group aboard a stagecoach faces danger from an Indian war party.

Notes: Thomas Mitchell won the 1939 Best Supporting Actor award for his performance in
STAGECOACH. He made several excellent films that year, among them GONE WITH THE WIND,
DESTRY RIDES AGAIN and MR. SMITH GOES TO WASHINGTON. A third version of
STAGECOACH is a Movie Made for Television. First shown in 1986★AOV★, it stars Willie Nelson,
Johnny Cash, Kris Kristofferson and Waylon Jennings.

★   ★   ★

▶ SUNSET PASS, THE (1933)
Paramount • Henry Hathaway

Randolph Scott, Kent Taylor

▷ SUNSET PASS, THE (1946)
RKO • William Berke

James Warren, Jane Greer

Plot: A government agent is assigned to break up a band of outlaws preying on trains.

Notes: A silent version of the Zane Grey novel, starring Jack Holt, was released by Paramount in
1929.

★   ★   ★

▶ TEXAS RANGERS, THE (1936)
Paramount • King Vidor

Fred MacMurray, Jack Oakie, Jean Parker,Lloyd
Nolan

▷ STREETS OF LAREDO, THE (1949)
Paramount • Leslie Fenton

William Holden, William Bendix, MacDonald Carey,
Mona Freeman

Plot: Two men join the Texas Rangers and hunt down an old friend who has become a dangerous
outlaw.

Notes: Legend has it that Fred MacMurray and Jack Oakie were the original choices for the first
"Road" film—the roles eventually went to Bing Crosby and Bob Hope.

★   ★   ★

★   ★   ★   ★   ★   ★   ★

▶ THREE GODFATHERS (1936)
MGM • Richard Boleslawski

Chester Morris, Lewis Stone, Walter Brennan

▷ THREE GODFATHERS (1948)★AOV★
MGM • John Ford

John Wayne, Harry Carey Jr., Ward Bond, Pedro Armendariz

Plot: Three outlaws escaping across the desert find and care for a baby.

Notes: The story was first done by Essanay Studios in 1909 under the title of BRONCO BILLY AND THE BABY. Other variations came out in 1916, 1920 and 1929. The 1948 film is dedicated to Harry Carey Sr., one of the stars of the 1920 film, which was directed by John Ford.

★ ★ ★

Dallas and The Ringo Kid. A young Claire Trevor and an equally youthful John Wayne in STAGECOACH—the breakthrough film for The Duke.

★ ★ ★

▶ UNDER THE TONTO RIM (1933)
Paramount • Henry Hathaway

Stuart Erwin, John Lodge

▷ UNDER THE TONTO RIM (1947)
RKO • Lew Landers

Tim Holt, Nan Leslie

Plot: A young man poses as an outlaw in order to catch the real criminals.

Notes: A silent version of the Zane Grey western, starring Richard Arlen and Mary Brian, was released by Paramount in 1928.

★ ★ ★

▶ VIRGINIAN, THE (1929)★AOV★
Paramount • Victor Fleming

Gary Cooper, Walter Huston, Richard Arlen

▷ VIRGINIAN, THE (1946)
Paramount • Stewart Gilmore

Joel McCrea, Brian Donlevy, Sonny Tufts

Plot: A rancher's friend goes to work for a cattle rustler—by film's end, the friend is hung by a posse and the rustler is killed in a gun duel by the rancher.

Notes: The 1929 version was Gary Cooper's first all-talking film. The story was previously made in 1914 and in 1923.

★ ★ ★

▶ WEST OF THE PECOS (1935)
RKO • Phil Rosen
Richard Dix, Martha Sleeper

▷ WEST OF THE PECOS (1945)
RKO • Edward Killy
Robert Mitchum, Barbara Hale

Plot: A girl, masquerading as a man to ensure her safety in rough country, meets a young man, wrongly accused of cattle rustling—together they unmask the real culprit.

Notes: "Perry Mason" aficionados will recognize Barbara Hale, who plays Della Street on the series, past and present.

▶ WINCHESTER '73 (1950)★AOV★
Universal-International • Anthony Mann
James Stewart, Shelley Winters, Dan Duryea

▷ WINCHESTER '73 (1967)
MMTV • Herschel Daugherty
Tom Tryon, John Saxon, Joan Blondell

Plot: The owner of a stolen rifle tracks the thief down—it is his own brother.

Notes: Playing small roles in the 1950 film are future stars Rock Hudson and Tony Curtis.

▶ YELLOW SKY (1948)
TCF • William Wellman
Gregory Peck, Anne Baxter, Richard Widmark

▷ JACKALS, THE (1967)
Robert D. Webb
Vincent Price

Plot: A band of outlaws reach a ghost town and seek to cheat its inhabitants, an old miner and his grand-daughter, out of what is rightfully theirs.

Notes: The setting of the first film is in the American West while the remake takes place in the South African Transvaal.

CHAPTER ELEVEN

DUAL DUELS AND OTHER SUCH THINGS: ACTION AND ADVENTURE FILMS REMADE

Who is your favorite movie fictional character? Is it Robin Hood, whose feats of derring-do in Merrie Old England have excited children of all ages or could it be the lovely Maid Marian, whose heart palpitates with love at the sight of the "Lord" of Sherwood Forest? And how about Tarzan, swinging from tree to tree, with his famous bellow—more studio than man-made—echoing through the jungles of "Africa" (in all probability a back lot over at MGM)? Or is your favorite character Jane, his lovely mate, who has given up a life of English ease to be with her own true love? Perhaps you've thrilled to Mr. Christian facing up to Captain Bligh aboard the HMS Bounty or to Long John Silver and his quest for buried treasure. And then there are Tom Sawyer, Huck Finn and Becky Thatcher, living life along the Mississippi—maybe one of them is more to your taste.

Since the advent of film, these and other fictional characters, the creations of best selling novelists, have quickened the hearts of millions, many coming back to the screen on more than one occasion, via the movie remake.

Played by some of our most revered performers, they have become flesh and blood beings, practically leaping off the screen and inviting us to come and share in their daring exploits. From the swashbuckling feats of Douglas Fairbanks Sr. and Errol Flynn to the sophisticated intrigues of James Bond, from silent to sound, in black and white and in living color, the adventure epic is still great fun for film goers, as witness such productions as RAIDERS OF THE LOST ARK and its sequels plus the sixty-seven film pairs listed in this chapter.

Although newer stars have taken the places of the old and although in some cases the plotline has been revamped to give the movie a more modern look, the old literary axiom still prevails, perhaps more so for some in the adventure genre than in any other: a story which makes the pulses race and the heart pound is, for better or for worse, worth a second (or third or fourth) go-round.

★   ★   ★   ★   ★   ★   ★

▶ ADVENTURES OF ROBIN HOOD, THE
(1938)★AOV★
Warners • William Keighley, Michael Curtiz

Errol Flynn, Olivia de Havilland, Basil Rathbone,
Claude Rains

▷ STORY OF ROBIN HOOD AND HIS MERRIE
MEN, THE (1952)★AOV★
Disney • Ken Annakin

Richard Todd, Joan Rice, Peter Finch

Plot: Robin Hood foils the enemies of King Richard while making love to Maid Marian.

Notes: A 1922 silent version of the Robin Hood saga, produced by and starring Douglas Fairbanks
Sr., was released by United Artists, the company founded by Fairbanks, Mary Pickford, Charles
Chaplin and D.W. Griffith. A cartoon version, filmed at Disney Studios in 1973, features the voices
of Phil Harris, Roger Miller and Peter Ustinov. Other remakes include PRINCE OF THIEVES
(1948), MEN OF SHERWOOD FOREST (1954) and SWORD OF SHERWOOD FOREST (1961).

★   ★   ★

▶ AGAINST ALL FLAGS (1952)★AOV★
Universal-International • George Sherman

Errol Flynn, Maureen O'Hara, Anthony Quinn

▷ KING'S PIRATE, THE (1967)
Universal • Don Weiss

Doug McClure, Jill St. John, Guy Stockwell,
Richard Deacon

Plot: An eighteenth century British soldier manages to infiltrate a pirate stronghold on orders of
his king.

Notes: Richard Deacon is well known to television watchers for his semi-regular stint on the "Dick
Van Dyke Show."

★   ★   ★

▶ ALI BABA AND THE FORTY THIEVES
(1943)
Universal • Arthur Lubin

Maria Montez, Jon Hall, Turhan Bey

▷ SWORD OF ALI BABA, THE (1965)

Universal • Virgil Vogel

Gavin MacLeod, Peter Mann, Jocelyn Lane

Plot: A prince, pretending to be a robber, regains his throne from an evil usurper.

Notes: Much of the footage of the original production was used in the remake. Gavin McLeod went
on to become the skipper of television's "Love Boat."

★   ★   ★

▶ BIRD OF PARADISE (1932)★AOV★
RKO • King Vidor

Joel McCrea, Dolores Del Rio, John Halliday

▷ BIRD OF PARADISE (1951)
TCF • Delmar Daves

Louis Jourdan, Jeff Chandler, Debra Paget

Plot: An adventurer, landing on a South Sea island, marries a native girl—this leads to trouble in
Paradise.

Notes: Delmar Daves produced the 1951 remake and also was responsible for writing its
screenplay.

★   ★   ★

★   ★   ★   ★   ★   ★   ★

▶ BLACK BEAUTY (1946)★AOV★
TCF • Max Nosseck
Mona Freeman, Richard Denning

▷ BLACK BEAUTY (1971)★AOV★
British/Tigon/Chilton • James Hill
Mark Lester, Walter Slezak

Plot: A horse has many adventures before being reunited with its original owner.

Notes: The films are based upon a famous children's story by Anna Sewell.

★   ★   ★

Errol Flynn and Olivia de Havilland as the mythical lovers of Sherwood Forest, Robin Hood and the fair Maid Marian in THE ADVENTURES OF ROBIN HOOD. Legend has it that the married Flynn's ardor for the fair Maid Olivia was for real.

★   ★   ★

▶ BLACK WATCH, THE (1929)
Fox • John Ford
Victor McLaglen, Myrna Loy

▷ KING OF THE KHYBER RIFLES (1953)★AOV★
TCF • Henry King
Tyrone Power, Michael Rennie, Terry Moore

Plot: A half caste officer staves off a rebel uprising at India's Khyber Pass, circa 1857.

Notes: "The Black Watch" refers to the name of a Scottish regiment. The 1929 film was director John Ford's first talkie.

★   ★   ★

▶ BLUE LAGOON, THE (1949)
GFD/Individual • Frank Launder
Jean Simmons, Donald Houston, Cyril Cusack

▷ BLUE LAGOON, THE (1980)★AOV★
Columbia • Randall Kleiser
Brooke Shields, Christopher Atkins, Leo McKern

Plot: A boy and girl, shipwrecked on a desert island, fall in love as they grow to maturity.

Notes: Because of production code laxity, the 1980 version contains more sexually explicit scenes than does the British made original.

★   ★   ★

☆   ☆   ☆   ☆   ☆   ☆   ☆

▶ BODY AND SOUL (1947)★ᴬᴼⱽ★
United Artists • Robert Rossen
John Garfield, Lilli Palmer, Canada Lee, Ann Revere

▷ BODY AND SOUL (1981)★ᴬᴼⱽ★
Cannon/Golan-Globus • George Bowers
Leon Isaac Kennedy, Jane Kennedy, Peter Lawford

Plot: A young boxer from the slums fights his way to the top by devious means and then learns that the crooked way is not always the best.

Notes: Leon Isaac Kennedy wrote the screenplay for the remake, which features former heavyweight champ Muhammed Ali in a cameo role.

★ ★ ★

▶ BUCCANEER, THE (1938)
Paramount • Cecil B. De Mille
Fredric March, Franciska Gaal, Akim Tamiroff, Anthony Quinn

▷ BUCCANEER, THE (1958)★ᴬᴼⱽ★
Paramount • Anthony Quinn
Yul Brynner, Claire Bloom, Charlton Heston, Charles Boyer

Plot: Pirate Jean Lafitte helps President Andrew Jackson repel a British invasion during the War of 1812.

Notes: During production on the 1958 version, Cecil B. De Mille became gravely ill. Direction of the project was taken over by his then son-in-law, Anthony Quinn. Mr. De Mille died a month after the premiere of the film.

★ ★ ★

▶ CALL OF THE WILD (1935)
Twentieth Century • William Wellman
Clark Gable, Loretta Young, Jack Oakie

▷ CALL OF THE WILD (1972)★ᴬᴼⱽ★
Massfilms • Ken Annakin
Charlton Heston, Michelle Mercier

Plot: A Yukon gold prospector fends off villains with the help of a wild dog he befriends.

Notes: Twentieth Century Pictures was founded by Darryl F. Zanuck in 1933. After releasing eighteen films, the company merged with Fox Films (1935). CALL OF THE WILD was Twentieth Century's last production.

★ ★ ★

▶ CAPTAIN BLOOD (1935)★ᴬᴼⱽ★

Warners • Michael Curtiz
Errol Flynn, Olivia de Havilland, Basil Rathbone

▷ FORTUNES OF CAPTAIN BLOOD, THE (1950)
Columbia • Gordon Douglas
Louis Hayward, Patricia Medina, George Macready

Plot: A British surgeon, wrongfully condemned for inciting a rebellion, takes to the high seas as a pirate.

Notes: Both films are based upon the novel by Rafael Sabatini. The 1935 production marked Errol Flynn's first starring vehicle. Flynn made his American film debut in THE CASE OF THE CURIOUS BRIDE (1935). His very first film, also for Warners, MURDER AT MONTE CARLO (1934) was British made. A French version of CAPTAIN BLOOD, starring Jean Marais, was released in 1960.

★ ★ ★

☆   ☆   ☆   ☆   ☆   ☆   ☆

▶ CAPTAINS COURAGEOUS (1937)★AOV★
MGM • Victor Fleming

Spencer Tracy, Freddie Bartholomew, Lionel
Barrymore, Melvyn Douglas

▷ CAPTAINS COURAGEOUS (1977)
MMTV • Harvey Hart

Karl Malden, Ricardo Montalban, Jonathan Kahn

Plot: A wealthy boy falls from a cruise liner and learns the true meaning of life when he is rescued and taken aboard a Portuguese fishing boat.

Notes: Spencer Tracy won the first of his two Oscars for his role as a Portuguese fisherman, complete with accent, in the 1937 movie. Both films are based upon a popular Rudyard Kipling novel.

★ ★ ★

Like father like son. Douglas Fairbanks Jr., sword in hand, gets ready to lead a forward charge in GUNGA DIN.

★ ★ ★

▶ CHARGE OF THE LIGHT BRIGADE, THE
(1936)★AOV★
Warners • Michael Curtiz

Errol Flynn, Olivia de Havilland, Patric Knowles,
Donald Crisp

▷ CHARGE OF THE LIGHT BRIGADE, THE
(1968)
United Artists • Tony Richardson

Trevor Howard, John Gielgud, Vanessa Redgrave

Plot: In the eighteen fifties, a cavalry officer leads a disastrous charge against an enemy using modern weaponry.

Notes: Appearing along with Vanessa Redgrave in the 1968 production are her brother Colin and her mother, actress Rachel Kempson.

★ ★ ★

★   ★   ★   ★   ★   ★   ★

▶ CORSICAN BROTHERS, THE (1942)★AOV★
United Artists • Gregory Ratoff
Douglas Fairbanks Jr., Akim Tamiroff, Ruth
Warrick

▷ CORSICAN BROTHERS, THE (1985)
MMTV • Ian Sharp
Trevor Eve, Geraldine Chaplin, Donald Pleasence

Plot: Siamese twins, separated at birth, unite to avenge the stealing of their parents' estate.

Notes: The films are based upon the novel by Alexandre Dumas. Ruth Warrick made her screen debut in CITIZEN KANE (1941). She is now working in television as one of the leading characters in the popular soap opera, "All My Children."

★ ★ ★

▶ COUNT OF MONTE CRISTO, THE
(1934)★AOV★
United Artists • Rowland V. Lee
Robert Donat, Elissa Landi, Louis Calhern

▷ COUNT OF MONTE CRISTO, THE
(1975)★AOV★
MMTV • David Greene
Richard Chamberlain, Tony Curtis, Trevor
Howard

Plot: A man, wrongfully imprisoned, escapes and takes his revenge on his enemies.

Notes: Two French language versions of the Alexandre Dumas novel were filmed, the first in 1954 starring Jean Marais and the second in 1961 starring Louis Jordan.

★ ★ ★

▶ CROWD ROARS, THE (1932)
Warners • Howard Hawks
James Cagney, Joan Blondell, Eric Linden, Ann
Dvorak

▷ INDIANAPOLIS SPEEDWAY (1939)
Warners • Lloyd Bacon
Pat O'Brien, Ann Sheridan, John Payne, Gale Page

Plot: A race car driver tries to keep his younger brother from following in his footsteps.

Notes: James Cagney and Joan Blondell appeared on Broadway in a 1929 play titled "Penny Arcade." Both were brought to Hollywood to recreate their roles in a 1930 film version of the play which was retitled SINNER'S HOLIDAY.

★ ★ ★

▶ DANGEROUS PARADISE (1930)
Paramount • William Wellman
Richard Arlen, Nancy Carroll

▷ VICTORY (1940)
Paramount • John Cromwell
Fredric March, Betty Field

Plot: A recluse helps a girl menaced by villains.

Notes: A silent version of the Joseph Conrad novel starring Jack Holt and Lon Chaney was released in 1919.

★ ★ ★

▶ EBB TIDE (1937)
Paramount • James Hogan

Ray Milland, Frances Farmer, Lloyd Nolan, Barry Fitzgerald

▷ ADVENTURE ISLAND (1947) ★ᴬᴼᵛ★
Paramount • Peter Stewart

Rory Calhoun, Rhonda Fleming, Paul Kelly

Plot: Sailors are stranded on a South Sea island with a fanatic.

Notes: A silent version of EBB TIDE was released in 1922 with James Kirkwood, Lila Lee and Noah Beery Sr. in leading roles. A biography of nineteen thirties film actress Frances Farmer, starring Jessica Lange, was released in 1982. It chronicles the star's tragic descent from fame and fortune to her commitment into a mental institution.

★ ★ ★

From Songs to Sarongs—this is your life, Dorothy Lamour. The ex-band singer in a scene from THE HURRICANE. The film's special effects caused as much comment at the time as Lamour did.

★ ★ ★

▶ FIVE CAME BACK (1939) ★ᴬᴼᵛ★
RKO • John Farrow

Chester Morris, Lucille Ball, Wendy Barrie, John Carradine

▷ BACK FROM ETERNITY (1956) ★ᴬᴼᵛ★
RKO • John Farrow

Robert Ryan, Anita Ekberg, Rod Steiger

Plot: A plane crashes in the jungle—when repaired, it is only able to take five people back.

Notes: In 1939, Lucille Ball was a contract player at RKO—twenty years later, she and Desi Arnaz owned much of her old studio.

★ ★ ★

☆   ☆   ☆   ☆   ☆   ☆   ☆

▶ FOUR FEATHERS, THE (1939)★AOV★
United Artists • Zoltan Korda

Ralph Richardson, John Clements, C. Aubrey
Smith, June Duprez

▷ FOUR FEATHERS, THE (1977)
MMTV • Don Sharp

Beau Bridges, Robert Powell, Simon Ward, Jane
Seymour

Plot: A man, sent the four feathers which symbolize cowardice, goes on to prove his valor.

Notes: Five versions of THE FOUR FEATHERS were made: two silents (1921, 1929), the two
listed above and a 1955 production starring Laurence Harvey titled STORM OVER THE NILE.

★ ★ ★

▶ GAWAIN AND THE GREEN KNIGHT (1973)
United Artists • Stephen Weeks

Robert Hardy, Murray Head

▷ SWORD OF THE VALIANT (1984)★AOV★
Cannon • Stephen Weeks

Sean Connery, Trevor Howard

Plot: A medieval squire takes on a challenge from the magical Green Knight.

Notes: Robert Hardy can be seen in the popular television series "All Things Great and Beautiful,"
taken from the stories of English veterinarian James Herriot.

★ ★ ★

▶ GUNGA DIN (1939)★AOV★
RKO • George Stevens

Cary Grant, Victor McLaglen, Douglas
Fairbanks Jr., Joan Fontaine, Sam Jaffe

▷ SERGEANTS THREE (1961)
United Artists • John Sturgis

Frank Sinatra, Dean Martin, Peter Lawford,
Sammy Davis Jr.

Plot: Three veteran soldiers have many adventures and are saved from their enemies by a water
boy.

Notes: GUNGA DIN is based upon a narrative poem by Rudyard Kipling. SERGEANTS THREE is a
reworking of the original with the location changed from India to the post-Civil War American
West; in it, Hollywood's famed "Rat Pack" play leading roles.

★ ★ ★

▶ HONKY TONK (1941)
MGM • Jack Conway

Clark Gable, Lana Turner, Frank Morgan, Claire
Trevor

▷ HONKY TONK (1974)
MMTV • Don Taylor

Richard Crenna, Stella Stevens, Margot Kidder

Plot: A con-man falls in love with an honest woman.

Notes: Richard Crenna began his long show business career in radio, playing a teenager on the "Our
Miss Brooks" weekly series. He also plays the same character in the 1955 film version of that same
program.

★ ★ ★

▶ HUCKLEBERRY FINN (1931)
Paramount • Norman Taurog

Jackie Coogan, Junior Durkin, Mitzi Green

▷ HUCKLEBERRY FINN (1939)★AOV★
MGM • Richard Thorpe

Mickey Rooney, Walter Connolly, William Frawley

Plot: Life along the Mississippi River with Huckleberry Finn and assorted friends.

Notes: Several later remakes followed: three titled THE ADVENTURES OF HUCKLEBERRY
FINN (1960, 1981, 1985) and two called HUCKLEBERRY FINN (1974★AOV★, 1975★AOV★).

★ ★ ★

▶ HURRICANE, THE (1937)★AOV★
Samuel Goldwyn • John Ford, Stuart Heisler
Dorothy Lamour, Jon Hall, Mary Astor, Raymond Massey

▷ HURRICANE, THE (1979)★AOV★
Paramount • Jan Troell
Jason Robards, Trevor Howard, Timothy Bottoms, Mia Farrow

Plot: Life on the island of Manikoora is upset by a vindictive governor and a violent storm.

Notes: The films are based upon the book by Charles Nordall and James Hall who also wrote "Mutiny on the Bounty."

★ ★ ★

Taylor and Taylor. Title-rolist Robert as Sir Walter Scott's hero, IVANHOE, and Elizabeth as the jewess Rebecca.

★ ★ ★

▶ IVANHOE (1952)★AOV★
MGM • Richard Thorpe
Robert Taylor, Joan Fontaine, Elizabeth Taylor, George Sanders

▷ IVANHOE (1982)★AOV★
MMTV • Douglas Canfield
James Mason, Anthony Andrews, Olivia Hussey

Plot: High adventure, love and derring-do in medieval England when knighthood was in flower.

Notes: The 1952 production was filmed in England—most of its major stars, excluding Nebraska-born Robert Talor, were English.

★ ★ ★

☆   ☆   ☆   ☆   ☆   ☆   ☆

▶ JAMAICA INN (1939)★AOV★
Mayflower • Alfred Hitchcock

Charles Laughton, Maureen O'Hara, Robert
Newton

▷ JAMAICA INN (1985)★AOV★
MMTV • Lawrence Gordon Clark

Jane Seymour, Patrick McGoohan

Plot: A nobleman is the secret head of a band of smugglers.

Notes: JAMAICA INN was adapted from a novel by English author Daphne du Maurier. Maureen
O'Hara made her debut in the 1939 film.

★ ★ ★

▶ JUNGLE BOOK, THE (1942)★AOV★
United Artists • Zoltan Korda, Andre de Toth

Sabu, Joseph Calleia, Rosemary de Camp

▷ JUNGLE BOOK, THE (1967)
Disney • Wolfgang Reitherman

Voices of Phil Harris, George Sanders, Sebastian
Cabot

Plot: A boy, abandoned in the forests of India, is raised by wolves.

Notes: Both films are loosely based upon stories by Rudyard Kipling. The producer of the 1942
film was Alexander Korda, brother of the director.

★ ★ ★

▶ KIDNAPPED (1938)
TCF • Alfred L. Werker

Warner Baxter, Freddie Bartholomew, John
Carradine

▷ KIDNAPPED (1959)★AOV★
Disney • Robert Stevenson

Peter Finch, James MacArthur, Peter O'Toole

Plot: A young boy, sold into slavery by his wicked uncle, is helped by an outlaw to regain his rightful
position in life.

Notes: James MacArthur is the son of the legendary actress Helen Hayes. He can currently be seen
in reruns of "Hawaii Five-O." Two other productions of the Robert Louis Stevenson novel were
released in 1948 and 1971. The 1948 film stars Roddy MacDowall and Dan O'Herlihy, while the
1971 version features Michael Caine, Trevor Howard and Jack Hawkins.

★ ★ ★

▶ KIM (1950)★AOV★
MGM • Victor Saville

Errol Flynn, Dean Stockwell, Pauk Lukas

▷ KIM (1984)
MMTV • John Davies

Peter O'Toole, Ravi Sheth, Bryan Brown

Plot: A young orphan has the adventure of his life while aiding a member of the British Secret
Service.

Notes: The films are based upon a novel by the prolific Rudyard Kipling.

★ ★ ★

▶ KING SOLOMON'S MINES (1937)★AOV★
Gainsborough • Robert Stevenson

Cedric Hardwicke, Paul Robeson, Roland Young

▷ KING SOLOMON'S MINES (1950)★AOV★
MGM • Compton Bennett

Stewart Granger, Deborah Kerr, Richard Carlson

Plot: An African chief is persuaded by a group of explorers to help them find a diamond mine.

Notes: Paul Robeson was a controversial show business personality. Singer, actor, activist, he was
most famous for his role in SHOW BOAT and his singing of "Old Man River."

★ ★ ★

★   ★   ★   ★   ★   ★   ★

▶ LASSIE COME HOME (1943)
MGM • Fred M. Wilcox
Roddy MacDowall, Donald Crisp, Elizabeth Taylor, Edmund Gwenn

▷ MAGIC OF LASSIE, THE (1978)★AOV★
Jack Wrather • Don Chaffey
James Stewart, Mickey Rooney, Alice Faye

Plot: After many miles and many adventures, the beloved collie finds her way back to her original master.

Notes: Jack Wrather, producer of the 1978 film, was co-producer, along with his wife, actress Bonita Granville, of the nineteen fifties " Lassie" television series.

★ ★ ★

▶ LIVES OF A BENGAL LANCER (1934)★AOV★
Paramount • Henry Hathaway
Gary Cooper, Franchot Tone, Richard Cromwell

▷ GERONIMO (1939)
Paramount • Paul Sloane
Preston Foster, Ellen Drew, Chief Thundercloud

Plot: Army heroics against Indians (different kinds in each version).

Notes: The first film takes place in India, the remake is set in the American west. In the latter film, Chief Thundercloud, an authentic Native American, plays GERONIMO.

★ ★ ★

▶ LORD OF THE FLIES (1963)★AOV★
British/Allan-Hogdon Productions • Peter Brook
James Aubrey, Tom Chapin

▷ LORD OF THE FLIES (1990)
Castle Rock/Nelson • Harry Hook
Paul Balthazar Getty, Chris Furrh, Daniel Pipoly

Plot: After their plane has crashed, some English schoolboys are stranded on a remote, uncharted island—with the passage of time, they become savages.

Notes: The films are based upon a popular novel by William Golding. Paul Balthazar Getty is related to oil tycoon J. Paul Getty.

★ ★ ★

▶ LORNA DOONE (1934)
British/ATP • Basil Dean
John Loder, Victoria Hopper, Margaret Lockwood

▷ LORNA DOONE (1951)
Columbia • Phil Karlson
Richard Greene, Barbara Hale

Plot: Farmers rebel against their landlords, the Doone family.

Notes: The 1951 film was shot in Yosemite National Park.

★ ★ ★

▶ MASTER OF BALLANTRAE, THE (1953)
Warners • William Keighley
Errol Flynn, Anthony Steel, Roger Livesey

▷ MASTER OF BALLANTRAE, THE (1984)
MMTV • Douglas Hickox
Richard Thomas, Michael York, John Gielgud

Plot: Two brothers vie for control of the family estate in Scotland after one has come home from fighting in the cause of Bonnie Prince Charlie.

Notes: The films are based upon a novel by Robert Louis Stevenson. Richard Thomas will be recognized by television fans as John-Boy on "The Waltons" television series.

★ ★ ★

★　　★　　★　　★　　★　　★　　★

▶ MISERABLES, LES (1935)★AOV★
TCF • Richard Boleslawski
Fredric March, Charles Laughton

▷ MISERABLES, LES (1952)
TCF • Lewis Milestone
Michael Rennie, Robert Newton

Plot: An escaped convict, imprisoned for the theft of a loaf of bread, is pursued by a relentless inspector of police.

Notes: The 1935 production of the Victor Hugo novel was Oscar-nominated but lost to MUTINY ON THE BOUNTY. There have been many other versions of LES MISERABLES: American-made, French-made and Italian-made, not to mention the Broadway show.

★　★　★

Captain Bligh (Oscar winner Charles Laughton) on the deck of his famous ship. Does the infamous captain expect a MUTINY ON THE BOUNTY?

★　★　★

▶ MOST DANGEROUS GAME, THE (1932)★AOV★
RKO • Ernest B. Shoedsack
Leslie Banks, Joel McCrea, Fay Wray

▷ RUN FOR THE SUN (1956)
United Artists • Roy Boulting
Richard Widmark, Jane Greer, Trevor Howard

Plot: A madman invites people to an island so that he can hunt them down like wild game.

Notes: Another version of this melodrama, titled A GAME OF DEATH, starring John Loder and Audrey Long, was released by RKO in 1945.

★　★　★

▶ MUTINY ON THE BOUNTY (1935)★AOV★
MGM • Frank Lloyd
Charles Laughton, Clark Gable, Franchot Tone

▷ MUTINY ON THE BOUNTY (1962)★AOV★
MGM • Lewis Milestone
Marlon Brando, Trevor Howard, Richard Harris

Plot: Mutineers on an eighteenth century vessel cast their captain adrift and settle on an island.

Notes: All three stars of the 1935 production were Oscar-nominated, as was the film. It won and so did Charles Laughton as Captain Bligh.

★　★　★

★   ★   ★   ★   ★   ★   ★

▶ OIL FOR THE LAMPS OF CHINA (1935)
Warners • Mervyn Le Roy
Pat O'Brien, Josephine Hutchinson, Lyle Talbot

▷ LAW OF THE TROPICS (1941)
Warners • Ray Enright
Constance Bennett, Jeffrey Lynn, Regis Toomey

Plot: A man works for an American oil company in a foreign land.

Notes: The locale of the first film is China, the second takes place in South America.

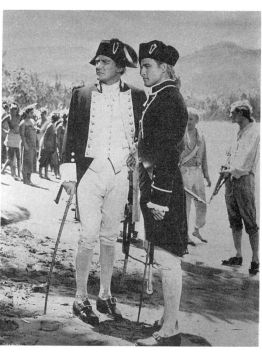

"Mr. Christian, I presume." Marlon Brando as Mr. Christian (the role played by Clark Gable in the original) will soon lock horns with Trevor Howard, playing Captain Bligh, in the 1962 remake of MUTINY ON THE BOUNTY.

★   ★   ★

▶ OLD MAN AND THE SEA, THE (1958)
Warners • John Sturges
Spencer Tracy, Harry Bellaver

▷ OLD MAN AND THE SEA, THE (1990)
MMTV • Jud Taylor
Anthony Quinn, Valentina Quinn, Francesco Quinn

Plot: An old fisherman dreams of hooking one great fish in his lifetime.

Notes: The films are based upon a novel by Ernest Hemingway who also wrote the screenplay for the 1958 production. Valentina and Francesco Quinn are the daughter and son of Anthony Quinn.

★   ★   ★

★   ★   ★   ★   ★   ★   ★

▶ ONE MILLION B.C. (1940)★AOV★
United Artists • Hal Roach, Hal Roach Jr.

Victor Mature, Carole Landis, Lon Chaney Jr.

▷ ONE MILLION YEARS B.C. (1966)
Hammer • Don Chaffey

Raquel Welch, John Richardson

Plot: Love, life and war among pre-historic tribes during the Stone Age.

Notes: The great filmmaker D.W. Griffith is said to have worked on the 1940 production. It is a fact that the dinosaur. although prominently featured in the films, had become extinct before the appearance on earth of the human being.

★ ★ ★

▶ PAINTED VEIL, THE (1934)
MGM • Richard Boleslawski

Greta Garbo, George Brent, Herbert Marshall, Warner Oland

▷ SEVENTH SIN, THE (1947)
MGM • Ronald Neame

Eleanor Parker, Bill Travers, George Sanders

Plot: A wife gives up her lover and helps her doctor husband in combatting an epidemic.

Notes: Based upon "The Painted Veil," a novel by Somerset Maugham, both films are set in China. Herbert Marshall, who played many romantic roles on screen, had an artificial leg. He lost his own during World War I.

★ ★ ★

▶ PRINCE AND THE PAUPER, THE (1937)★AOV★
Warners • William Keighley

Errol Flynn, Claude Rains, Alan Hale, Billy and Bobby Mauch

▷ CROSSED SWORDS (1977)★AOV★
British • Richard Fleischer

Oliver Reed, Mark Lester, Ernest Borgnine, George C. Scott, Charlton Heston

Plot: A young prince switches identities with a poor boy who looks exactly like him.

Notes: The Mauch Twins play the title roles in the 1937 film while Mark Lester plays both roles in the 1977 version of the Mark Twain story.

★ ★ ★

▶ PRISONER OF SHARK ISLAND (1936)
TCF • John Ford

Warner Baxter, Gloria Stuart

▷ ORDEAL OF DR. MUDD, THE (1980)★AOV★
MMTV • Paul Wendkos

Dennis Weaver, Susan Sullivan

Plot: Life of the doctor who treated the assassin of Abraham Lincoln.

Notes: Both Dennis Weaver and Susan Sullivan appeared in successful TV shows: Weaver in "Gunsmoke" and "McCloud", and Sullivan in "Falcon Crest."

★ ★ ★

▶ PRISONER OF ZENDA, THE (1937)
David Selznick • John Cromwell

Ronald Colman, Madeleine Carroll, Douglas Fairbanks Jr.

▷ PRISONER OF ZENDA, THE (1952)★AOV★
MGM • Richard Thorpe

Stewart Granger, James Mason, Deborah Kerr

Plot: An Englishman impersonates a kidnapped king.

Notes: A third sound version was filmed by Universal in 1979★AOV★ starring Peter Sellers and Elke Sommer. Two silent versions were released, the first in 1913, the second in 1922.

★   ★   ★   ★   ★   ★   ★

▶ QUO VADIS? (1951)★AOV★
MGM • Mervyn Le Roy
Robert Taylor, Deborah Kerr, Peter Ustinov

▷ QUO VADIS? (1985)★AOV★
MMTV • Franco Rossi
Klaus Maria Brandauer, Frederic Forrest

Plot: A Roman commander under Nero falls in love with a Christian and both are sentenced to death.

Notes: The 1951 film was shot in Rome. Two silent versions of the story were filmed, one in 1912 and the other in 1925. The last noted stars Emil Jannings, winner of the first Best Actor Academy Award.

★   ★   ★

▶ ROME EXPRESS (1932)
Gaumont • Walter Forde
Conrad Veidt, Esther Ralston

▷ SLEEPING CAR TO TRIESTE (1948)
GFD/Two Cities • John Paddy Carstairs
Albert Lieven, Jean Kent

Plot: Several passengers aboard a train traveling across Europe are involved in criminal activities.

★   ★   ★

▶ SCARLET PIMPERNEL, THE (1934)★AOV★
United Artists • Harold Young
Leslie Howard, Merle Oberon, Raymond Massey

▷ SCARLET PIMPERNEL, THE (1982)★AOV★
MMTV • Clive Donner
Anthony Andrews, Jane Seymour, Ian McKellen

Plot: An Englishman leads a double life—apparently leading a dissolute existence, he is, in reality, rescuing innocent victims of the French Revolution.

Notes: Leslie Howard lost his life under mysterious circumstances during World War II. It was rumored that he was on a secret mission for the British government.

★   ★   ★

▶ SEA WOLF, THE (1941)★AOV★
Warners • Michael Curtiz
Edward G. Robinson, John Garfield, Ida Lupino

▷ WOLF LARSEN (1958)
Allied Artists • Harmon Jones
Barry Sullivan, Peter Graves, Gita Hall

Plot: The psychopathic captain of a freighter holds his passengers captive.

Notes: Other sound versions of the Jack London novel were released in 1930 and in 1975. Silent productions were filmed in 1913, 1920 and 1925.

★   ★   ★

▶ SEVEN SAMURAI (1954)★AOV★
Japanese • Akira Kurosawa
Toshiro Mifore, Takashi Shimura

▷ MAGNIFICENT SEVEN, THE (1960)★AOV★
United Artists • John Sturges
Yul Brynner, Steve McQueen, Robert Vaughn

Plot: Seven men are hired to protect a town from bandits.

Notes: The famous western version of the Japanese film takes place in Mexico. Robert Vaughn, featured in the 1960 film, is best known for his role as Napoleon Solo in Television's "Man from U.N.C.L.E."

★   ★   ★

☆   ☆   ☆   ☆   ☆   ☆   ☆

▶ SHANGHAI EXPRESS (1932)
Paramount • Josef von Sternberg
Marlene Dietrich, Clive Brook, Anna May Wong

▷ PEKING EXPRESS (1951)
Paramount • William Dieterle
Joseph Cotten, Corinne Calvet, Edmund Gwenn

Plot: Two ex-lovers meet on a train which is waylaid by outlaws.

Notes: Another version of this adventure yarn was released in 1942. NIGHT PLANE FROM CHUNG KING stars Ellen Drew and Robert Preston. In this film the passengers take the plane, not the train. To coincide with the war going on, one of the passengers is an enemy agent.

★　★　★

▶ SHE (1935)
RKO • Irving Pichel
Randolph Scott, Helen Gahagan

▷ SHE (1965)
ABP/Hammer • Robert Day
Peter Cushing, Ursula Andress

Plot: An expedition comes upon a city where a queen lives who cannot die until she has known love.

Notes: The 1935 version is set in the Arctic, the 1965 film reverts back to its original African locale. The first filming of this epic took place in 1925, the last was Italian-made in 1985. Helen Gahagan, wife of Melvyn Douglas, later went into politics and served in Congress until she was unseated by Richard Nixon.

★　★　★

▶ SINGAPORE (1947)
Universal • John Brahm
Fred MacMurray, Ava Gardner

▷ ISTANBUL (1957)
Universal • Joseph Pevney
Errol Flynn, Cornell Bouchers

Plot: A smuggler returns to the scene of the crime to reclaim the jewels he has hidden and finds the wife he thought dead suffering from amnesia and married to another man.

Notes: Featured in the 1957 version are Nat King Cole, who sings two songs and Werner Klemperer, known to television fans as Colonel Klink on the "Hogan's Heroes" series.

★　★　★

▶ SIXTEEN FATHOMS DEEP (1934)★AOV★
Armond Schaefer
Lon Chaney Jr., Sally O'Neil

▷ 16 FATHOMS DEEP (1948)
Irving Allen
Lloyd Bridges, Lon Chaney Jr.

Plot: A sponge fisherman goes against a greedy money-lender.

Notes: In the first film, Lon Chaney Jr. is the hero, in the second, he is the villain.

★　★　★

▶ SLIM (1937)
Warners • Ray Enright
Pat O'Brien, Henry Fonda, Margaret Lindsay

▷ MANPOWER (1941)
Warners • Raoul Walsh
Edward G. Robinson, George Raft, Marlene Dietrich

Plot: Two electric linesmen fall in love with the same woman.

Notes: Playing a small role in the 1937 film is a twenty-three year old actress named Jane Wyman.

★　★　★

☆　☆　☆　☆　☆　☆　☆

▶ SON OF FURY (1942)

TCF • John Cromwell

Tyrone Power, Gene Tierney, George Sanders, Frances Farmer

▷ TREASURE OF THE GOLDEN CONDOR, THE (1952)★AOV★

TCF • Delmar Daves

Cornel Wilde, Constance Smith, George Macready

Plot: A man deprived of his inheritance goes to the South Seas and later returns to regain his rights.

Notes: Cornel Wilde began his show business career on Broadway. One of his roles was in a Laurence Olivier production of "Romeo and Juliet." After being featured in a few films, he played Frederic Chopin in A SONG TO REMEMBER (1945) and was Oscar- nominated for his portrayal of the Polish composer.

★ ★ ★

▶ SPAWN OF THE NORTH (1938)
Paramount • Henry Hathaway

Henry Fonda, George Raft, Dorothy Lamour, John Barrymore

▷ ALASKA SEAS (1953)
Paramount • Jerry Hopper

Robert Ryan, Gene Barry, Jan Sterling

Plot: Conflict between American and Russian salmon fishermen.

Notes: The exteriors for the 1938 film were shot in Alaska, making the film appear more realistic. This plus an all-star cast made for a rousing hit at the box-office.

★ ★ ★

▶ SWISS FAMILY ROBINSON, THE (1940)★AOV★
RKO • Edward Ludwig

Thomas Mitchell, Edna Best, Freddie Bartholomew

▷ SWISS FAMILY ROBINSON, THE (1960)★AOV★
Disney • Ken Annakin

John Mills, Dorothy McGuire, James MacArthur

Plot: A shipwrecked family builds a home on a desert island.

Notes: John Mills, the well-known English actor, is the father of actresses Hayley and Juliet Mills. A Movie Made for Television version of the famous novel, starring Martin Milner and Cameron Mitchell, was released in 1975.

★ ★ ★

▶ TALE OF TWO CITIES, A (1935)★AOV★
MGM • Jack Conway

Ronald Colman, Elizabeth Allen, Basil Rathbone

▷ TALE OF TWO CITIES, A (1958)★AOV★
Rank • Ralph Thomas

Dirk Bogarde, Dorothy Tutin, Christopher Lee

Plot: A British subject in the midst of the French Revolution aids its victims and sacrifices his life in the name of justice.

★ ★ ★

▶ TARZAN, THE APE MAN (1932)★AOV★
MGM • W.S. Van Dyke
Johnny Weissmuller, Maureen O'Sullivan

▷ TARZAN, THE APE MAN (1959)
MGM • Joseph M. Newman
Denny Miller, Joanna Barnes

Plot: An English gentlewoman finds adventure and true love in the arms of a jungle man.

Notes: A third version of this first of the "Tarzan" series (based on the writings of Edgar Rice Burroughs) was produced by John Derek in 1981★AOV★ as a vehicle for his wife Bo. There have been thirty-three Tarzan films released thus far. Besides Weissmuller and Miller, six others have played the character: Glenn Morris, Herman Brix (a.k.a. Bruce Bennett), Lex Barker, Gordon Scott, Jock Mahoney and Mike Henry.

★ ★ ★

▶ THREE MUSKETEERS, THE (1935)★AOV★
Rowland V. Lee
Walter Abel, Paul Lukas, Margot Grahame, Heather Angel

▷ THREE MUSKETEERS, THE (1948)★AOV★
MGM • George Sidney
Gene Kelly, Lana Turner, June Allyson, Van Heflin

Plot: Conspiracies, duels and feats of derring-do during the reign of French Emperor Louis XIII.

Notes: There have been four filmings of the Alexandre Dumas novel thus far: the two listed, one made in 1939 starring Don Ameche plus the comedy of The Ritz Brothers and another released in 1973★AOV★ featuring Michael York.

★ ★ ★

▶ TRADER HORN (1930)
MGM • W.S. Van Dyke
Edwina Booth, Duncan Renaldo

▷ TRADER HORN (1973)
MGM • Reza Badiyi
Rod Taylor, Anne Heywood

Plot: A white trader of goods in Africa incurs tribal hostility.

Notes: Director Van Dyke's 1929 location trek to Africa lasted seven months. Edwina Booth became ill while filming and never completely recovered. She successfully sued MGM for damages.

★ ★ ★

▶ TREASURE ISLAND (1934)★AOV★
MGM • Victor Fleming
Wallace Beery, Jackie Cooper, Lewis Stone

▷ TREASURE ISLAND (1950)★AOV★
Disney • Bryan Haskin
Robert Newton, Bobby Driscoll

Plot: An old pirate map leads an English lad and a one-legged reprobate on a long journey in search of buried treasure.

Notes: A 1920 silent version of the Robert Louis Stevenson novel features actress Shirley Mason in the juvenile lead as Jim Hawkins. A 1972 filming of the story stars Orson Weles as Long John Silver.

★ ★ ★

▶ WAGES OF FEAR, THE (1953)★AOV★
Filmsonor/CICC • Henri-Georges Clouzot
Yves Montand

▷ SORCERER, THE (1977)
Universal • William Friedkin
Roy Scheider

Plot: Four men in Latin America take to the road bringing truckloads of nitroglycerine to help put out an oil fire.

★ ★ ★

▶ WICKED LADY, THE (1945)★AOV★
GFD/Gainsborough • Leslie Arliss
Margaret Lockwood, James Mason, Patricia Roc,
Michael Rennie

▷ WICKED LADY, THE (1983)★AOV★
Cannon • Michael Winner
Faye Dunaway, Alan Bates, John Gielgud

Plot: An English gentlewoman meets a highwayman and takes to a life of crime.

Notes: The remake was co-authored by Leslie Arliss, writer-director of the first film and son of the eminent actor, George Arliss.

★ ★ ★

▶ ZERO HOUR (1957)
Paramount • Hall Bartlett
Dana Andrews, Linda Darnell, Sterling Hayden

▷ TERROR IN THE SKY (1971)
MMTV • Bernard Kowalski
Leif Ericson, Roddy McDowall, Keenan Wynn, Doug McClure

Plot: A dangerous situation arises when the pilot and several passengers on a commercial flight suffer from food poisoning.

Notes: The disaster storyline has been used on many occasions, most prominently in the 1981 satire, AIRPLANE.

★ ★ ★

★   ★   ★   ★   ★   ★   ★

CHAPTER TWELVE

CLASSIC FILMS REMADE: EVERYTHING OLD IS NEW AGAIN

The dictionary describes a classic as a work of enduring quality, one which forms a part of mankind's permanent achievement—its universal theme is enjoyed by all and transcends the boundaries of countries and custom.

Many literary works have become part of this heritage of mankind. Deemed classics, they have also translated into film with varying degrees of success—some have been remade (a few more than once), also with varying degrees of success.

There is really no one genre into which we can place all of the films based upon classics produced throughout the years—most are better represented in the several genres already studied thus far. The film pairings chosen for this chapter, however, are part of a certain type of classic, different and older than the others, several going back to the sixteenth century writings of Shakespeare and some even farther back to Biblical times. In other words, some works of the Bard, a dash of Sophoclean antiquity and a flavoring of epic costume drama add up to this potpourri of entertainment.

★   ★   ★   ★   ★   ★   ★

▶ CLEOPATRA (1934)★AOV★
Paramount • Cecil B. De Mille

Claudette Colbert, Henry Wilcoxon, Warren
William

▷ CLEOPATRA (1963)★AOV★
TCF • Joseph L. Mankiewicz

Elizabeth Taylor, Richard Burton, Rex Harrison

Plot: Love along the Nile as Cleopatra turns her her attention to Mark Antony.

Notes: An addenda to the above plot outline should read "and Taylor turns her attention to Burton," for it was on the set of the 1963 opus that the two met. The story of this production was chronicled by its producer, Walter Wanger, in the book, "My Life With Cleopatra."

★   ★   ★

Claudette Colbert as CLEOPATRA, B.L.T. (Before Liz Taylor). How many remember this version?

★   ★   ★

▶ HAMLET (1948)★AOV★
Rank/Two Cities • Laurence Olivier

Laurence Olivier, Jean Simmons

▷ HAMLET (1969)★AOV★
British • Tony Richardson

Nicol Williamson, Gordon Jackson, Marianne Faithful

Plot: Hamlet's intellectual introspection delays the avenging of his father's death, thus leading to further tragedy.

Notes: Olivier won Best Actor Oscar for his performance as the melancholy Dane. The picture was also honored. A Russian version of the Shakespeare classic was released in 1964.

★   ★   ★

☆   ☆   ☆   ☆   ☆   ☆   ☆

▶ JULIUS CAESAR (1953)＊ᴬᴼⱽ＊
MGM • Joseph L. Mankiewicz

Marlon Brando, Greer Garson, James Mason,
Deborah Kerr, John Gielgud

▷ JULIUS CAESAR (1970)＊ᴬᴼⱽ＊
British/Commonwealth • Stuart Burge

Richard Johnson, Jason Robards, Charlton
Heston, Diana Rigg

Plot: Conspiracies and politics abound in ancient Rome as Julius Caesar is assassinated and Mark
Antony triumphs in the events which follow.

Notes: Ten years after directing JULIUS CAESAR, Mankiewicz turned his hand to CLEOPATRA.
This proved a big mistake as the latter film was lambasted by the critics. Both the 1953 film and
its star, Marlon Brando, who was coached for his role as Mark Antony by John Gielgud, were Oscar-
nominated.

★   ★   ★

*Political Power and Honor in
Ancient Rome. Greer Garson
and Louis Calhern in a scene
from JULIUS CAESAR.*

★   ★   ★

▶ KING LEAR (1971)＊ᴬᴼⱽ＊
Columbia/Filmways-Laterna • Peter Brook

Paul Scofield, Irene Worth

▷ KING LEAR (1987)
US/Swiss • Jean Luc Godard

Peter Sellers, Burgess Meredith

Plot: An old king divides his kingdom between his daughters and then becomes senile, with tragic
results.

Notes: The 1971 version was photographed in Denmark. The remake, an updating of the classic
story by Shakespeare, features such diverse personalities as Woody Allen, Molly Ringwald, Norman
Mailer and the director himself.

★   ★   ★

☆   ☆   ☆   ☆   ☆   ☆   ☆

▶ MACBETH (1948)★AOV★
Republic • Orson Welles

Orson Welles, Dan O'Herlihy, Roddy McDowall,
Jeanette Nolan, Edgar Barrier

▷ MACBETH (1971)★AOV★
Playboy/Caliban • Roman Polanski

Jon Finch, Francesca Annis

Plot: A Scottish lord and his ambitious wife thirst for power and they kill their king while he is asleep; this leads to several more murders and their own undoing.

Notes: A Movie Made for Television version of the Shakespearean tragedy, starring Maurice Evans and Judith Anderson, was released in 1960.

★   ★   ★

▶ MAN FOR ALL SEASONS, A (1966)★AOV★
Columbia • Fred Zinnemann

Paul Scofield, Wendy Hiller, Susannah York,
Robert Shaw, Orson Welles

▷ MAN FOR ALL SEASONS, A (1988)★AOV★
MMTV • Charlton Heston

Charlton Heston, Vanessa Redgrave, John Gielgud

Plot: Sir Thomas Moore's conflict with Henry VIII over the latter's divorce and break with the Pope leads to his execution.

Notes: Paul Scofield and Fred Zinnemann won Best Actor and Best Director Oscars. The film was also honored.

★   ★   ★

▶ MIDSUMMER NIGHT'S DREAM, A (1935)★AOV★
Warners • Max Reinhardt, William Dieterle

James Cagney, Dick Powell, Olivia de Havilland,
Joe E. Brown, Mickey Rooney

▷ MIDSUMMER NIGHT'S DREAM, A (1968)
British • Peter Hall

Diana Rigg, David Warner, Ian Richardson

Plot: Lovers, tradesmen and fairies frolic in the woods of Athens.

Notes: The players in the 1968 production were members of England's Royal Shakespeare Company. A ballet version of the Shakespearean comedy, performed by the New York Ballet Company, was released in 1966.

★   ★   ★

▶ OEDIPUS REX (1957)★AOV★
Canadian • Tyrone Guthrie

Douglas Rain, Eric House, Douglas Campbell

▷ OEDIPUS THE KING (1967)★AOV★
British • Philip Saville

Christopher Plummer, Orson Welles, Lilli Palmer,
Donald Sutherland

Plot: Sophocles' classic play of a king who has unknowingly murdered his father and married his mother.

Notes: An Italian version of this Greek tragedy starring Alida Valli and Silvana Mangano was released in 1967.

★   ★   ★

☆   ☆   ☆   ☆   ☆   ☆   ☆

▶ OTHELLO (1952)
Mercury/Films Marceau • Orson Welles
Orson Welles, Michael MacLiammoir, Suzanne
Cloutier

▷ OTHELLO (1965)
BHE • Stuart Burge
Laurence Olivier, Derek Jacobi, Maggie Smith

Plot: Othello is tricked into believing that his wife has been unfaithful to him.

Notes: OTELLO∗AOV∗, an opera by Verdi, based upon the play by Shakespeare, was released in 1986. Directed by Franco Zeffirelli, it stars Placido Domingo.

★ ★ ★

▶ ROMEO AND JULIET (1936)
MGM • George Cukor
Norma Shearer, Leslie Howard, John Barrymore,
Basil Rathbone

▷ ROMEO AND JULIET (1968)∗AOV∗
Paramount • Franco Zeffirelli
Leonard Whiting, Olivia Hussey, Michael York

Plot: The members of two powerful families are sworn enemies. The son of one falls in love with the daughter of the other. A misunderstanding results in the tragic death of the couple.

Notes: At the time of filming, Norma Shearer was in her thirties and Leslie Howard was in his forties—Romeo and Juliet are both teenagers. It worked due to the magic of its stars and did well at the box-office. Another version of the Shakespearean tragedy was filmed in 1954∗AOV∗ starring Laurence Harvey and Susan Shentall. A Royal Ballet version starring Margot Fonteyn and Rudolf Nureyev was filmed in 1966∗AOV∗.

★ ★ ★

▶ SAMSON AND DELILAH (1949)∗AOV∗
Paramount • Cecil B. De Mille
Hedy Lamarr, Victor Mature, Angela Lansbury,
George Sanders

▷ SAMSON AND DELILAH (1984)∗AOV∗
MMTV • Lee Philips
Antony Hamilton, Belinda Bauer, Max von Sydow,
José Ferrer, Victor Mature

Plot: The Biblical story of Delilah who cuts strongman Samson's hair and delivers him to his enemies, the Philistines.

Notes: An interesting sidelight to the remake is that in it, Victor Mature, the original Samson, is seen as that character's father.

★ ★ ★

▶ THREE SISTERS (1966)
Actors Studio • Paul Bogart
Shelley Winters, Geraldine Page, Kim Stanley

▷ THREE SISTERS (1970)
British • Laurence Olivier
Laurence Olivier, Joan Plowright, Alan Bates

Plot: Upon the death of their father at the turn of the century, three sisters in a small Russian town dream of life in the big city.

Notes: The 1966 film is a taped recreation of the Actors Studio Broadway production of the play by Anton Chekov.

★ ★ ★

★   ★   ★   ★   ★   ★   ★

CHAPTER THIRTEEN

FROM SILENCE TO SOUND: EVERYTHING OLD IS NEW AGAIN

The "shot" heard round the world! Only one of the many ways to describe the premiere of THE JAZZ SINGER at New York's Warner Theater on October 6, 1927.

On that fall evening, the Broadway audience saw and heard Al Jolson not only sing, but talk. Although the sound sequences of the landmark film were few and although silents continued to be made throughout 1928 and well into 1929, the handwriting was on the wall—whether folks like Charlie Chaplin liked it or not (and he didn't, resisting spoken dialogue until his 1940 triumph, THE GREAT DICTATOR), the talking picture, for better or for worse, was here to stay.

By late 1929, most of Hollywood had hopped on the band wagon. The major studios began preparing for "The Talkies"—constructing sound stages, putting in necessary equipment and nervously testing the voices of their established stars. Several of the industry's most popular and highly paid performers, who had mesmerized audiences by a look and a gesture, suddenly saw themselves and their careers fading into oblivion as the revolution continued. Concurrently, an exodus from the Broadway stage took place as Hollywood offered its trained voices the sun, the moon, the stars, lucrative contracts and balmy weather to boot, to board the Twentieth Century Limited at New York's Grand Central Station and make the train trek westward. Among these were performers who would take their places among the immortals of the screen: Fredric March, Paul Muni, James Cagney, Edward G. Robinson, Bette Davis, Claudette Colbert, Tallulah Bankhead.

With so much change taking place and with expenses mounting during those early days of sound, the moguls came up with a "novel" idea: why not combine new material with old and save money? The studio heads reasoned that the public would welcome sound versions of silent favorites as well as newly commissioned works. And say what you will about the movie moguls of old (and plenty has been said), they knew their business and were right on the mark: the old became new again, with dialogue added.

★   ★   ★   ★   ★   ★   ★

Several of the silents made into talkies have not been listed in this chapter because the two or more later versions produced have assumed more importance than the originals. There are fifty-five pairings in this chapter, however, diverse in content, but linked together by the thread of a great silent becoming a sound film.

They are to be enjoyed in this diversity.

★　★　★　★　★　★　★

▶ ABIE'S IRISH ROSE (1928)
Paramount • Victor Fleming, Jules Furthman
Nancy Carroll, Charles "Buddy" Rogers, Jean Hersholt

▷ ABIE'S IRISH ROSE (1946)
United Artists • Edward Sutherland
Joanne Dru, Richard Norris, J.M. Kerrigan, Michael Chekov

Plot: Families clash as a Jewish boy marries an Irish colleen.

Notes: The stage version of ABIE'S IRISH ROSE opened on Broadway in 1922 and closed six years later. Bing Crosby Productions was responsible for the sound version. Joanne Dru was married to both crooner Dick Haymes and later to actor John Ireland. She is also the sister of TV host Peter Marshall.

★　★　★

▶ ALOMA OF THE SOUTH SEAS (1926)
Paramount • Maurice Torneur
Gilda Gray, Warner Baxter, William Powell

▷ ALOMA OF THE SOUTH SEAS (1941)
Paramount • Alfred Santell
Dorothy Lamour, Jon Hall, Philip Reed

Plot: Two men on a tropical island vie for the love of a native girl.

Notes: Additions to the remake, besides a few plot alterations, include some underwater scenes and a volcanic eruption.

★　★　★

▶ ANNA CHRISTIE (1923)★AOV★
First National • John G. Wray
Blanche Sweet

▷ ANNA CHRISTIE (1930)★AOV★
MGM • Clarence Brown
Greta Garbo, Marie Dressler, Charles Bickford

Plot: A waterfront woman of easy virtue falls in love with a young sailor.

Notes: Garbo's first talkie. She was Oscar-nonimated, but lost.

★　★　★

▶ BEAU BRUMMELL (1924)★AOV★
Warners • Harry Beaumont
John Barrymore, Mary Astor

▷ BEAU BRUMMELL (1954)
MGM • Curtis Bernhardt
Stewart Granger, Elizabeth Taylor, Peter Ustinov

Plot: A nineteenth century dandy enjoys a good relationship with the Prince of Wales—this ends and when he dies, he is penniless.

Notes: Besides being filmed in England, the remake of BEAU BRUMMELL boasts a cast of mostly English-born performers.

★　★　★

▶ BEAU GESTE (1926)
Paramount • Herbert Brenon
Ronald Colman, Neil Hamilton, Victor McLaglen, Noah Beery Sr., Ralph Forbes

▷ BEAU GESTE (1939)★AOV★
Paramount • William Wellman
Gary Cooper, Ray Milland, Brian Donlevy, Robert Preston, Susan Hayward

Plot: Three brothers join the Foreign Legion, suffer under a brutal sergeant, and die in battle.

Notes: Brian Donlevy was Oscar-nominated for his role as the sadistic sergeant in the 1939 production. A 1966 remake stars Telly Savalas, Guy Stockwell and Doug McClure.

★　★　★

☆　　☆　　☆　　☆　　☆　　☆　　☆

▶ BEN HUR (1926)★AOV★
MGM • Fred Niblo
Ramon Novarro, Francis X. Bushman, Carmel
Myers

▷ BEN HUR (1959)★AOV★
MGM • William Wyler
Charlton Heston, Jack Hawkins, Stephen Boyd

Plot: A Jew suffers under his Roman masters during the days of Christ.

Notes: The 1959 production won twelve Oscars, among them Best Film, Best Director (Wyler), Best Actor (Heston), Best Supporting Actor (Hugh Griffith) and Best Scoring (Miklos Rozsa).

★　★　★

▶ BLOOD AND SAND (1922)★AOV★
Paramount • Fred Niblo
Rudolph Valentino, Nita Naldi, Lila Lee

▷ BLOOD AND SAND (1941)★AOV★
TCF • Rouben Mamoulian
Tyrone Power, Linda Darnell, Rita Hayworth

Plot: A matador falls under the spell of a femme fatale and ignores the girl who has always loved him.

Notes: The 1941 film won an Oscar for its cinematographers, who used the Technicolor process to its then greatest advantage in filming the bullfighting sequences.

★　★　★

▶ BRIDGE OF SAN LUIS REY, THE (1929)
MGM • Charles Brabin
Lili Damita, Ernest Torrence, Duncan Renaldo

▷ BRIDGE OF SAN LUIS REY, THE (1944)★AOV★
United Artists • Rowland V. Lee
Lynn Bari, Francis Lederer, Akim Tamiroff, Louis Calhern

Plot: Five people die when a Peruvian bridge collapses. Their reasons for being on the bridge make up the plot of the film.

Notes: Both films are based upon the Pulitzer-Prize winning novel by Thorton Wilder.

★　★　★

▶ BROKEN BLOSSOMS (1919)★AOV★
United Artists • D.W. Griffith
Lillian Gish, Donald Crisp, Richard Barthelmess

▷ BROKEN BLOSSOMS (1936)
British/Twickenham • John Brahm
Dolly Haas, Emlyn Williams

Plot: A man beats his daughter to death and a Chinese man, who loves her, kills the father and then himself.

Notes: D.W. Griffith began to direct the remake, but left because of production disagreements. Brahm took over.

★　★　★

▶ CAMERAMAN, THE (1928)★AOV★
MGM • Edward Sedgwick
Buster Keaton, Marcelline Day

▷ WATCH THE BIRDIE (1950)
MGM • Jack Donohue
Red Skelton, Arlene Dahl, Ann Miller

Plot: The antics of a comical cameraman.

Notes: The script of the second production was altered to fit the talents of Red Skelton, who plays three roles in the film: a camera bug, his father and his grandfather.

★　★　★

▶ CAT AND THE CANARY, THE (1927)★AOV★
Universal • Paul Leni
Creighton Hale, Laura La Plante

▷ CAT AND THE CANARY, THE (1939)
Paramount • Elliott Nugent
Bob Hope, Paulette Goddard, Gale Sondergaard

Plot: Relatives of an eccentric gather together in an old house for the reading of his will.

Notes: Another filming of the old chestnut, titled THE CAT CREEPS, was released in 1930 and a 1978★AOV★ version under the original title was shot in Great Britain. As a result of her performance in the 1939 film, Paulette Goddard was given a ten year contract at Paramount.

★ ★ ★

Adventures in the Foreign Legion. Title-rolist Gary Cooper as BEAU GESTE, flanked by "brothers" Robert Preston (left) and Ray Milland (right).

★ ★ ★

▶ DARK ANGEL (1925)
Samuel Goldwyn • George Fitzmaurice
Ronald Colman, Vilma Banky

▷ DARK ANGEL (1935)
Samuel Goldwyn • Sidney Franklin
Fredric March, Merle Oberon, Herbert Marshall

Plot: A man, blinded in World War I, tries to discourage his fiance, who has not been told of his condition, from marrying him.

★ ★ ★

▶ DON JUAN (1926)★AOV★

Warners • Alan Crosland
John Barrymore, Mary Astor

▷ ADVENTURES OF DON JUAN, THE (1949)★AOV★
Warners • Vincent Sherman
Errol Flynn, Viveca Lindfors, Alan Hale

Plot: The exploits in and out of the bedroom of the famous lover who lived at the time of the Borgias.

Notes: DON JUAN was released with a synchronized score, the success of which led to further experimentation and the start of the talkies.

★ ★ ★

☆   ☆   ☆   ☆   ☆   ☆   ☆

▶ FARMER'S WIFE, THE (1928)★AOV★
British/BIP • Alfred Hitchcock
James Thomas, Lillian Hall-Davies

▷ FARMER'S WIFE, THE (1940)
British/Pathe • Norman Lee, Leslie Arliss
Basil Sydney, Michael Wilding, Nora Swinburne

Plot: After several disappointments, a farmer seeking a wife finds that he really does not have to look further than than his own home—he marries his housekeeper.

Notes: One of Hitchcock's few comedies. He also wrote the 1928 screenplay.

★   ★   ★

▶ FORBIDDEN PARADISE (1924)
Paramount • Ernst Lubitsch
Pola Negri, Rod La Rocque

▷ ROYAL SCANDAL, A (1945)
TCF • Otto Preminger
Tallulah Bankhead, William Eythe, Anne Baxter, Vincent Price

Plot: Amorous exploits at the court of Catherine The Great of Russia.

Notes: The 1945 production was to have been directed by Lubitsch but due to ill health, he handed the project over to Preminger.

★   ★   ★

▶ FOUR HORSEMEN OF THE APOCALYPSE THE (1921)
Metro • Rex Ingram
Rudolph Valentino, Alice Terry, Alan Hale, Wallace Beery

▷ FOUR HORSEMEN OF THE APOCALYPSE, THE (1961)★AOV★
MGM • Vincente Minnelli
Glenn Ford, Ingrid Thulin, Charles Boyer, Paul Henreid

Plot: The members of a family fight a war on opposing sides.

Notes: The setting of the remake is updated to World War II. Metro Pictures had been formed in 1919. It was taken over by Loew's Incorporated in order to get its product distributed. In 1924, Loew's Incorporated and Goldwyn Pictures merged. With Louis B. Mayer's name included (he became studio head), the new enterprise called itself Metro-Goldwyn-Mayer (MGM).

★   ★   ★

▶ FOUR SONS (1928)
Fox • John Ford
Margaret Mann, James Hall, Francis X. Bushman

▷ FOUR SONS (1940)
TCF • Archie Mayo
Don Ameche, Alan Curtis, Eugenie Leontovich, Robert Lowery

Plot: In wartime, a widow's four sons fight on opposite sides.

Notes: The silent version is set during World War I, the remake in World War II.

★   ★   ★

▶ FOUR WALLS (1928)
MGM • William Nigh
Joan Crawford, John Gilbert

▷ STRAIGHT IS THE WAY (1934)
MGM • Paul Sloane
Karen Morley, Franchot Tone, Gladys George

Plot: A man, jailed for manslaughter, is released from prison and becomes involved in a gangland murder.

Notes: Joan Crawford, star of the first film, was married for a brief time during the nineteen thirties to Franchot Tone, the star of the remake.

★   ★   ★

★　★　★　★　★　★　★

▶ GENERAL, THE (1926)★ᴀᴏᴠ★
United Artists • Clyde Bruckman, Buster Keaton
Buster Keaton, Marion Mack

▷ SOUTHERN YANKEE, A (1948)
MGM • Edgar Sedgwick
Red Skelton, Arlene Dahl, Brian Donlevy

Plot: Hijinks during the Civil War as a southern man finds himself behind enemy lines.

Notes: The story is supposedly based on a true incident. Buster Keaton was involved in the making of the 1948 film.

Type-casting? John Barrymore as the legendary DON JUAN. The lady receiving his attentions is a very young Mary Astor at the beginning of a long career. (See Chapter One for a picture of Mary in her middle years.)

▶ GLORIOUS BETSY (1928)
Warners • Alan Crosland
Conrad Nagel, Dolores Costello, Betty Blythe

▷ HEARTS DIVIDED (1936)
Warners • Frank Borzage
Marion Davies, Dick Powell, Claude Rains, Edward Everett Horton

Plot: What happens when Napoleon's brother falls in love with an American woman.

Notes: Dolores Costello, star of the first production was, for a time, the wife of John Barrymore, while Marion Davies, star of the remake, was the long-time mistress of newspaper tycoon William Randolph Hearst.

★　★　★

☆   ☆   ☆   ☆   ☆   ☆   ☆

▶ GRAND DUCHESS AND THE WAITER, THE (1926)
Paramount • Malcolm St. Clair

Adolphe Menjou, Florence Vidor

▷ HERE IS MY HEART (1934)

Paramount • Frank Tuttle

Bing Crosby, Kitty Carlisle

Plot: A wealthy man disguises himself as a waiter to be close to the princess he loves.

Notes: Kitty Carlisle is the widow of playwright Moss Hart. Still active, the actress-singer bills herself as "Kitty Carlisle Hart."

▶ HOTEL IMPERIAL (1927)
Paramount • Mauritz Stiller

Pola Negri, James Hall

▷ FIVE GRAVES TO CAIRO (1943)
Paramount • Billy Wilder

Franchot Tone, Anne Baxter, Erich von Stroheim

Plot: A hotel in a war zone is alternately occupied by opposing forces.

Notes: The 1943 production was updated to World War II with Erich von Stroheim playing famed General Erwin Rommel. The love theme in the first film becomes a spy theme in the remake. In between the two came HOTEL IMPERIAL (1939) starring Ray Milland.

▶ HUNCHBACK OF NOTRE DAME, THE (1923) ★AOV★
Universal • Wallace Worsley

Lon Chaney Sr., Patsy Ruth Miller

▷ HUNCHBACK OF NOTRE DAME, THE (1939) ★AOV★
RKO • William Dieterle

Charles Laughton, Maureen O'Hara, Cedric Hardwicke

Plot: A deformed bell ringer feels a strange attraction for a lovely gypsy girl.

Notes: As has been noted, two later versions of the Victor Hugo novel were made, one in 1957 starring Anthony Quinn and Gina Lollobrigida, the other a 1982 Movie Made for Television starring Anthony Hopkins and Lesley-Anne Down.

▶ IRON MASK, THE (1929) ★AOV★
United Artists • Allan Dwan

Douglas Fairbanks Sr., Belle Bennett

▷ MAN IN THE IRON MASK, THE (1939) ★AOV★
United Artists • James Whale

Louis Hayward, Joan Bennett

Plot: Louis XIV, the true king of France, locked in an iron mask and languishing in prison, has his throne usurped by his evil twin brother. In time it is restored to him by some of his loyal followers.

Notes: There was no relationship between Belle and Joan Bennett. The screen play of the 1929 film was written by Douglas Fairbanks Sr. under an assumed name.

▶ KING OF KINGS (1927) ★AOV★
Pathe • Cecil B. De Mille

H.B. Warner, Joseph Schildkraut, Jacqueline Logan, Ernest Truex

▷ KING OF KINGS (1961) ★AOV★
MGM • Nicholas Ray

Jeffrey Hunter, Robert Ryan, Siobhan McKenna, Rita Gam

Plot: The life of Jesus Christ.

Notes: The 1961 film is narrated by Orson Welles.

★   ★   ★   ★   ★   ★   ★

▶ KISS ME AGAIN (1925)
Warners • Ernst Lubitsch
Marie Provost, Monte Blue, Clara Bow

▷ THAT UNCERTAIN FEELING (1941)★AOV★
United Artists • Ernst Lubitsch
Merle Oberon, Melvyn Douglas, Burgess Meredith

Plot: A bored wife is tempted to stray, but soon realizes that she still loves her husband and stays with him.

Notes: Melvyn Douglas made his first film in 1931. Thirty-three years later, he received a Best Supporting Actor Oscar for his performance in HUD.

★ ★ ★

Charles Laughton in make-up and padding as the tragic Quasimodo in the second version of THE HUNCHBACK OF NOTRE DAME.

★ ★ ★

▶ LIGHT THAT FAILED, THE (1923)
Paramount • George Medford
Percy Marmount, Jacqueline Logan

▷ LIGHT THAT FAILED, THE (1939)
Paramount • William Wellman
Ronald Colman, Ida Lupino, Walter Huston

Plot: An artist is going blind as the result of a war wound but wants to complete a portrait of the girl he has come to love.

Notes: The first filming of the Rudyard Kipling novel took place in 1916.

★ ★ ★

★   ★   ★   ★   ★   ★   ★

▶ LITTLE LORD FAUNTLEROY (1921)
United Artists • Jack Pickford, Alfred E. Greene

Mary Pickford, Claude Gillingwater

▷ LITTLE LORD FAUNTLEROY (1936)★AOV★
United Artists • John Cromwell

Freddie Bartholomew, C. Aubrey Smith, Mickey Rooney, Dolores Costello

Plot: A boy, living in America, discovers that he is the grandson of a Duke.

Notes: In an unusual bit of casting, Mary Pickford is seen as both the young lord and his mother. Co-director Jack Pickford was Mary's brother. Another version of LITTLE LORD FAUNTLEROY surfaced in a 1980 Movie Made for Television starring Ricky Schroder★AOV★.

★ ★ ★

▶ LONDON AFTER MIDNIGHT (1927)
MGM • Tod Browning

Lon Chaney Sr., Conrad Nagel, Marcelline Day

▷ MARK OF THE VAMPIRE (1935)★AOV★
MGM • Tod Browning

Lionel Barrymore, Jean Hersholt, Elizabeth Allan, Bela Lugosi

Plot: Vampires terrorize a rural village.

Notes: Many readers will remember Jean Hersholt as the kindly Dr. Christian of radio and screen fame. To honor the actor for his many humanitarian services to the film industry, "The Jean Hersholt Humanitarian Award" was initiated at the 1956 Academy Award festivities. It is a special Oscar given occasionally to a deserving member of the industry.

★ ★ ★

▶ MAIN STREET (1923)
Warners • Harry Beaumont

Florence Vidor, Monte Blue

▷ I MARRIED A DOCTOR (1936)
Warners • Archie Mayo

Pat O'Brien, Josephine Hutchinson

Plot: A city-bred girl marries a rural doctor and tries to adjust to life in a small town.

Notes: The films are based upon the best-selling novel, "Main Street," by Sinclair Lewis. Pat O'Brien is remembered by movie buffs for his portrayal of legendary Notre Dame football coach Knute Rockne (appearing with O'Brien in the film is Ronald Reagan as Rockne's star player, George Gipp).

★ ★ ★

▶ MANSLAUGHTER (1922)
Paramount/Famous Players • Cecil B. De Mille

Leatrice Joy, Thomas Meighan

▷ MANSLAUGHTER (1930)
Paramount • George Abbott

Claudette Colbert, Fredric March

Plot: A District Attorney falls in love with a wealthy girl whom he has convicted of manslaughter.

Notes: Leatrice Joy, the star of the 1922 production, was married for a time to silent screen idol John Gilbert.

★ ★ ★

★　　★　　★　　★　　★　　★　　★

▶ MARK OF ZORRO (1920)★AOV★
United Artists • Fred Niblo

Douglas Fairbanks Sr., Noah Beery Sr.,
Marguerite de la Motte

▷ MARK OF ZORRO (1940)
TCF • Rouben Mamoulian

Tyrone Power, Basil Rathbone, Linda Darnell

Plot: The son of a California noble man returns to find the territory under the control of a dictator. He becomes a masked avenger and the evil doers are routed.

Notes: Another case of a screenplay being written by Fairbanks Sr. under an assumed name. The silent opened at New York's Capitol Theater to great acclaim.

"Let my people go." A confrontation between Yul Brynner as the Pharaoh of Egypt and Charlton Heston as Moses in THE TEN COMMANDMENTS— courtesy of Cecil B. De Mille.

▶ MARRIAGE CIRCLE, THE (1924)★AOV★
Warners • Ernst Lubitsch

Monte Blue, Florence Vidor, Adolphe Menjou

▷ ONE HOUR WITH YOU (1932)
Paramount • Ernst Lubitsch

Maurice Chevalier, Jeanette MacDonald, Genevieve Tobin

Plot: The marriage of a chic couple is threatened by the arrival on the scene of a third party, a flirtatious lady.

Notes: George Cukor was the original director of the 1932 film. Producer Lubitsch took over so much of the project that Cukor left and Lubitsch completed the film and received the credit.

★　★　★

▶ PECK'S BAD BOY (1921)★AOV★
Famous Players/Lasky • Sam Wood

Jackie Coogan, Raymond Hatton

▷ PECK'S BAD BOY (1934)★AOV★
Fox • Edward Cline

Jackie Cooper, Jackie Searle

Plot: Adventures of an inveterate mischief-maker.

Notes: Jackie Cooper, child star of the nineteen twenties, is still active both in front of the camera as an actor and behind the scenes as a director.

☆   ☆   ☆   ☆   ☆   ☆   ☆

▶ PEG O' MY HEART (1922)
MGM • King Vidor

Laurette Taylor

▷ PEG O' MY HEART (1933)
MGM • Robert Z. Leonard

Marion Davies, Onslow Stevens

Plot: An English nobleman falls in love with an Irish girl much to the consternation of his family.

Notes: Laurette Taylor made very few films, but enjoyed an illustrious career on Broadway. One of her most famous roles was in the Tennessee Williams play, "The Glass Menagerie."

★ ★ ★

▶ PHANTOM OF THE OPERA, THE
(1925)★AOV★
Universal • Rupert Julian

Lon Chaney Sr., Mary Philbin, Norman Kerry

▷ PHANTOM OF THE OPERA, THE
(1943)★AOV★
Universal • Arthur Lubin

Nelson Eddy, Claude Rains, Susannah Foster

Plot: A disfigured man in a mask who has fallen in love with a singer, kidnaps her from the Paris Opera House.

Notes: An exact replica of the Paris Opera House was constructed at Universal for the 1925 production. Chaney's make-up as the title-rolist was so menacing it is said that some theater patrons fainted at each showing of the film. Other filmings of the classic were released in 1962 and 1983. As of this writing, the stage version is still going strong via Broadway and road company productions.

★ ★ ★

▶ QUALITY STREET (1927)
MGM • Sidney Franklin

Marion Davies, Conrad Nagel

▷ QUALITY STREET (1937)★AOV★
RKO • George Stevens

Katharine Hepburn, Franchot Tone, Fay Bainter

Plot: A woman masquerades as her own niece to find out whether the soldier she has not seen since he went off to war ten years previously still loves her.

Notes: The films are based upon a play by Sir James M. Barrie. Joan Fontaine plays a small role in the 1937 production.

★ ★ ★

▶ REBECCA OF SUNNYBROOK FARM
(1917)★AOV★
Paramount • Marshall Neilan

Mary Pickford, Eugene O'Brien

▷ REBECCA OF SUNNYBROOK FARM (1932)

Fox • Alfred Santell

Marian Nixon, Ralph Bellamy

Plot: A high spirited girl comes to live with her strait-laced aunts.

Notes: The original story was altered to a show business theme in 1938★AOV★ when Shirley Temple was assigned the role.

★ ★ ★

☆   ☆   ☆   ☆   ☆   ☆   ☆

▶ SCARLET LETTER, THE (1926)
MGM • Victor Seastrom
Lillian Gish, Lars Hanson

▷ SCARLET LETTER, THE (1934)★AOV★
Majestic • Robert G. Vignola
Colleen Moore, Hardie Albright

Plot: A Puritan woman in Salem, who has had a baby out of wedlock, wears a scarlet "A" (for adultery) rather than reveal that the child's father is the local minister.

Notes: Other versions of the Nathaniel Hawthorne novel were filmed during the silent era and again in 1973★AOV★.

★ ★ ★

▶ SEVENTH HEAVEN (1927)
Fox • Frank Borzage
Janet Gaynor, Charles Farrell

▷ SEVENTH HEAVEN (1937)
TCF • Henry King
James Stewart, Simone Simon

Plot: A Paris sewer worker marries a young girl, goes off to war and returns sightless.

Notes: Janet Gaynor and Frank Borzage both won Oscars. The actress and Charles Farrell were a popular team during the silent era and also during the early days of the talkies. They co-starred in fourteen films. Charles Farrell enjoyed a brief career on television as Gale Storm's father in "My Little Margie."

★ ★ ★

▶ SNOW WHITE (1916)

Paramount • J. Searle Dawley
Marguerite Clark, Creighton Hale

▷ SNOW WHITE AND THE SEVEN DWARFS (1937)
Disney • Frank Hand
Animation

Plot: Snow White goes to live with the Seven Dwarfs and after a near fatal accident, finds her true love.

Notes: On several occasions, Walt Disney said that the 1916 production of SNOW WHITE had made a deep impression on him. The 1937 film can therefore technically be termed a "remake."

★ ★ ★

▶ SQUAW MAN, THE (1914)
Famous Players/Lasky • Cecil B. De Mille
Dustin Farnum

▷ SQUAW MAN, THE (1931)
MGM • Cecil B. De Mille
Warner Baxter, Lupe Velez

Plot: An Indian girl marries an Englishman, has a child, kills her husband's enemy and commits suicide.

Notes: The 1914 production was the first feature length film to be made in Hollywood. In 1918, De Mille made a second version of his landmark movie with Elliott Dexter in the title role.

★ ★ ★

☆   ☆   ☆   ☆   ☆   ☆   ☆

▶ STELLA DALLAS (1925)
Samuel Goldwyn • Henry King

Belle Bennett, Ronald Colman, Douglas
Fairbanks Jr., Lois Moran

▷ STELLA DALLAS (1937)★AOV★
Samuel Goldwyn • King Vidor

Barbara Stanwyck, John Boles, Anne Shirley

Plot: Mother love and sacrifice so that a daughter can have the better things in life.

Notes: Barbara Stanwyck and Anne Shirley were both Oscar nominated, Stanwyck for Best
Actress and Shirley for Best Supporting Actress. They lost to Luise Rainer and Alice Brady. A
third, updated version of the story by Olive Higgins Prouty was released in early 1990. Directed
by John Erman, this Touchstone production stars Bette Midler and John Goodman.

★ ★ ★

▶ STUDENT PRINCE, THE (1926)
MGM • Ernst Lubitsch

Norma Shearer, Ramon Novarro

▷ STUDENT PRINCE, THE (1954)
MGM • Richard Thorpe

Edmund Purdom, Ann Blyth

Plot: A student prince in Heidelberg falls in love with a barmaid, but both know they can never
marry.

Notes: Mario Lanza was set to star in the 1954 version. He had already recorded the sound track
when his temperament and weight problems cost him his job—it is Lanza's voice that is heard while
Purdom is "singing."

★ ★ ★

▶ TEN COMMANDMENTS, THE (1923)★AOV★
Famous Players/Lasky • Cecil B. De Mille

Richard Dix, Rod La Rocque, Theodore Roberts,
Leatrice Joy, Nita Naldi

▷ TEN COMMANDMENTS, THE (1956)★AOV★
Paramount • Cecil B. De Mille

Charlton Heston, Edward G. Robinson, Anne
Baxter, Yvonne De Carlo

Plot: The life of Moses from birth to his leading the Israelites into the promised land.

Notes: The 1956 production received an Academy Award nomination but did not win. It was filmed
at a cost of thirteen million dollars, one reason being that some of its scenes were shot on location
at Mount Sinai.

★ ★ ★

▶ THIEF OF BAGDAD, THE (1924)★AOV★
United Artists • Raoul Walsh

Douglas Fairbanks Sr., Julanne Johnston, Anna
May Wong

▷ THIEF OF BAGDAD, THE (1940)★AOV★
United Artists • Michael Powell, Ludwig Berger,
Tim Whelan

Sabu, Conrad Veidt, June Duprez

Plot: Magic is used by a thief to thwart the evil Caliph of Bagdad.

Notes: The technicolor photography of the 1940 film won an Oscar. An Italian version of the
Arabian Nights fantasy was released in 1961★AOV★ starring Steve Reeves. The latest is a 1978
Movie Made for Television starring Peter Ustinov and Terrence Stamp★AOV★.

★ ★ ★

☆   ☆   ☆   ☆   ☆   ☆   ☆

▶ TOL'ABLE DAVID (1921)★AOV★
First National • Henry King
Richard Barthelmess, Ernest Torrence

▷ TOL'ABLE DAVID (1930)
Columbia • John Blystone
Richard Cromwell, Noah Beery Sr.

Plot: A man driving a postal truck rids his small community of the thieves who want to steal the mail.

Notes: Noah Beery Sr., featured in the 1930 production, was the brother of MGM star Wallace and the father of actor Noah Jr.

★ ★ ★

▶ TRAIL OF THE LONESOME PINE, THE (1923)
Paramount • Charles Maigne
Antonio Moreno, Mary Miles Minter

▷ TRAIL OF THE LONESOME PINE, THE (1936)
Paramount • Henry Hathaway
Fred MacMurray, Henry Fonda, Sylvia Sidney

Plot: A city dweller falls in love with a Kentucky girl and is caught up in an Ozark Mountain feud.

Notes: The 1936 remake was the first outdoor film shot in three-color Technicolor. A 1916 version, directed by Cecil B. De Mille and starring Thomas Meighan, was released by Paramount.

★ ★ ★

▶ WAY DOWN EAST (1920)★AOV★
United Artists • D.W. Griffith
Lillian Gish, Lowell Sherman, Richard Barthelmess

▷ WAY DOWN EAST (1935)
Fox • Henry King
Henry Fonda, Rochelle Hudson, Andy Devine

Plot: A girl, who has been seduced, is abandoned by her New England community. She is rescued from drowning by a young farmer and finds happiness with him.

Notes: The remake was completed just before the merger of Twentieth Century and Fox.

★ ★ ★

▶ WAY OF ALL FLESH, THE (1927)
Paramount • Victor Fleming
Emil Jannings, Belle Bennett

▷ WAY OF ALL FLESH, THE (1940)
Paramount • Louis King
Akim Tamiroff, Gladys George

Plot: A bank messenger is fleeced by a blonde and becomes a derelict—he is too ashamed to come home.

Notes: Both the 1927 film and Emil Jannings were Oscar-nominated. Only Jannings won. During the early years of the motion picture industry, performers were nominated for more than one role. This was the case with Jannings. His second nomination came for THE LAST COMMAND.

★ ★ ★

▶ WEST OF ZANZIBAR (1928)
MGM • Tod Browning
Lon Chaney Sr., Lionel Barrymore, Mary Nolan

▷ KONGO (1932)
MGM • William Cowan
Walter Huston, Conrad Nagel, Lupe Velez, Virginia Bruce

Plot: An embittered ivory trader revenges himself upon the man who has stolen his wife.

Notes: Walter Huston played the role of the revenge-crazed man on the Broadway stage during the nineteen twenties.

★ ★ ★

☆ ☆ ☆ ☆ ☆ ☆ ☆

▶ WHAT PRICE GLORY? (1926)
Fox • Raoul Walsh
Victor McLaglen, Edmund Lowe, Dolores Del Rio

▷ WHAT PRICE GLORY? (1952)★AOV★
TCF • John Ford
James Cagney, Dan Dailey, Corinne Calvet

Plot: Two boisterous soldiers go head to head when they vie for the affections of a French girl during World War I.

Notes: The films are based upon a play by Maxwell Anderson.

★ ★ ★

▶ WHITE SISTER, THE (1924)
Metro • Henry King
Lillian Gish, Ronald Colman

▷ WHITE SISTER, THE (1933)
MGM • Victor Fleming
Helen Hayes, Clark Gable, Lewis Stone

Plot: A woman becomes a nun after hearing that the man she loves is a casualty of war. Though he returns, she keeps her vow to the church.

Notes: Lillian Gish and her sister Dorothy were famous stars of the silent screen era. Lillian was still active during the nineteen seventies and eighties. Louis Stone is best remembered as Judge Hardy in the "Andy Hardy" series.

★ ★ ★

▶ WOMAN OF AFFAIRS, A (1928)
MGM • Clarence Brown
Greta Garbo, John Gilbert, John Mack Brown

▷ OUTCAST LADY (1934)
MGM • Robert Z. Leonard
Constance Bennett, Herbert Marshall, Hugh Williams

Plot: A young woman lives recklessly and finally loses her life in a car crash.

Notes: Garbo and Gilbert were a romantic item both on screen and off. They made four films together. There are several stories as to why Gilbert's screen career came to a close during the nineteen thirties. One concerns the pitch of his voice, another lists, as the main cause, some allegedly offensive remarks made by him in the presence of Louis B. Mayer.

★ ★ ★

▶ ZAZA (1923)
Paramount • Allan Dwan
Gloria Swanson, H.B. Warner

▷ ZAZA (1938)
Paramount • George Cukor
Claudette Colbert, Herbert Marshall

Plot: A French music hall performer falls in love with a married aristocrat.

Notes: ZAZA was filmed in 1915 by famous Players/Lasky with Pauline Frederick in the title role. The Gloria Swanson version was filmed at the Astoria Studios in New York City. Claudette Colbert, star of the 1938 version, is of French descent and was born in Paris.

★ ★ ★

★   ★   ★   ★   ★   ★   ★

CHAPTER FOURTEEN

DOUBLE EXPOSURES: WHEN STARS REPRISE THEIR ROLES

I have saved a most interesting phenomenon for last, that of a star reprising a role some years after appearing in the original production.[*] A rare policy, yes, but one which was followed upon occasion with a good deal of success for the most part, during the days when the studios controlled the film industry.

A more common practice was that of a director doing a repeat filming of a hit production on which he had previously worked. Such legendary filmmakers as Cecil B. De Mille, Ernst Lubitsch, Frank Capra, Raoul Walsh and William Wyler are only a few of the directorial guiding spirits who went the remake route in the hope that lightning would strike twice in the form of another hit. Those named above usually had carte blanche in the selection of projects—contract directors, however, were assigned films by their studios.

In the case of a star, it was the studio system calling the shots all the way. Studio heads and chiefs of production were the ones who assigned roles to contract players (which most stars were in the early days) and if "the brass" wanted a certain star to remake a certain story, who was the contractee to disagree?

Twenty repeat performers are listed in this chapter including the great silent star Lon Chaney Sr., the young and lovely Ingrid Bergman, the throaty-voiced Alice Faye, James Bond himself, Sean Connery and Clark Gable, the man voted "King of Hollywood" during the nineteen thirties. Also prominent in these pairings are the team of Dorothy Lamour and Ray Milland who were signed to co-star in both an original film and its remake and George Arliss, a famous stage actor and silent screen star, who had the distinction of performing in both the silent original and the sound remake of not one but two films.

---

[*] Two character actors also had the unusual opportunity of playing the same role in both an original film and its remake—because they are not leading performers in either, the pairings are listed in their respective genres (a third, Jack Oakie, is listed in the body of this chapter because of Alice Faye's involvement in the same film). The two are Lionel Stander, who appears in THE MILKY WAY and its musical remake, THE KID FROM BROOKLYN, and Edward Everett Horton, who plays the same role in both versions of Philip Barry's HOLIDAY.

★   ★   ★   ★   ★   ★   ★

Unlike the pairings listed in previous pages, the thirty- eight films written about in this chapter have been put into chronological order according to the year of the original's release so that the reader may get a better perspective of the stars and stories which make up this most interesting aspect of the film remake.

One final thought—will the stars of this generation do repeat performances of their films in the twenty-first century for the next generation?

Something to ponder, it must be admitted.

☆   ☆   ☆   ☆   ☆   ☆   ☆

▶ DISRAELI (1921)
United Artists • Henry Kolker
George Arliss, Florence Arliss

▷ DISRAELI (1929)★AOV★
Warners • Alfred E. Greene
George Arliss, Florence Arliss, Joan Bennett

Plot: Incidents in the life of the Victorian Prime Minister of England.

Notes: George Arliss won an Academy Award for his performance in the 1929 film. Florence Arliss appeared in several motion pictures with her husband—her billing usually read "Mrs. George Arliss."

★ ★ ★

▶ MAN WHO PLAYED GOD, THE (1922)
United Artists • Harmon Wright
George Arliss, Mary Astor

▷ MAN WHO PLAYED GOD, THE (1932)
Warners • John G. Adolfi
George Arliss, Bette Davis

Plot: A concert pianist, who has become deaf, finds satisfaction in helping others.

Notes: The 1922 production marked the debut of Mary Astor while the 1932 movie gave Bette Davis her big break in Hollywood. Warner Brothers filmed the story for the third time two decades later as SINCERELY YOURS (1955), starring Liberace.

★ ★ ★

▶ ARAB, THE (1924)
MGM • Rex Ingram
Ramon Novarro, Alice Terry

▷ BARBARIAN, THE (1933)
MGM • Sam Wood
Ramon Novarro, Myrna Loy

Plot: An American woman in the Middle East falls in love with a handsome Arab.

★ ★ ★

▶ UNHOLY THREE, THE (1925)
Tod Browning
Lon Chaney Sr., Victor McLaglen, Mae Busch

▷ UNHOLY THREE, THE (1930)
MGM • Jack Conway
Lon Chaney Sr., Lila Lee, Elliott Nugent

Plot: In a circus setting, a ventriloquist, a dwarf and a strong man opt for a life of crime.

Notes: The 1930 production was Lon Chaney Sr.'s first and only sound film. He died just before its release.

★ ★ ★

▶ SEA BEAST, THE (1926)
Warners • Millard Webb
John Barrymore, Dolores Costello

▷ MOBY DICK (1930)
Warners • Lloyd Bacon
John Barrymore, Joan Bennett

Plot: Captain Ahab, minus a leg, sets sail in search of the white whale responsible for his loss.

Notes: A third version of the Herman Melville adventure story starring Gregory Peck, was released in 1956★AOV★.

★ ★ ★

▶ LOVE (1927)
MGM • Edmund Goulding
Greta Garbo, John Gilbert

▷ ANNA KARENINA (1935)★AOV★
MGM • Clarence Brown
Greta Garbo, Fredric March, Basil Rathbone,
Maureen O'Sullivan

Plot: The wife of a Russian aristocrat and a cavalry officer fall in love.

Notes: Two more versions of ANNA KERENINA were filmed. The 1948 production★AOV★ stars
Vivien Leigh, Kieron Moore and Ralph Richardson. The 1985 Made for Television Movie stars
Jacqueline Bisset, Paul Scofield and Christopher Reeve.

★ ★ ★

*Electricity is in the air as Jean
Harlow faces up to Clark Gable in
RED DUST.*

★ ★ ★

▶ RED DUST (1932)★AOV★
MGM • Victor Fleming
Clark Gable, Jean Harlow, Mary Astor

▷ MOGAMBO (1953)★AOV★
MGM • John Ford
Clark Gable, Ava Gardner, Grace Kelly

Plot: A man is caught between two women, one of whom is married.

Notes: Both Ava Gardner and Grace Kelly were Oscar-nominated. CONGO MAISIE, a 1940 MGM
release starring Ann Sothern and John Carroll, is loosely based upon the original story.

★ ★ ★

▶ GREAT EXPECTATIONS (1934)★AOV★
Universal • Stuart Walker
Phillips Holmes, Jane Wyatt, Francis L. Sullivan

▷ GREAT EXPECTATIONS (1946)★AOV★
Rank/Cineguild • David Lean
John Mills, Martita Hunt, Francis L. Sullivan, Jean Simmons

Plot: A mysterious benefactor helps a young orphan grow up to become a gentleman of means.

Notes: Another version of the Charles Dickens novel was a 1974 Movie Made for Television starring James Mason, Michael York, Sarah Miles and Margaret Leighton. Jean Simmons plays the young Estella in the 1946 film. In a 1989 mini-series, she played the elderly Miss Favorsham.

Same star, same role, different co-star. Clark Gable, twenty-one years later, with Ava Gardner in MOGAMBO.

▶ KING OF BURLESQUE (1935)★AOV★
TCF • Sidney Lanfield
Alice Faye, Jack Oakie, Warner Baxter

▷ HELLO FRISCO HELLO (1943)
TCF • H. Bruce Humberstone
Alice Faye, Jack Oakie, John Payne

Plot: A show business impresario mingles with high society, but then returns to his roots and the people who love him.

Notes: Alice Faye and Jack Oakie appear together in several other Twentieth Century-Fox musicals. "You'll Never Know," featured in the 1943 production, won that year's Best Song Academy Award.

★ ★ ★

▶ INTERMEZZO (1936)★AOV★   ▷ INTERMEZZO (1939)★AOV★
Swedish • Gustav Molander   David O. Selznick • Gregory Ratoff
Ingrid Bergman, Gosta Ekman   Ingrid Bergman, Leslie Howard

Plot: A married violinist falls in love with a gifted young piano student.

Notes: On the strength of her performance in the 1936 film, Ingrid Bergman was brought to America by Selznick.

★ ★ ★

Loretta Young is smiling as an irate Tyrone Power tries to make a point in LOVE IS NEWS.

★ ★ ★

▶ JUNGLE PRINCESS (1936)   ▷ HER JUNGLE LOVE (1938)
Paramount • William Thiele   Paramount • George Archainbaud
Dorothy Lamour, Ray Milland   Dorothy Lamour, Ray Milland

Plot: A British visitor, stranded on a South Sea island, falls in love with a beautiful native girl.

Notes: JUNGLE PRINCESS was Dorothy Lamour's first film. She had been a band and radio singer before being signed by Paramount.

★ ★ ★

▶ LOVE IS NEWS (1937)   ▷ THAT WONDERFUL URGE (1948)
TCF • Tay Garnett   TCF • Robert B. Sinclair
Tyrone Power, Loretta Young, Don Ameche   Tyrone Power, Gene Tierney, Reginald Gardiner

Plot: An heiress, tired of a newspaperman's invasion of her privacy, tries to embarrass him by issuing a statement saying that she has married him.

Notes: In between the two films listed came SWEET ROSIE O'GRADY, starring Betty Grable and Robert Young. This 1943 musical has the same basic story, but takes place in the Gay Nineties, with Betty as an ex-burlesque queen trying to hide her past.

★ ★ ★

★   ★   ★   ★   ★   ★   ★

▶ SWAMP WATER (1941)
TCF • Jean Renoir
Walter Brennan, Walter Huston, Dana Andrews, Anne Baxter

▷ LURE OF THE WILDERNESS (1952)
TCF • Jean Negulesco
Walter Brennan, Jeffrey Hunter, Jean Peters

Plot: A hunter helps a wrongly accused man hiding out in the Okefenokee swamps to prove his innocence.

Notes: Jean Peters was married to eccentric billionaire Howard Hughes from 1956 to 1971.

★   ★   ★

Astaire may be holding Marjorie Reynolds in his arms but it's Crosby who gets her at the finale in HOLIDAY INN.

★   ★   ★

▶ HOLIDAY INN (1942) ★AOV★
Paramount • Mark Sandrich
Bing Crosby, Fred Astaire, Marjorie Reynolds, Virginia Dale

▷ WHITE CHRISTMAS (1954) ★AOV★
Paramount • Michael Curtiz
Bing Crosby, Danny Kaye, Rosemary Clooney, Vera-Ellen

Plot: Music and romance are the order of the day as a hotel opens for business.

Notes: Both films feature the music of Irving Berlin. First performed in HOLIDAY INN, "White Christmas" won the 1942 Best Song Oscar.

★   ★   ★

☆　☆　☆　☆　☆　☆　☆

▶ CONEY ISLAND (1943)
TCF • Walter Lang
Betty Grable, George Montgomery, Cesar Romero

▷ WABASH AVENUE (1950)
TCF • Henry Koster
Betty Grable, Victor Mature, Phil Harris

Plot: Two rival showmen are in love with a pretty singer.

Notes: The first film is set in New York's Coney Island, while the second takes place in Chicago. Phil Harris, band leader and alumnus of the Jack Benny Show, is the husband of Alice Faye, who along with Betty Grable, was a top star at Twentieth Century-Fox during the nineteen thirties and forties.

★　★　★

Betty Grable and Phil Harris in WABASH AVENUE. In real life Harris was (and still is) married to Alice Faye, Betty's chief "rival" at Twentieth Century-Fox.

★　★　★

▶ DAY THE EARTH STOOD STILL, THE (1951)★AOV★
TCF • Robert Wise
Patricia Neal, Michael Rennie, Hugh Marlowe

▷ STRANGER FROM VENUS (1954)★AOV★

British • Burt Balaban
Patricia Neal, Helmut Dantine

Plot: An alien lands his space craft on earth in order to bring its inhabitants a message of peace.

★　★　★

▶ SKIN GAME, THE (1971)★AOV★
Warners • Paul Bogart
Louis Gossett, James Garner, Susan Clark

▷ SIDEKICKS (1974)
MMTV • Burt Kennedy
Louis Gossett, Larry Hagman, Blythe Danner

Plot: In the days of the Civil War, a white con-man keeps on passing his black counterpart off as a runaway slave in order to collect the bounty.

Notes: Larry Hagman, son of musical comedy star Mary Martin, is known the world over as J.R. Ewing on the long running television series "Dallas." Louis Gossett won a Best Supporting Actor award in 1982 for his role in AN OFFICER AND A GENTLEMAN.

★　★　★

★   ★   ★   ★   ★   ★   ★

▶ RIO BRAVO (1959)★AOV★
Warners • Howard Hawks

John Wayne, Dean Martin, Rick Nelson, Angie Dickinson

▷ EL DORADO (1967)★AOV★
Paramount • Howard Hawks

John Wayne, Robert Mitchum, James Caan, Charlene Holt

Plot: Four men try to prevent a jail break in a western frontier town.

Notes: Late actor-singer Rick Nelson was the son of veteran performers Ozzie Nelson and Harriet Hilliard and the father of Tracy Nelson, star of the current (1990) TV series "Father Dowling Mysteries."

"Reach for the sky, ya mangy critters." Sheriff John Wayne and deputies Dean Martin and Rick Nelson are quick on the draw in RIO BRAVO. Its remake, EL DORADO, was the last film directed by the legendary Howard Hawks.

▶ THUNDERBALL (1965)★AOV★
United Artists • Terence Young

Sean Connery, Claudine Auger

▷ NEVER SAY NEVER AGAIN (1983)★AOV★
Warner/Woodcote/Taliafilm • Irvin Kershner

Sean Connery, Klaus Maria Brandauer, Max von Sydow

Plot: The western hemisphere is threatened with destruction by a criminal organization which has hijacked a plane carrying nuclear bombs—James Bond to the rescue.

Notes: THUNDERBALL was the fourth Bond movie released. Its special effects won an Oscar.

★   ★   ★

EPILOGUE

THE END OF AN ODYSSEY

And so it goes. As we wend our way into the nineteen nineties, there will be many uncertainties in life, but we can be sure of three things: death, taxes and the movie remake. In spite of the myriad of changes which have taken place in the entertainment industry, over the years, many filmmakers are still saying "once is not enough." Hardly a year goes by without the film goer or television watcher experiencing a feeling of déjà vu and the next decade promises even more of the same.

Movie remakes mean different things to different people. For the filmmaker, the operative word is money: cash receipts at the box-office, television sales and possible world-wide distribution. New versions of old films have usually provided a good source of revenue for the movie capital and also, within the past couple of decades, for the television industry, which has gone the remake route via several Movies Made for Television (MMTVs)—if this was not so, it is doubtful as to whether the remake would be a fact of life.

For performers in the days that the studios held sway, stardom meant assignment at the whim of others (read studio brass). For today's stars, however, a far different scenario has emerged. It is essential, therefore, in this age of independent production and no multi-picture contracts, for them to select properties which they think (and hope) will become box-office hits. Several of todays performers have elected to follow in the footsteps of those who have gone before, from Barbra Streisand in the 1976 third version of A STAR IS BORN, playing the role made famous by both Janet Gaynor and Judy Garland, to Bette Midler as STELLA in a 1990 reworking of Barbara Stanwyck's memorable 1937 triumph, STELLA DALLAS, itself a remake of a 1925 silent starring Belle Bennett and Ronald Colman.

And finally for the film buff, historian and young movie goer, the remake is a fascinating link to the past, one which can give those who love and revere the art of movie-making a feel for both the productions and stars that used to be and those that are to be.

Love, as the beautiful old Ira Gershwin lyric goes, is here to stay. So, for better or for worse, is the movie remake.

INDEX

☆ ☆ ☆ ☆ ☆ ☆ ☆

☆   ☆   ☆   ☆   ☆   ☆   ☆

☆   ☆   ☆   ☆   ☆   ☆   ☆

☆   ☆   ☆   ☆   ☆   ☆   ☆

☆ ☆ ☆ ☆ ☆ ☆ ☆

☆   ☆   ☆   ☆   ☆   ☆   ☆

★   ★   ★   ★   ★   ★   ★

★ ★ ★ ★ ★ ★ ★

☆   ☆   ☆   ☆   ☆   ☆   ☆